A History of the Grand Traverse Region

A HISTORY

OF THE

Grand Traverse Region

By Dr. M. L. LEACH,

PUBLISHED IN THE

GRAND TRAVERSE HERALD,

TRAVERSE CITY, MICHIGAN,

1883.

There is indubitable evidence that the Mound-Builders wrought the copper mines of Lake Superior—that the work was carried on by large bodies of men through a period of hundreds of years—but the evidence that they established permanent settlements there is wanting. The most reasonable theory is that the laborers spent the summer in the mines, but retired for the winter to a more genial clime. Hence, it becomes an interesting problem to determine the northern limit of their permanent abode.

It is evident that they had populous settlements in some of the more fertile districts of the southern part of the State. Farther north their remains are found less frequently, and are of a less imposing character. Characteristic earth works, (whether built for defense or for civil or religious purposes is uncertain,) are found in Ogemaw county. Mounds are known to exist in Manistee county. That outlying colonies extended north to the Grand Traverse country, scarcely admits of a doubt. Around Boardman Lake, near Traverse City, several small mounds formerly existed, some of which have been destroyed in the search for relics. One small burial mound has been opened within the village limits.

The sites of several ancient manufactories of stone arrow-heads have been found. In excavating for a street, on the bank of Boardman River, in Traverse City, such a location was discovered, marked by the presence of great numbers of chips of flint, or hornstone, the refuse of the material used for making the arrow-heads. At Charlevoix, the soil for a foot or more in depth, on the top of the bluff, north of the mouth of the river, contains great numbers of these flint chips, together with some unfinished arrow-heads that were spoiled in making and thrown away. Another well marked site of an arrow-head manufactory, is on the farm of John Miller, on the north shore of Pine Lake, about a mile from the village of Boyne City.†

Fragments of ancient pottery, having the markings common to the pottery attributed to the Mound Builders, is found at the locality last mentioned, and also within the village limits of Boyne City, as well as sparingly in other places.

At Charlevoix, in excavating a cellar, an ancient grave was opened, in which was found a great number of beautifully finished flint arrow-heads, and a quantity of copper beads. In the same locality, some boys amusing themselves by running up and down the steep bank of the "Old River," discovered a piece of copper protruding from the gravelly bank. An examination resulted in the finding of two knives and two bodkins, or piercing instruments, all of copper.

The evidence seems conclusive that the Mound-Builders, the most ancient inhabitants of the territory of the United States of whom we have any knowledge, had extended their scattered frontier settlements into the Grand Traverse country. Here, perhaps, mining expeditions from the more populous south called to make their final preparations for the northern summer trip, and here some of the returning miners were accustomed to spend the winter.

That ancient people have long since disappeared. Of the reason and manner of their disappearance, no record remains, except, perhaps, a vague and shadowy tradition, which seems to imply that they retired towards the south, before the fierce and savage race that succeeded them in the occupancy of the country.

---

*The writer has in his possession the fragments of a burned human skull, found in a mound, in such a situation as to warrant the above statement. Two bodies had been laid in shallow graves, and a mound partly built above them. On a level spot, on the partly built mound, a body had been burned, and then the bed of ashes, with the burned bones lying upon it, had been covered with earth by the completion of the mound.
M. L. L.

† It may be objected that the Indians made and used flint arrow-heads and stone axes, and that therefore the finding of these relics is no evidence of the former presence of the Mound-Builders. I freely admit the possibility that in the cases mentioned the arrow-heads were made by the Indians, but I am fully convinced that at least three-fourths of all the stone implements and ornaments found in the United States are the work of the Mound-Builders. In regard to the pottery of the Grand Traverse country, its marking and general appearance place it with the pottery of the Mound-Builders. As to the copper ornaments and implements, the fact is well established that the Indians knew nothing of the copper mines, and did not put copper to any practical use till the white men taught them how.
M. L. L.

CHAPTER II.

Migrations of the Ottawas—First meeting of the Ottawas and Chippewas—The Three Brothers—The Underground Indians—The Mush'quah tas—An Unpardonable Insult—A Tribe Blotted Out.

When northern Michigan first became known to the white man, the Ottawas, a tribe of the Algonquin family, occupied the region now known as the Grand Traverse country. Their origin as a tribe, is veiled in the obscurity of the past. Tradition says that they came from the east, advancing up the Ottawa River, in Canada, and then westward by way of the north shore of Lake Huron and the Manitoulin Islands. The reason for the migration is not known. There may have been no special reason beyond the common exigencies of savage life, which necessitate removal, or they may have been influenced by the proximity of their fierce and powerful neighbors, the Iroquois, with whom they were always at war. The advance westward was slow and gradual, being interrupted by pauses of varying duration. At the great Manitoulin Island the tribe for a long time made their home.

At the Sault St. Marie they first met the Chippewas, who inhabited the country bordering on Lake Superior. The two tribes were mutually surprised to find that, though previously each had had no knowledge of the existence of the other, their languages were so nearly alike that they could converse intelligibly. A council was held, the subject was discussed and the history of each tribe rehearsed, but the tradition does not tell us that the mystery of the likeness of the languages and the probable consanguinity of the tribes was solved.

The Ottawas were brave and warlike. As they advanced westward, they fought and vanquished those who opposed their progress; with those that were friendly they smoked the pipe of peace. Friendly intercourse with the Chippewas and Pottawattamies resulted in the formation of a sort of loose confederacy of the three tribes, who styled themselves "The Three Brothers." During the period of the earlier intercourse of the whites with the Indians of the Northwest, these tribes seem to have held undisputed possession of nearly the whole of the Lower Peninsula.

The Ottawas remained for some time established in the vicinity of the Straits, before they extended their settlements along the shore of Lake Michigan. During this period, though they were at peace with their immediate neighbors, they gratified their thirst for battle by frequent warlike expeditions against distant tribes. They often passed south around the head of Lake Michigan, and westward beyond the Mississippi, sometimes, it is said, extending their forays almost to the foot of the Rocky Mountains. They brought home many western prisoners. Some of these were called by the Ottawas Under-ground Indians, on account of their custom of digging pits in the ground for dwellings. The Under ground Indians were brave and intelligent, and made excellent counsellors. The captors often intermarried with their captives, and the descendents of the latter, in many cases, were closely related to the royal families of the Ottawas. Some of the most noted Ottawa chiefs of later times were descended from the Under-ground Indians.

At that time a portion of the present county of Emmet was the home of a small tribe, called the Mush quah-tas.* Their principal village was situated in a beautiful valley, in the northeast part of the township now called Friendship. The name of the tribe signifies "The

People Who Roam Over the Prairies."* They were of Algonquin stock, as is proved by the fact that their language resembled the Ottawa, while the tribal name and their recognized affinity to the Underground Indians seem to point to a western origin. The Muhs-quah-tas were intelligent, peaceable, and industrious, cultivating large fields of corn, and seldom going on the war path. They had been on friendly terms with the Ottawas since the arrival of the latter in the country, though it is probable that some degree of concealed ill-will existed on both sides. It was a sad day for the Mush-quah-tas, when, by their own foolish act, these friendly relations were disturbed.

There was a small village of the Mush-quah-tas on the lake shore, at what is now called Seven Mile Point. A small party of Ottawas, returning in their canoes from an expedition against the Sacs, having lost some of their comrades, as they came near the village commenced wailing for the dead, according to the Indian custom. The Mush-quah-tas, hearing the distant sounds of grief, instead of preparing to join in the mourning, as would have been proper, rashly determined to express in an emphatic manner their disapproval of the marauding expeditions of their neighbors and their contempt for those who engaged in them. Accordingly as the canoes touched the beach, their occupants were pelted by the young men and boys of the village, with balls of ashes wrapped up in forest leaves. The Ottawas retired, sullen and burning with the spirit of revenge, and soon reported the occurrence to their own people. To the proud Ottwas, the insult was such as could only be wiped out with blood. A joint council of the Ottawas and Chippewas was held, in which it was determined, if possible, to annihilate the Mush-quah-tas.

Living in the principal village of the Mush-quah-tas, was an old man and his two married sons. Whether the old man, hearing of the affair at Seven Mile Point, shrewdly surmised that the insulted Ottawas would seek a bloody revenge, or, as the tradition seems to imply, was impressed with a true prophetic presentiment of coming evil, he faithfully warned the people that their village would soon be overwhelmed by enemies, and earnestly counselled retirement to a place of safety. Finding his counsel disregarded, he, with his sons and their families, removed to the shore of Little Traverse Bay, fixing his temporary abode near the present site of Harbor Springs.

It may have been that a calm summer's night had nearly passed away. The first faint glimmering of light in the east, heralds the approach of morn. The village of the Mush-qua-tas is still wrapt in slumber. The sleeping mother gently clasps her baby to her breast, unconscious of approaching danger. The maiden dreams of her lover; the young man of glorious feats of the chase or of war. The old brave lives over again the experiences of the youth or dreams of the happy hunting ground to which he is hastening. Dark forms, crouching in the shadows, are stealthily approaching—on this side a long line of Ottawa braves, on that their friends and allies, the Chippewas. The lines close round the doomed village. Some of the crouching figures are already at the very doors. So noiseless and stealthy has been the approach that not even the watchful dogs have been alarmed. Suddenly there bursts upon the night air a sound to make the blood curdle—a deafening chorus of demoniac yells, as if uttered in concert by a legion of frantic furies. Full well the startled Mush-quah-tas know the fearful import of that sound, the warhoop of their enemies. Full well they know there is no avoiding the death struggle. The old brave reaches for his war club, and the young man strings his bow, but their assailants are quick and powerful, and the stone hatchets are wielded with terrible effect. Crushed and mangled, they go down, slain but not conquered. The maiden covers her face with her garment, and quietly bows her head to the fatal blow. The mother loosens her clasp of her frightened infant, seizes the nearest weapon, and, with the fierceness of a tigress at bay, springs upon her foes. Her blows tell, but fierceness can not long avail against strength and numbers. She falls mortally wounded. Her dying eyes are turned lovingly upon her child. A brawny warrior seizes it by the feet, whirls it high in air, dashes it with crushing force upon the earth, and flings its bleeding and lifeless body upon its mother's bosom. The surprised Mush-quah-tas, taken at a disadvantage, make a brave fight, but victory does not long waver in the balance. As the sun rises upon the scene, all the inmates save one of that doomed village lie stark and bleeding on the ground, or are consuming in the rapidly burning wigwams. The revenge of the insulted Ottawas is complete.

This battle, says the Ottawa tradition, was one of the most terrible ever fought in this region. Only a young man escaped, who carried the news of the disaster to the three families at Little Traverse Bay. Some of the Mush-quah-tas living in the small outlying villages escaped. The remnant of the tribe removed toward the south, and established themselves near the St. Joseph River, where for a time they enjoyed a degree of prosperity. But they were not safe. After intercourse had been opened between the French and the Ottawas, and the latter had been supplied with guns and axes by the French traders, it occurred to them that these implements would be effective in battle. Anxious to put them to the test, they resolved to try their effectiveness on their old enemies, the Mush-quah-tas, who as yet were unacquainted with firearms. Accordingly an expedition was fitted out, destined for the St. Joseph. As the Ottawas approached the village of their enemies, each man carrying a gun, the Mush-quah-tas mistook the weapons for clubs, and came out with their bows and arrows, anticipating an easy victory. But they were soon undeceived, and suffered a second crushing defeat, from the effects of which they never recovered. The tribal organization was dissolved, and the few Mush-quah-tas remaining alive were scattered among the neighboring tribes.†

After the destruction of the principal village of the Mush-quah-tas and the removal of the remnant of the tribe to the St. Joseph, the Ottawas gradually extended their settlements towards the south, along the shore of Lake Michigan.

In the forest were plenty of beaver, marten, and otter, but not many deer. At the approach of winter, they generally went south to hunt, returning in the spring. The fish in the lakes, during the proper season, furnished an abundant supply of food. They were caught in gill nets made of twine manufactured from the inner bark of the slippery elm (*Ulmus fulva*). The manufacture of the twine was a part of the work of the women. The bark was macerated in the lye of wood ashes, to remove the mucilage, beaten to separate the fibers, and spun by hand. It was the work of the women, also, to dress the game, cure the skins, cultivate their limited cornfields, pound the corn in wooden mortars and prepare the hominy, gather the fuel, and perform the general drudgery of the household. The men, when not engaged in fishing or the chase, or in forays into the homes of distant tribes, (for all distant tribes were considered lawful plunder,) reclined in listless idleness in the shelter of their bark wigwams, or engaged in the athletic sports common among the Algonquin people.

We see in the Ottawas what may be called a fair average example of Indian character. In common with others, they were brave, suspicious, treacherous, generous as friends and cruel and implacable as enemies. Marquette says that they were addicted beyond all other tribes to foulness, incantations, and sacrifices to evil spirits, but the estimates of Indian character of all the early Jesuit missionaries should be taken with many grains of allowance

As a tribe the Ottawas were never strong in numbers Their own tradition says they were more numerous at the time of Pontiac's war than ever before, and that that period was the most glorious of their existence yet historical records seem to show that they could not bring more than a few hundred warriors into the field

*This name should be accented on the last syllable and the a pronounced with the long sound, as in late M L L

†The version of this affair given by Judge Hatch in his historical address differs in some particulars from the foregoing I have told the story as it has been told to me by persons of Indian descent, who are thoroughly familiar with the traditions of the Ottawas M L L

CHAPTER III

Jesuit Missionaries—Principal Missions—Point St Ignace—Father Marquette—First White Men in the Grand Traverse Country—L'Arbre Croche—Schemes of Pontiac—Massacre at Mackinac—Father Jonois—The English Prisoners Carried to L'Arbre Croche—The Release

When, about the year 1650, the Huron settlements at the southeastern extremity of the Georgian Bay of Lake Huron were broken up by the victorious Iroquois, and the people scattered in various directions, a remnant, known as the Tobacco Nation, migrated towards the northwest, and fixed their abode on the Island of Mackinac. There they were joined by a band of Ottawas, from the Isle des Allumettes of the Ottawa River, the ancient home of the Ottawa nation, and, it is said, by some Ottawas and other Algonquins from the western shore of Lake Huron After remaining several years at Mackinac, and finding themselves still harassed by their enemies, they moved again westward, and took possession of the islands at the entrance of Green Bay. From thence they migrated southward and westward, coming in contact with the Illinois, and afterward, on the banks of the Mississippi, with the Sioux Quarreling with the Sioux and being driven from their country, they retreated to Point St Esprit, near the Islands of the Twelve Apostles, in the southwestern part of Lake Superior.

The Jesuit missionaries, who had done some of their most successful work among the Hurons, followed the flying remnants of their flock into the depths of the northwestern wilderness Two principal missions were established, one named St. Esprit, at the point of that name, on Lake Superior, the other at Sault St Marie About 1760, a third mission was founded at Green Bay

The Mission at St. Esprit was of short duration About 1671, the Sioux commenced open hostilities upon the Hurons and Ottawas, and so terrified them that they abandoned their settlement and fled Marquette, who was in charge of the mission, followed his panic stricken flock They coasted Lake Superior, passed the mission at the Sault, and descended the St Mary's river The Hurons stopped in the vicinity of Mackinac, fixing their abode on Point St. Ignace The Ottawas continued on to the Great Manitoulin Island The Hurons were afterwards joined at St Ignace by bands of Ottawas from those occupying the country in the vicinity of the Straits A new mission was now established at St Ignace, and placed in charge of Marquette

The missions were centers from which radiated influences that, in a wonderful degree, affected the lives and fortunes of the Indians Each was in reality a sort of triple establishment, consisting of the mission proper, under the control and management of the zealous, determined, and wily Jesuits, a military post, kept by an officer and a few French soldiers, and a straggling village, inhabited by a motley company—traders, adventurers, and voyageurs—Frenchmen, Indians, and half-breeds Unlike the English, the French colonists readily adapted themselves to the manners and customs of the Indians A few Frenchmen brought their wives to the western wilderness, but no disgrace attached to the marrying of an Indian woman, and in many localities families of mixed blood became the rule, rather than, as in the English border settlements, the exception to the rule

The salvation of souls, the aggrandizement of the Society of Jesus, and the glory of France were the objects aimed at by the leading spirits of the mission, to which the greed of gain, manifested in much sharp practice in trade, was scarcely subordinated. So cleverly was the intercourse with the Indians planned and executed, through a long series of years, that the northwestern tribes became the firm friends and allies of France. During the war between France and England, ending with the surrender of Canada to the English in 1760, commonly called in this country the French and Indian war, though living far distant from the principal theater of action, they rendered valuable service to the French. It is said that even on the farthest shores of Lake Superior, the wigwams of Indian braves were garnished with English scalps.

The Grand Traverse country came properly within the territory over which the mission at St. Ignace essayed to establish politico ecclesiastical control For two years after the establishment of the mission, Marquette was its animating spirit Popular belief credits him with having preached the gospel to the Ottawas along the eastern shore of Lake Michigan, but is not sustained by the record There is no evidence that he ever visited the beautiful wilderness country bordering on Grand Traverse and Little Traverse bays, or that he even coasted along the shore It is probable that his arduous duties at the mission left no time for extended journeys, and that he found ample opportunity for the fullest exercise of his persuasive powers on the residents and visitors of St Ignace

With Marquette it had long been a cherished project to visit the great river of the west, the Mississippi, wonderful accounts of which he had received, while at St. Esprit, from the Illinois and the Sioux, who visited him there. When, after two years' residence at St. Ignace, he was permitted to set out on his tour of discovery, in company with Joliet, he passed westward to Green Bay, and then to the Mississippi by way of the Fox and Wisconsin rivers Returning, he passed up the Illinois and Des Plaines rivers, crossed the portage to the Chicago, and from the mouth of that stream coasted along the western shore of the lake to Green Bay After spending the winter and summer there, he set out on a visit to the Illinois, taking the route of the western shore of the lake and the portage to the Des Plaines On his return, in the spring of 1675, he started to coast for the first time along the eastern shore of the lake A disease from which he had long been a sufferer, assumed increased violence, and it soon became evident that he could not long survive At the mouth of a little river, supposed to be somewhere north of the stream that bears his name, he peacefully passed away, and was buried by his faithful attendants, Pierre and Jacques, who then pursued their lonely journey to St. Ignace. A year afterwards, a party of Ottawas returning from their annual winter hunt, opened the grave, washed and dried the bones, enclosed them in a box of birch bark, and carried them to St Ignace, where they were received with solemn ceremony, and buried beneath the floor of the little chapel of the mission

It is possible that some devoted and adventurous missionary, burning with a desire to promote the spiritual welfare of the Ottawas of the Grand Traverse country, had visited them in their own vil lages, or that some trader, bent on schemes of profit, had coasted along its western border, or even penetrated the interior, previous to the death of Marquette, but, if so, there is no record of it. As far as we know, Pierre and Jacques, lonely and sorrowful, returning in their canoe to St. Ignace, were the first white men to look upon the placid waters of the two beautiful bays, one of which gives its name to the country. The next was La Salle's lieutenant, Henri de Tonty, who, with a party of men, passed southward along the shore, late in the autumn of 1679, and, after great hardship and suffering, joined his commander at St. Joseph.

Since the death of Marquette, nearly a century had rolled away, when the stirring events of Pontiac's war furnished material for an interesting chapter of the history of what was then the northwestern wilderness. Some of those events fall properly within the scope of the present narrative.

In the Grand Traverse country and the region adjacent, some important changes had taken place. A military post had been established at Mackinaw, not on the island of that name, but on the south side of the Straits, at the place which, since the military occupation of the island, has been known as Old Mackinaw. Around the fort had grown up a little French village. It is said there were thirty families living within the palisade, and as many more in the immediate vicinity. The Hurons had left St. Ignace, and settled at Detroit and Sandusky, where they had taken the name of Wyandots. The mission had been transferred from St. Ignace to L'Arbre Croche, (The Crooked Tree,) south of the Straits. L'Arbre Croche seems to have been used by the French as a general name for the Ottawa settlements along the shore of Lake Michigan, in the western part of what now constitutes the county of Emmet. The village of L'Arbre Croche proper, so named from a crooked pine tree, a conspicuous and convenient landmark for the voyageurs coasting in their canoes along the shore, was on the site of Middle Village of the present day. Another landmark, conspicuous to the hardy voyageurs of those days, was a huge cross, of cedar timber, standing on the brow of the bluff, at what is now, from the circumstance, called Cross Village. Whether it was erected by Father Junois, or some one who preceded him, is not known. By whomsoever erected, it has stood there till the present day, being repaired or renewed by the willing hands of the Catholic Ottawas, when natural decay made repair or renewal necessary.

The Ottawas of L'Arbre Croche, under their head chief, Ne-saw-kee, could muster two hundred and fifty warriors. Many of them were nominal Catholics. Profiting by the instruction of the missionaries, they had made some advancement in civilization, and cultivated the ground to a greater extent than formerly. *

South of L'Arbre Croche, in the western part of the Michigan peninsula, there were other settlements of Ottawas, and there was a strong band in the vicinity of Detroit, under the immediate chieftianship of the renowned Pontiac.

The principal village of the Chippewas in the northern part of the peninsula, was on Mackinac island. The village contained a hundred warriors. There was another smaller village at Thunder Bay, where dwelt their chief, Minavavana. There were also numerous settlements of the Chippewas in the Saginaw valley and on Grand River.

A part of the Wyandots, as we have already seen, were living at Detroit, and the Pottawattamies occupied the southwestern portion of the peninsula. Theoretically, the peninsula, or, at least, the northern part of it, belonged to the Ottawas and Chippewas, the former claiming the western and the latter the eastern portion, the boundary between them being an imaginary line drawn due south from the fort at Mackinaw.

At the close of the French and Indian war, in accordance with the terms of capitulation agreed to by the French at Montreal, all the military posts of the northwestern wilderness passed into the hands of the English. The Indians throughout the region were the enemies of the English and the firm friends of the French. It was with ill concealed displeasure that they saw the English come among them. The haughty and sometimes brutal treatment received from the latter, so different from the easy familiarity and kindness of the French, instead of tending to allay the irritation, had only the effect of increasing it. The first English traders at Mackinaw, who came after the removal of the French garrison and before the English troops arrived, ventured there at their peril. They succeeded in propitiating the Chippewas, but the Ottawas of L'Arbre Croche, a strong body of whom were at Mackinaw, were bent on mischief. The traders saved their goods, and perhaps their lives, only by arming their followers, barricading themselves in a house, and holding the Ottawas at bay, till the arrival of the troops assured some degree of security.

Pontiac, an Ottawa by birth or adoption, having won distinction at the head of a numerous body of his braves at the memorable battle of the Monongabela, contributing not a little to the defeat of Braddock's army, now smarting under wrongs both fancied and real, and foreseeing the probable ruin of his people before the increasing strength of the English, conceived the bold plan of cutting off all the frontier military posts, almost at a single blow. So well were the arrangements of the wily chieftain carried out that, in a short time, with the exception of the garrison at Detroit, not a British soldier remained in the region of the great lakes.

The fall of Mackinaw, next to Detroit the most important post in the western country, has been a theme of thrilling interest both to the historian and the writer of romance. In the events grouped around the tragic fate of the garrison, the people of the region the history of which we are endeavoring to trace bore a conspicuous part.

When, towards the end of May, 1763, the Chippewas of Mackinaw heard that Pontiac had already struck Detroit, they at once resolved on the immediate destruction of the English at the fort. Their number had recently been largely increased by the arrival of several bands from other localities. Though confederate with the Ottawas of L'Arbre Croche, they determined to proceed independently of the latter, securing all the plunder and glory to themselves.

It was the fourth of June, the birthday of King George. The Chippewas came to the fort, inviting the officers and men to come out and witness a game of baggattaway, their favorite ball-play, which had been arranged between them and the Sacs, several bands of whom, from the Wisconsin River, were encamped in the vicinity. The unsuspecting commander allowed the gates to be thrown wide open, and some of the soldiers went out to watch the game. The Indian women collected near the entrance, each with a weapon concealed under her blanket. When the excitement of the game had apparently reached its height, the ball received a blow that sent it over the palisade, into the area of the fort. It seemed an accident, but was really a well executed part of the plan of attack. In an instant there was a rush of players through the gateway, as if to recover the ball, but, as they passed the women, each snatched a weapon, and fell upon the nearest unsuspecting and defenseless Englishman. The bloody work was quickly completed, and a general cry was raised of "All is finished." There were at the fort thirty-four officers and soldiers, constituting the garrison, and four traders.

Of these, one officer, fifteen soldiers, and one trader were killed. The others were made prisoners. Of the prisoners, five soldiers were soon afterwards killed by an infuriated brave who had not been present at the assault, and took this method of expressing his approval of what had been done, and of his hatred of the English.

It is uncertain what would have been the fate of the remaining prisoners, had there been no check to the doings of the Chippewas. Probably most of them would have met death by torture. Their lives had not been spared from motives of humanity or clemency. The French had looked coolly on, neither helping the Indians nor offering protection to the English. The latter, however, found a friend in Father Jonois, the Catholic missionary at L'Arbre Croche. But by far the most effectual aid came from the incensed Ottawas. Confederates of the Chippewas, it was their right to be consulted in matters of such moment as the destruction of the English, or, at least, to be invited to join in the execution of the project. Regarding themselves as slighted and wronged, if not insulted, they resolved to revenge themselves by taking the control of matters into their own hands.

A party of seven Chippewas, with four prisoners, started in a canoe for the Isles du Castor, (Beaver Islands.) When about eighteen miles on their way, an Ottawa came out of the woods and accosted them, inquiring the news, and asking who were their prisoners. As the conversation continued, the canoe came near the shore, where the water was shallow, when a loud yell was heard, and a hundred Ottawas, rising from among the trees and bushes, rushed into the water, and seized the canoe and prisoners. The astonished Chippewas remonstrated in vain. The four Englishmen were led in safety to the shore. The Ottawas informed them that their captors were taking them to the Isles du Castor merely to kill and eat them, which was probably not far from the truth. The four prisoners soon found themselves afloat in an Ottawa canoe, and on their way back to Mackinaw, accompanied by a flotilla of canoes, bearing a great number of Ottawa warriors.

Arrived at Mackinaw, the Ottawas, fully armed, filed into the fort, and took possession of it. A council of the two tribes followed, in which the wounded feelings of the Ottawas were somewhat soothed by a liberal present of plunder, taken from the whites. The prisoners seem to have been divided, the Ottawas, because they were the stranger party, or for other reasons, being allowed to keep the greater number. The Ottawas soon after returned to L'Arbre Croche, taking with them Capt. Etherington, Lieut. Leslie, and eleven men. They were disarmed, but, probably through the influence of Father Jonois, treated kindly. Father Jonois performed a journey to Detroit in their behalf, bearing a request to Major Gladwyn for assistance, but that officer, beleaguered by a horde of savages, could do nothing.

In the mean time, Capt. Etherington, had found means to communicate with Lieut. Gorell, commanding the little garrison at Green Bay, requesting him to come with his command immediately to L'Arbre Croche. Gorell had the fortune to secure the good will of the Menomonies, ninety of whom volunteered for an escort. As the fleet of canoes on the way approached the Isles du Castor, warning was received that the Chippewas were lying in wait to intercept them. Immediately the Menomonies raised the war song, and stripped themselves for battle. The alarm, however, proved to be false. When the party reached L'Arbre Croche, they were received with honor, and presented the pipe of peace. After a series of councils, to which the Chippewa chiefs were invited, the latter reluctantly consented not to obstruct the passage of the soldiers to Montreal. Accordingly, on the eighteenth of July, the English, escorted by a fleet of Indian canoes, left L'Arbre Croche, and, going by way of the Ottawa River, reached Montreal the thirteenth of August.

* Parkman, in his History of the Conspiracy of Pontiac says that the name of the Ottawa chief at L'Arbre Croche has not survived in history or tradition. This is a mistake. His name, Nee-saw-kee is familiar to the Ottawas of to-day. His grandson, Nee-saw-wa-quat, a chief of the Little Traverse Indians died in 1857. M. L. L.

CHAPTER IV.

The Period Following Pontiac's War—The War of 1812—Military Operations on the Island of Mackinac—Indian Barbarities—Golden Age of the Ottawas of L'Arbre Croche—Extent of their Settlements—Indian Houses—Gardens—Hunting Grounds—The Jesuits Again—Churches Built.

From the massacre at Mackinac in 1763 up to the close of the war of 1812, a period of fifty-two years, we are able to gather from history and tradition only meager accounts of events occurring strictly within the limits of the Grand Traverse country. It was not at any time the theater of active war. The Ottawas were still the only inhabitants, except here and there an adventurous fur trader, or possibly a zealous Roman Catholic missionary.

That the Ottawas of L'Arbre Croche were concerned, directly or indirectly, in most of the Indian troubles of the northwestern frontier, occurring during the period alluded to, scarcely admits of a doubt. They were probably represented at the grand Indian council held near the mouth of Detroit River, in 1786. Some of their warriors, no doubt, were present at the battles in which Harmer and St. Clair were defeated, and some of their braves may have fallen before Wayne's victorious army, on the banks of the Maumee. One of their noted chiefs, Saw-gaw-kee, a son of the former head chief Nee-saw-kee, was a firm believer in the Shawnee prophet Waw-wa-gish-e-maw, or, as he is called by the historians, Elkswatawa. It does not appear that either Tecumseh or the the prophet visited L'Arbre Croche in person, but the influence of the prophet was sufficient to induce a deputation of Ottawas from that vicinity to visit the distant Indian villages on Lake Superior, with a message he professed to have received from the Great Spirit, intended to rouse them against the Americans.

When, in 1812, war was declared between the United States and Great Britain, Capt. Roberts, commanding the British post on St. Joseph's Island, was able in a short time to gather round him a thousand Indian warriors, for the capture of the American fort on the island of Mackinac. It is probable that nearly the whole force of the Ottawa warriors of L'Arbre Croche and the scattered bands around Grand Traverse Bay, was engaged in that enterprise. The affair ended in the complete success of the British, happily without the shedding of blood. Two years later, when the Americans under Col. Croghan, attempted to retake the fort, they were foiled mainly by the large force of Indians the British commander had again been able to gather to his standard. In this attempt the Americans suffered severe loss. The most shocking barbarities were practiced on the bodies of the slain. They were literally cut to pieces by their savage conquerors. Their hearts and livers were taken out, and cooked and eaten, and that too, it is said, even in the quarters of the British officers. More than forty years afterwards, when the Indians had become friendly towards the Americans, and the settlements of the latter had reached the Grand Traverse country, Asa-bun, an Indian of Old Mission, used to be pointed out as one who had been seen running about with a human heart in his hands, which he was devouring. Another, a chief by the name of Aish-qua gwon-a-ba, was credited by the settlers, whether justly or not, with keeping a number of scalps, the trophies of his prowess at Mackinac, carefully hidden away in a certain trunk.

In reviewing the history of the Indian tribes of the United States, one can not avoid the conclusion that the greatest hindrance to the increase of population, and, indirectly, to the development of an indigenous civilization, was not so much the privations incident to a peaceful savage state as to the destruction of life by constantly recurring wars. There seems little doubt that if the number of deaths by violence during a given time could be ascertained, it would be found not to fall far below the number of births for the same period. This remark applies more especially to the Indians as the Europeans found them; not to those of the present time, where whites and Indians live in mingled or adjacent communities, in the border settlements. The sudden partial transition from their mode of life to that of their white neighbors and the adoption of many of the worst vices of the white men with few of their virtues, are doing more to hasten the extinction of the race than was done by all the Indian wars of which we have any knowledge.

If, as their tradition asserts, the Ottawas were at the height of their power and glory at the time of Pontiac's war, a later period was the golden age of those at L'Arbre Croche, with reference to the prosperity that comes from peaceful pursuits.

At the close of the war of 1812, the occupation of the warrior passed away. Quarrels with their Indian neighbors of the south and west, and with the Iroquois of the east, had already ceased. Thenceforth there was no opportunity to take an enemy's scalp. The arts of war gave place to the peaceful pursuits of savage life. There followed as much prosperity as savage life improved by the first dawnings of civilization, in a country well fitted by nature for the habitation of a people in just that stage of advancement, was capable of producing. The lakes, streams, and forests, with their cultivated gardens of no mean extent, supplied an abundance of food; their peltries, bartered at Mackinac, procured various articles of comfort and luxury. The baleful effects of fire-water were yet but seldom felt; the ruinous influence of vicious white men had not yet begun to warp the Indian character. The concurrent testimony of witnesses still living goes to show that, previous to the time when the first adventurous white men erected their cabins in the Grand Traverse country, there was a degree of physical comfort, moral culture, and social and domestic happiness among the Indians far exceeding what the observation of a more recent period would would lead one to believe. Their condition was much better than that of the ordinary American savage of the average historical writer.

Their principal and most permanent settlements were at Cross Village, Middle Village, Seven Mile Point, and Little Traverse; but between the first and last of these places, wigwams, singly and in groups, were scattered at intervals all along the shore. A few families had their home at Bear Creek, on the south side of Little Traverse Bay. There were gardens on the height of land, a mile or more back from the shore, not far south of the present village of Norwood, and a camping place, frequently occupied, on the shore. There were gardens on the peninsula in Grand Traverse Bay and a village at Old Mission. West of the bay, a small band had their home on the point afterwards known as New Mission, and another on the shore of Lake Michigan, at or near the site of the present village of Leland.

Their dwellings were of various sizes and shapes, and were constructed of a variety of materials. The most substantial and permanent, consisted of a frame of cedar poles, covered with cedar bark. One of these, called o-maw-gay-ko-gaw-mig, was square or oblong, with perpendicular walls, and a roof with a slope in opposite directions, like the simplest form of frame houses among white men. Another, the ke-no-day-we-gaw-mig, had perpendicular end walls, but the side walls in the upper part were bent inward, meeting along the middle line, thus forming the roof in the shape of a broad arch. Houses of this kind were sometimes fifty or sixty feet long, and had places for three fires. The ne-saw-wah-e-gun and the wah-ge-no-gawn, were light but very serviceable houses, consisting of frames of poles covered with mats. The former was cone-shaped; the latter regularly convex at the top. The mats, ten or twelve feet long and three or four wide, were made of the long, slender leaves of the cat-tail flag, (*Typha,*) properly cured and carefully sewed together. When suitably adjusted on the frames, with the edges lapping, they made a serviceable roof. Being light, and, when rolled up, not inconvenient to carry, they were used for traveling tents. Houses of mats were often used for winter residence in the woods, and were not uncomfortable. The ah-go-beem-wah-gun was a small summer house for young men, usually constructed of cedar bark, on an elevated platform resting on posts, reached only by ascending a ladder. Winter houses in the woods, were sometimes built of slabs, or planks, of split timber. They were often cone-shaped, and were made tight and warm. They were called pe-no-gawn.* In the woods, even in winter, they sometimes lived in temporary wigwams of evergreen boughs, which they managed to make comfortable.

The Indian houses were without windows. The fire was built upon the ground, in the center if the lodge was small; or there was a row of fires down the middle line, in a long ke-no-day-we-gaw-mig. A hole in the roof, above each fire, served for the escape of the smoke. A raised platform, a foot or a foot and a half high, covered with mats, along the sides of the room, served for a seat during the day and for a sleeping place at night. The mats, some of them beautifully ornamented with colors, were made of rushes found growing in shallow lakes, ingeniously woven together with twine manufactered from the bark of the slippery elm.

In their gardens they cultivated corn, pumpkins, beans, and potatoes. Apple trees, the seed for which was originally obtained from the whites—either the Jesuit missionaries or the fur traders—were planted in every clearing. Wild fruits, especially choice varieties of wild plums, were grown from seed introduced from their distant southern hunting grounds. At the time of the present writing, fruit trees of their planting are found growing wild in the young forests that have sprung up on abandoned fields. The gardens were frequently some distance from the villages. The owners resorted to them at the proper season, to do the necessary work, living for the time in portable lodges or in temporary structures erected for the occasion.

Though they hunted more or less at all times, winter was the season devoted more especially to that pursuit. Then the greater part of the population left the villages, and scattered through the forest. The chain of inland lakes in Antrim county, having its outlet at Elk Rapids, was a favorite resort, on account of the facilities for fishing, as well as for hunting and trapping. Many plunged into the deeper solitudes of the forest, and fixed their winter abode on the Manistee, the Muskegon, or the Sauble. Others embarked in canoes, and coasted along Lake Michigan to its southern extremity, from there making their way to the marshes of the Kankakee and the hunting grounds of northern Indiana and Illinois. Several families had their favorite winter camping place on the northeastern shore of Boardman Lake, within the present corporate limits of

Traverse City. Here the women and children remained, while the hunters made long trips in the woods, returning to camp, with the spoils of the chase, several times during the winter. One principal advantage of the location, was the abundance of pickerel in the lake—an abundance that seems fabulous to the white fisherman of the present day. They were caught with spears, through holes cut in the ice, and were an important addition to the winter supply of food.

In spring, traders came from Mackinac, and sometimes from other places, to barter goods for furs. Not infrequently, however, the Indian hunter, accompanied by his wife and children, preferred to visit the center of trade with his peltries, in person. Then, sometimes, there was a brief but fearful indulgence of the Indian's appetite for strong drink. At home sobriety usually prevailed.

How long the Jesuits continued active work at L'Arbre Croche after the time of Father Jonois, is not known. There seems to have been a long period during which the Indians were left to themselves. The great cedar cross remained standing on the brow of the bluff at Cross Village, a memorial of the devotion and zeal of the early missionaries, but their teachings had been forgotten. It is said that when the ground was afterwards re-occupied, only one Indian could be found who could prove himself a christian by making the sign of the cross.

In 1825, the Catholics sent a missionary to re-occupy the long-abandoned field. Seven Mile Point was chosen as a center of operations, and a church was immediately built. The building was about twenty feet by forty in size, constructed, like the better class of Indian houses, of the most suitable materials readily obtainable—cedar timbers for the frame, and for the covering cedar bark. Seven Mile Point not proving a satisfactory location, in 1827 the mission was moved to Little Traverse. At the latter place a church, of cedar logs, was built the following year. About the same time, a similar church was built at Cross Village. The work of the missionaries was successful, a considerable number of Indians readily becoming Catholics.

About 1839 and 1840, the population was greatly diminished by a sudden exodus, caused by distrust of the Indian policy of the United States government. Fearing to be forcibly removed beyond the Mississippi, fully one half of the Indians, it is said, took refuge in Canada.

In the preceding pages, the author has endeavored to narrate succinctly the events known to have occurred in the Grand Traverse region while it was yet a strictly Indian country, and to portray truthfully the situation as it was when the first adventurous white men essayed to establish permanent homes within its borders. In those that follow, it will be our duty to trace, as faithfully as the material at hand will enable us to do, the varied fortunes of the early pioneers.

*All these names of Indian houses are pronounced with the accent on the last syllable. In Indian words, g always has the hard sound.
M. L. L.

CHAPTER V.

The two Missionaries—Consultation With the Indians—Site for Mission Chosen at Elk River—The Track of a White Man's Horse—House Built—Sorrowful News—Visit From Indian Agent—Removal to Mission Harbor—School Opened—A Mixture of Races—Two Civilizing Agencies.

In May, 1839, a Mackinaw boat, with four men at the oars and two passengers, rounded the point that, jutting out from the peninsula into the east arm of Grand Traverse Bay, forms the little cove known as Mission Harbor. The passengers were Rev. John Fleming and Rev. Peter Dougherty, missionaries of the Presbyterian Board. They had spent the previous winter at Mackinac, and now came to the country of Grand Traverse Bay, which to the white man was then almost a *terra incognita*, for the purpose of establishing a mission among the Indians. They had brought supplies from Mackinac, including doors and windows for a house.

On all sides the country was seen in its primeval wildness and beauty. The shores were fringed to the water's edge with foliage of various shades of green. In the crystal flood on which their frail craft floated, the shore scenes were reflected, as in a mirror of liquid silver. Of the presence of man there were no signs visible, save a few bark wigwams, in a narrow break in the fringe of forest, from one of which a thin column of blue smoke curled lazily upward.

The adventurers landed, near where the wharf has since been built. They found only one Indian in the village. He informed them that the band were encamped at the mouth of the river, on the opposite side of the bay. The Indian made a signal with a column of smoke, which had the effect of bringing over a canoe, full of young men, who came to inquire who the strangers were and what was wanted.

The next day, a chief, with a number of men, came over. Messrs. Fleming and Dougherty informed him that they had come, by direction of their agent at Mackinac, and by permission of their great father, the president, to establish a school among them for the instruction of their children, and to teach them a knowledge of the Savior. The reply was that the head chief, with his men, would come in a few days, and then they would give an answer.

On the arrival of the head chief, Aish-qua gwon-a-ba,* a council was held, for the purpose of considering the proposal of the missionaries. At its close, Messrs. Fleming and Dougherty were informed that the Indians had decided to unite the bands living in the vicinity, and locate near the river, on the east side of the bay. If the missionaries would go with them, they would show them the intended location of their new villages and gardens, so that they could select a good central site for their dwelling and school.

About the 20th of the month, the white men, in their boat, accompanied by a fleet of Indian canoes, crossed the bay, landing at the mouth of the river, where the village of Elk Rapids is now situated. The Indians proposed to divide their settlement into two villages. After looking over the ground, the missionaries chose a location, something more than a quarter of a mile from the river, on the south side.

The day after the missionaries landed at Elk River, the Indians came to their tent in great excitement, saying there were white men in the country. They had seen a horse's track, which contained the impression of a shoe. Their ponies were not shod. Shortly after, a white man came into the camp. He proved to be a packman, belonging to a company of United States surveyors, who were at work on the east side of Elk and Torch lakes. He had lost his way, and wanted a guide, to pilot him back to his company. An Indian went with him several miles, returning in the afternoon with the man's hatchet in his possession, having taken it on the refusal of the latter to pay him for his services. The next day, the whole company of surveyors came in, and encamped for a short time at the river.

Immediately after deciding upon the location, Messrs. Fleming and Dougherty commenced cutting logs for the construction of a dwelling and schoolhouse. Hard work and the discomforts of a wilderness, the latter of which were doubly annoying to the inexperienced missionaries, filled up the next few days. Among other evils from which they could not escape, the sand flies were a terrible torment. Finally, the body of the house was raised, the doors and windows brought from Mackinac were put in their places, and the gables and roof were covered with sheets of cedar bark, purchased of the Indians.

Then an unexpected blow fell upon the devoted missionaries, crushing the hopes and changing the life prospects of one, and plunging both into deep sorrow. A messenger came from Mackinac, with intelligence that Mr. Fleming's wife had suddenly died, at that place. The bereaved husband, with the four men who had come with them, immediately embarked in their boat for Mackinac. He never returned to the mission. Mr. Dougherty was left alone. With the exception of the surveyors at work somewhere in the interior, he was the only white person in the country.

After the departure of his comrade, Mr. Dougherty, with the assistance of Peter Greensky, the interpreter, busied himself with the work of finishing the house, and clearing away the brush in the vicinity. Once or twice the cedar bark of the roof took fire from the stove pipe, but fortunately the accident was discovered before any serious damage was done. The old chief Aish-qua-gwon-a-ba and his wife, perhaps to show their friendliness and make it less lonely for the missionary, came and staid with him several days in his new house.

About the 20th of June, Henry R. Schoolcraft, Indian agent at Mackinac, arrived, in a small vessel, accompanied by his interpreter, Robert Graverat, and Isaac George as Indian blacksmith. From information received at Mackinac, Mr. Schoolcraft had come impressed with the notion that the harbor near the little island, on the west side of the peninsula, (Bowers' Harbor,) would be a suitable point at which to locate the blacksmith, carpenter, and farmer, that, by the terms of the recent treaty, the government was obligated to furnish for the benefit of the Indians. Looking over the ground, and consulting the wishes of the Indians, he finally came to the conclusion that Mission Harbor was a more suitable place. Accordingly Mr. George was left to commence operations, and Mr. Schoolcraft returned to Mackinac.

Soon after the departure of Mr. Schoolcraft, Ah-go-sa, the chief at Mission Harbor, accompanied by the principal men of his band, visited Mr. Dougherty, saying that most of the Indians at that place were unwilling to move over to the east side of the bay, and offering to transport him and his goods across to Mission Harbor, and furnish him a house to live in, if he would take up his residence with them. Convinced that, all things considered, the harbor was a more elegible site for the mission, Mr. Dougherty at once accepted the proposal. Leaving what things were not needed for immediate use, and loading the balance in Indian canoes, he was ferried across the bay to the scene of his future labors—the place where he had first landed, not many weeks before, and which, under the name of Old Mission, has since become famous as a center of development of the agricultural interests of northwestern Michigan.

The next day, arrangements were made for opening a school, with interpreter Greensky as teacher, in the little bark wigwam that the Indians had vacated for Mr. Dougherty's use. Then followed a hard summer's work. Mr. Dougherty and Mr. George commenced the construction of a house for themselves. The logs for the building were cut close along the border of the harbor, floated to a point near where they were to be used, and then dragged to the site of the building by hand. Of course, the work could never have been accomplished without the aid of the Indians. The house was covered with shingles, such as the two inexperienced men were able to make, and a few boards brought from Mackinac with their fall supplies. The building was so nearly completed that the men found themselves comfortably housed before winter fairly set in.

Desiring not to be left alone, while the Indians were absent on their annual winter hunt, Mr. Dougherty induced the chief Ah-go-sa and two others, with their families, to remain till sugar-making time in the spring, by offering to help them put up comfortable houses for winter. There is some uncertainty about the style of these houses. We are informed that the offer was, to help them put up log or slab shanties. If finally the latter was determined on, the slabs must have been rough planks, split out of suitable logs with beetle and wedges, and smoothed with an ax. Whether the shanties were built cone-shaped or not, by placing the planks on end in a circle, with the tops inclining inward, like the Ottawa pe-bo-ne-gawn, does not appear. Before they were finished, the weather had become so cold that boiling water had to be used to thaw the clay for plastering the chinks in the walls. Mr. Dougherty's house stood on the bank of the harbor, east of the site afterwards occupied by the more commodious and comfortable Mission house. The chief's shanty was built on the south side of the little lake lying a short distance northwest of the harbor. The cabins for the other two Indian families were located a little way south of where the mission church was afterwards built.

In the fall, Mr. John Johnston arrived at the Mission, having come by appointment of Mr. Schoolcraft, to reside there as Indian farmer. During the winter, the mission family consisted of the four men—Dougherty, George, Greensky, and Johnston. Mr. Johnston had brought with him a yoke of oxen, for use in Indian farming. There was no fodder in the country, unless he may have brought a little with him. Be that as it may, he found it necessary to browse his cattle all winter.

In the spring of 1840, the log house which had been built at Elk Rapids the previous year was taken down, and the materials were transported across the bay and used in the construction of a schoolhouse and wood-shed. Until the mission church was built, a year or two after, the schoolhouse was used for holding religious services, as well as for school.

In the fall of 1841, besides Indian wigwams, there were five buildings at the mission—the school-house and four dwellings. All were built of logs, and all, except Mr. Dougherty's house, were covered with cedar bark. The dwellings were occupied by Mr. Dougherty, missionary, Henry Bradley, mission teacher, John Johnston, Indian farmer, and David McGulpin, assistant farmer. Mr. George was still there, and there had been another addition to the community in the person of George Johnston, who had come in the capacity of Indian carpenter. As regards race, the little community, the only representative of christian civilization in the heart of a savage wilderness, was somewhat mixed. John Johnston was a half Indian, with a white wife; McGulpin was a white man, with an Indian wife. All the others, except Greensky the interpreter, were whites.

As the little community represented two races, so also it represented two distinct agencies, working in harmony for the improvement of the physical, intellectual, and moral condition of the Indians. The blacksmith, carpenter, and farmer were employes of the United States government, appointed by the Indian agent at Mackinac, and subject to his control. It was their duty to instruct the Indians in the simpler and more necessary arts of civilization. The missionary and his assistants, the interpreter and teacher, were employed by the Presbyterian Board, and supported by missionary funds. The only assistance they received from the government was an allowance for medicines dispensed to the Indians.

*This name ould be accented on the fourth syllable, giving the a the long sound. M. L. L.

CHAPTER VI.

Mrs. Dougherty—The Dame Family—Lewis Miller—The Mission School—First Frame Building—Church Built—First White Settlers—Scattering of the Indians—Removal of the Mission—Manual Labor School—The Mission Discontinued.

In the fall of 1841, an event occurred that must have created a little flutter of excitement in the quiet and isolated settlement at the Mission. It was on a pleasant morning in September that the little schooner Supply came into the harbor, having on board as passengers, besides Mr. and Mrs. Dougherty and their infant daughter Henrietta, two persons whose names have since become intimately associated with the events of the early history of the Grand Traverse country. Those two persons were Deacon Joseph Dame and Lewis Miller.

We are not informed at what time Mrs. Dougherty first came to the mission. On the occasion referred to, she and her husband were returning from a visit to Mackinac, where they had gone some time previously, in order to be within reach of suitable assistance at the period of Mrs. Dougherty's confinement.

Deacon Dame had received the appointment of Indian farmer, as successor to John Johnston, and came to enter upon the duties of his office. With him were Mrs. Dame, their eldest son, Eusebius F., and two daughters, Almira and Mary. Another daughter, Olive M., came the following year.

Lewis Miller was an orphan, left alone to make his way in the world. His birthplace was Waterloo, Canada West; the date of his birth September 11th, 1824. The year 1839 found him in Chicago. From that City, in 1840, he made his way to Mackinac. Here he became acquainted with the Dames. A strong friendship grew up between him and Mr. and Mrs. Dame. When, in 1841, Deacon Dame received his appointment as Indian farmer, and commenced preparations for removal to his new field of labor, Miller, then seventeen years of age, resolved to accompany him, more for the novelty of the thing than from any definite purpose with reference to the future. Except the children who came with their parents, he was the first white settler in the Grand Traverse country who did not come in consequence of an appointment from the Presbyterian Board or the Mackinac Indian agency.

Eusebius and Almira Dame were in their teens; Mary was younger. During some portion of the time for the next year or two, the three, with young Miller, were pupils in the mission school. A true picture of that school, could one have been handed down to us, would be a picture of absorbing interest. Except the Catholic mission school at Little Traverse, it was the first in the Grand Traverse country.

Imperfectly we may picture to ourselves the small, roughly built, log schoolhouse, with its covering of cedar bark; a few Indian children, half dressed, according to civilized notions, looking with wondering eyes upon the mysterious characters of the books put into their hands; the four white pupils, conscious of the disadvantage of isolation from the great world of learning and refinement, yet ambitious to excel; the patient, hopeful teacher, sowing the seeds of truth according to the divine injunction, not knowing "whether shall prosper, either this or that, or whether both shall be alike good." Then we may picture the surroundings—the scattered group of log houses and Indian wigwams; the forest, lovely in the tender green of early summer or gorgeous in gay autumn colors; the bay, placid and shimmering in the golden sunlight or lashed into foam by the furious north wind; the Indians, idle and listless, arrayed in scanty costume or decked with a profusion of savage finery; the few white people, intent on the labors of their several stations and apparently content in the discharge of duty, yet sometimes casting regretful glances backward to other days and other homes. And we may wonder how, when the Indians had gone to their hunting grounds, and winter had come down from the north in all his fury, shutting them up within the limits of their little settlement almost as effectively as locking them in a prison, they managed to keep cheerful during the dreary, monotonous months, till the opening spring permitted the re-establishment of communication with the outside world.

About 1842, the construction of a more commodious dwelling and a mission church was commenced by Mr Dougherty. The dwelling, since known as the mission house, was the first frame building erected in the Grand Traverse country. The church had solid walls, of hewn cedar timbers laid one upon another and kept in place by the ends being fitted into grooves in upright posts. The timbers were brought from the east side of the bay, in a huge log canoe, or dug out, called the Pe-to-be go, which was thirty feet long, and, it is said, was capable of carrying twenty barrels of flour. At the present writing, forty years after the completion of these structures, the mission house, enlarged and improved, is occupied as a dwelling by Mr. D. Rushmore. The church is owned by the Methodist Episcopal society of Old Mission, and is still used as a house of worship. The little log schoolhouse, in which Mr. Bradley taught Miller and the young Dames, in connection with his classes of Indian boys and girls, was accidentally burned several years ago.

During the next ten years, some changes occurred at the mission. Mr. Bradley as teacher was succeeded by a gentleman by the name of Whiteside. Not liking the position, Mr. Whiteside soon resigned, and was followed by Mr. Andrew Porter.

Changes were also made, from time to time, among the employes of the Indian agency. Some of them remained in the country, after their connection with the agency had terminated, and turned their attention to farming or other pursuits. Among such appear the names of John Campbell, Robert Campbell, Wm. R. Stone, and J. M. Pratt. Among the earlier settlers not connected with the mission or the agency, were H. K. Coles, John Swaney, and Martin S. Wait. O. P. Ladd and his brother in-law, Orlin Hughson, settled on the peninsula as early as 1850, but remained only two or three years. E. P. Ladd, having come on a visit to his sister, Mrs. Hughson, in May, 1852, was so well pleased with the country that he at once determined to make his home here. G. A. Craker arrived in April of the same year, and immediately hired out to Mr. Dougherty.

The little group of wigwams and log cabins at the harbor, had grown to a village of considerable size. The Indians had generally abandoned their early style of wigwams, and were living in houses built of hewn logs and whitewashed on the outside. Seen from a distance, the village presented a pretty and inviting appearance; a close inspection did not always confirm first impressions. According to their original custom, the Indians lived in the village, and cultivated gardens some distance away.

The gardens, or patches of cultivated ground, were of all sizes, from one acre to six. The Indians had no legal title to the soil. By the terms of treaty, the peninsula had been reserved for their exclusive occupation for a period of five years, and after that they were to be permitted to remain during the pleasure of the government. The period of five years had long since expired. Their landed property was held by sufferance, and was liable at any moment to be taken away. The project of removing them beyond the Mississippi was at one time seriously entertained by the government, or at least it was so understood. The prospect was not pleasing to the Indians. A deputation sent to examine their proposed new home in the west, reported unfavorably. They determined not to be removed, preferring to take refuge in Canada, as a large part of the Indian population of Emmet county had done several years before.

At this juncture, the adoption of the revised State constitution of 1850 made citizens of all civilized persons of Indian descent, not members of any tribe. Here was a way out of the difficulty. They could purchase land of the government, settle down upon it, and claim the protection of the State and the general government as citizens. The land on the peninsula was not yet in market; that on the west shore of the bay was. By the advice of Mr. Dougherty, several families agreed to set apart a certain amount, out of their next annual payment, for the purchase of land. A list of names was made, and the chief was authorized to receive the money from the agent at Mackinac, which he brought to Mr. Dougherty for safe keeping. Having made their selections, on the west side of the bay, some of their most trusty men were sent to the land office, at Ionia, the following spring, to make the purchase.

If the general government ever seriously entertained the project of removing the Indians of the Grand Traverse country beyond the Mississippi, it was abandoned, and several townships, in what are now the counties of Leelanaw, Charlevoix, and Emmet, were withdrawn from market and set apart as reservations for their benefit. Within the limits of these reservations, each head of a family and each single person of mature age was permitted to select a parcel of land, to be held for his own use, and eventually to become his property in fee simple.

As already indicated, the lands on the peninsula were not yet in market. The Indians held possession of considerable portions, but could give no legal title to the soil. They could, however, sell their possessory rights, and white men, recognizing the eligibility of the location for agricultural pursuits, were not backward in becoming purchasers, taking the chance of obtaining a title from the government at a future time.

The combined effect of the several circumstances narrated above, was to cause a gradual scattering of the Indians of the mission settlement. Those who had purchased land on the west side of the bay, removed to their new homes. Others removed to the lands they had selected in the reserved townships. Seeing that the Indian community at the mission would finally be broken up, Mr. Dougherty wisely concluded to change the location of the mission itself. Accordingly purchase was made of an eligible tract of land, suitable for a farm and manual labor school, on Mission Point, near the place now called Omena, in Leelanaw county, to which he removed early in the spring of 1852.

Considering the scattered condition and migratory habits of the Indians, it was thought that the most effective work for their christianization and civilization could be done by gathering the youth into one family, where they would be constantly and for a term of years under the direct supervision and influence of teachers. And then, a well managed industrial school, it was thought, could not fail to exert, in some degree, a beneficial influence on the parents and youth of the vicinity, who did not attend, by a practical exhibition of the advantages of education and industry. In this respect, the new location of the mission was well chosen, being in the vicinity of those families who had purchased land of the government, and who, it might reasonably be expected, would profit by its example.

Mission Point had been occupied by a band of Indians, called, from the name of their chief, Shawb-wah-sun's band, some of whose gardens were included in the tract purchased by Mr. Dougherty. There were apple trees growing there, at the time of the purchase, as large as a man's body. Tradition says that the band had inhabited the western shore of the bay for a long time, and had once been numerous and powerful.

The manual labor school was opened in the fall following the removal. The number of pupils was limited to fifty—twenty five of each sex. Young children were not received, except in one instance, when the rule was suspended in favor of two homeless orphans.

When received into the school, the pupils were first washed and clothed. The common clothing of both sexes consisted of coarse but decent and serviceable material. The boys were employed on the farm; the girls in housework and sewing. At five o'clock in the morning, the bell rang for all to rise. At six, it called all together for worship. Soon after worship, breakfast was served, the boys sitting at one table, the girls at another. After breakfast, all repaired to their daily labor, and worked till half past eight, when the school bell gave warning to assemble at the school-room. The boys worked under the supervision of Mr. Craker. Every boy had suitable tools assigned him, which he was required to care for and keep in their proper places. Mr. Craker kept the tools in order, so that they were always ready for use, and each boy could go to his work promptly. A considerable portion of the mission farm was cleared, and afterwards cultivated, by the labor of the boys. The girls were divided into classes, or companies, to each of which was assigned some particular department of domestic labor, changes being made weekly, so that all could be instructed in every department.

In the school-room were two teachers—one for the boys and another for the girls. Miss Isabella Morrison, of New Haven, Ct., was for many years the girls' teacher. After her resignation, the place was filled by Miss Catherine Gibson, till the mission was discontinued. Miss Gibson was from Pennsylvania. In the boys' department, the teachers were successively Miss Harriet Cowles, Miss Beach, Mr. John Porter, and Miss Henrietta Dougherty. Miss Cowles came from near Batavia, N. Y., Miss Beach from White Lake, N. Y., and Mr. Porter from Pennsylvania.

Concerning the mission, it only remains to mention, that the financial embarrassment of the Board, growing out of the war of the rebellion, necessitated the discontinuance of the work. The school was finally broken up, and the mission farm passed into other hands.

Looked at from the christian standpoint, the mission, seems to have been moderately successful. A good understanding was always maintained between the missionaries and the Indians. Mr. Dougherty testifies that the latter were uniformly kind. Both at Old Mission and Mission Point, a considerable number were hopefully converted.

CHAPTER VII.

Personal Incidents and Reminiscences—Wading the Boardman—A New Way to Dry a Shirt—Sleeping in Barrels—A Tribute to Mr. Dougherty—The Dougherty Family—Romance of the Early Days—The First Wedding—Bridal Trip in a Birch Canoe—Lewis Miller as an Indian Trader—Marriage at Mackinac and Tempestuous Voyage Home—"Where is the Town?"

During the period of Mr. Dougherty's residence at Old Mission, there being no physician in the country, he was often applied to for medicine and advice for the sick. On one occasion, after Mr. Boardman had established himself at the head of the bay, at the place where Traverse City now stands, he was called to prescribe for Mrs. Duncan, who was keeping the boarding-house at that place. He found Mrs. Duncan very sick. Two or three days after, not having heard from his patient in the interval, he became anxious for her safety, and resolved to get some information in regard to her condition, and to send a further supply of medicine, or repeat his visit.

There were some men from Boardman's establishment getting out timber at the harbor on the west side of the peninsula, (Bowers' Harbor,) which they were conveying home in a boat. Hoping to get th desired information from them, and to send the necessary medicine by their hand, he walked across the peninsula to their place of labor. The men had gone home with a cargo. Thinking he might get to Boardman's in time to return with them on their next trip, he started for the head of the bay on foot, making his way as rapidly as possible along the beach. There was no bridge over Boardman river near the boarding-house, and, on his arrival, the skiff used for crossing was on the other side. There was no time to lose. Not to be delayed, he quickly entered the stream, and waded across, the cold water coming up to his chin. Fortunately, he found his patient much improved; unfortunately, the boat in which he had hoped to return was already nearly out of sight, on its way back to the peninsula.

Mr. Dougherty would have been hospitably entertained, could he have been persuaded to remain, but he felt that he must return home. Not stopping to put on a dry suit that was offered him, he partook of a hasty lunch, and set out on his return. Some one set him across the river in the skiff. As soon as he was out of sight in the woods, he resolved to dry his clothes, without hindering himself in the journey. Taking off his shirt, he hung it on a stick carried in the hand, spreading it to the sun and air, as he walked rapidly along. The day was warm, and the sun shone brightly. When the shirt was partly dry, he exchanged it for his flannel, putting on the shirt, and hanging the flannel on the stick. It was near sundown when he reached home, thoroughly fatigued, but happy in the thought that his patient was getting well. The next day, he was so sore and stiff as to be scarcely able to move.

Some years later, after the removal of the mission to the west side of the bay, Mr. Dougherty had an adventure that may serve to illustrate the wild character of the country, and the shifts to which the settlers were sometimes reduced.

While seeking supplies for his school, one spring, he heard that a vessel, carrying a cargo of provisions, had been wrecked on the shore of Lake Michigan, somewhere south of Sleeping Bear Point, and that consequently there was flour for sale there at a reasonable price. In those days, the wrecking on the shore of a vessel with such a cargo, while it was, as now, a misfortune to the owners and underwriters, was not unfrequently a blessing of no small magnitude to the inhabitants. The captain of the unfortunate craft was usually willing and even anxious to sell, at a moderate price, such provisions as could be saved from the wreck, and the people were only too glad to buy.

Starting early one morning, Mr. Dougherty walked across the country, to the Indian village of Che-ma-go-bing, near the site of the present village of Leland. From Che-ma-go-bing he followed the shore round the bay since marked on the maps as Good Harbor, past the place afterwards called North Unity, and round the point separating Good Harbor from what was then known as Sleeping Bear Bay, but since called Glen Arbor Bay, his point of destination being the residence of John Lerue, who he knew lived on the shore somewhere in that region.

The walk was long and fatiguing. When the shades of evening fell upon the landscape, he had not reached Mr. Lerue's cabin. At ten o'clock he came to a small shed on the beach, where some cooper had been making barrels for the fishermen on the coast. It was now too dark to travel, and he resolved to pass the night there. The air was chilly, but everything was very dry, and he feared to make a fire, lest the shed should be burned. One less conscientious than Mr. Dougherty, and less careful of the rights of others, would not have hesitated for such a reason, but he preferred a night of discomfort to the risk of injuring a fellow-being. A backwoodsman of more experience would, no doubt, have found a method to make everything safe, while enjoying the luxury of a camp fire.

Looking about for the best means of protection from the cold, he found two empty barrels, each with a head out. It occurred to him that these might be converted into a sleeping apartment. It required some little ingenuity to get into both at once, but after considerable effort he succeeded. Bringing the second barrel so near that he could reach the open end, he worked his head and shoulders into the first, and placing his feet and legs in the second, drew it up as close to the first as possible. In telling the story years afterwards, Mr. Dougherty declared that he slept, and could not recollect his dreams, but, as his business was urgent, the luxury of his bed did not keep him long the next morning. He was out early, and soon found Mr. Lerue's house, which was not far off.

He now learned, what would have saved him a toilsome journey, had he known it a day earlier, that the flour had been removed to Northport, which was only a few miles from the mission. After breakfast, Mr. Lerue guided him across the point that separates the bays, and he set out for Northport. Arriving there after dark, he was disappointed with the information that the flour had all been sold. After a night's rest, not in barrels on the beach, he had no alternative but to return home empty-handed.

Mr. Dougherty was a graduate of Princeton theological seminary. He was a person of strong convictions, energetic and persevering in labor, in manner gentle and pleasing. His life work was well done. Blest with a companion of superior natural and educational endowments, and the sincerity, sweet disposition, and polished manners of the ideal christian lady, the social atmosphere of his home produced a healthful moral effect on all who came within the sphere of its influence. Mr. and Mrs. Dougherty were fortunate in their children, of whom there were nine—one son and eight daughters. Two of the daughters died in childhood. The other children grew up to be an honor to their parents and a blessing to the communities in which their lots were cast. At the proper age, most of them were sent east, for a few years, for the sake of the educational advantages that could not be had at home. The society of the early days of the Grand Traverse country was largely indebted to the Doughertys for the refinement that distinguished it from the coarseness too often found in border settlements.*

Those early days had their romance, as well as their stern realities of hardship and endurance. The first wedding in the Grand Traverse country would, no doubt, form a pleasing episode in the history we are tracing, were all the incidents of the affair placed at the disposal of some one capable of weaving them into shape with an artistic hand.

It has been already mentioned that Deacon Dame's oldest daughter, Olive M., came to Old Mission the next summer following the arrival of the family. She had passed the winter in Wisconsin, where she had been betrothed to Mr. Ansel Salisbury. In the fall after her arrival, Mr. Salisbury came to Old Mission to claim his bride.

Mr. Dougherty was anxious that the Indians of his flock should profit by acquaintance with the institutions of christian civilization. The opportunity to show them a form of marriage recognized by the white man's law and the church, was too important to let slip; consequently, by the consent of all parties, it was arranged that the ceremony should take place in public.

At a convenient hour in the morning, the little schoolhouse was filled with a mixed company of whites and Indians. There was no newspaper reporter present, to describe the trousseau of the bride or the costumes of distinguished guests. We must draw upon the imagination for a picture of the same. We see the bride in simple attire, as became the occasion and the surroundings. There are the Indian women, in their brightest shawls and elaborately beaded moccasins, and the Indian men, some of them clothed in a style only a degree or two removed from the most primitive undress, all looking gravely on, apparently unmoved, yet keenly observant of all that passes. The whites are dressed in their Sunday best, which, to tell the truth, is in most cases somewhat rusty, their hilarity scarcely veiled by the gravity inspired by the solemnity of the occasion. The hymeneal rite is simple and impressive—the more impressive from the simple earnestness of its administration. Then we see the group of friends on the shore, waving adieus amid smiles and tears, as the newly married couple float away in their canoe, on the bridal tour.

Mrs. Dame accompanied her daughter as far as Mackinac. The craft in which the company embarked, was a large birch bark canoe, navigated by four Indians. They proceeded directly across the bay to the east shore. There the Indians got out a long line manufactured from basswood bark, and running along the beach, towed the canoe rapidly after them. At night they had reached the mouth of Pine River, where they made their camp. The next morning, the Indians hoisted a large, square sail, and, running before a fair wind, they reached Mackinac at night. Mrs. Dame returned in the canoe, with the Indians, to Old Mission. Mr. and Mrs. Salisbury remained a few days at Mackinac, and then embarked on a steamboat for their home in Wisconsin.

It has already been stated that Lewis Miller came to Old Mission in company with the Dame family, more for the novelty of the thing than because of any definite plan for the future. At that time, the fur trade, having its center at Mackinac, was still profitable. When young Miller had been at the Mission about a year, he entered into an arrangement with Mr. Merrick, a merchant of Mackinac, to open trade with the Indians on the bay. Mr. Merrick was to furnish the goods; Miller to conduct the business. A wigwam, rented of an Indian, served for a storehouse at the Mission.

To carry on trade with the Indians successfully and profitably, involved a great deal of hard labor. Frequent journeys had to be made to Mackinac, and to various points along the shore, at all seasons of the year. When the lake was open, Indian canoes or Mackinac boats were used; when it was closed, there was no way but to travel on snowshoes, on the ice or along the beach.

The winter journeys were always attended with hardship; sometimes with danger. Mr. Miller was usually accompanied by a man in his employ, and not unfrequently by two—half-breeds or Indians. When overtaken by night, a camping place was selected on the shore, where there was plenty of fuel at hand, and where some thicket would, in a measure, break the fury of the wintry wind. With their snow shoes for shovels, the travelers cleared away the snow down to the surface of the ground—not an easy task when, as was sometimes the case, it was three feet or more in depth. Then evergreen boughs were set up around the cleared space, as a further protection from the wind, and a thick carpet of twigs was spread on the ground. A fire was built, the kettle hung above it, and tea made. After supper the tired wanderers, each wrapped in two or three Mackinac blankets, lay down to rest. On one of his journeys to Mackinac, in the depth of winter, Mr. Miller and his companions waded Pine river, where Charlevoix is now situated, both going and returning.

Stopping over at Little Traverse, when on a boat journey in December, Mr. Miller was informed by the Indians that a vessel had gone ashore, near the "Big Stone," on the south side of Little Traverse bay. It was already dark, but, procuring a boat and two Indians to row, he lost no time in crossing the bay to the scene of the disaster. He found the vessel without difficulty. There was no one remaining on board, but a light could be seen, among the trees, some distance back from the beach. Making his way to it, he found gathered round a camp fire the crew of the vessel, which proved to be the Champion, and eighteen passengers. Had he dropped from the clouds into their midst, the company would have been scarcely more surprised. He was immediately overwhelmed with questions as to who he was, where he came from, and especially where *they* were. Neither captain, crew, nor passengers had any definite notion of the locality they were in. Learning their exact position, they set about making arrangements to get out of the wilderness. The captain willingly sold to Mr. Miller, at a low price, such supplies as the latter wished to purchase. Some of them bought boats of the Indians, and made their way to Mackinac. A party, led by the captain, crossed Grand Traverse bay, landing in the vicinity of Omena, and proceeded south, on foot, along the shore of Lake Michigan. As far as known, crew and passengers all eventually reached their homes, but not without undergoing considerable hardship. Fortunately there were no women or children on board the Champion.

The first bride who came to the Grand Traverse country on her wedding tour, was Mrs. Lewis Miller, whose maiden name was Catherine Kiley. She was a native of London, Eng., and, like her husband, had been left an orphan. Somehow she had found her way to America, and then to the outpost of civilization at Mackinac. During Mr. Miller's frequent visits to that place, an attachment had grown up between them, which finally resulted in marriage. The wedding took place in September, 1845.

Immediately after the marriage, they set sail in the little sloop Lady of the Lake, for their home in the wilderness. Mr. Miller had chartered the vessel for the occasion, and had loaded her with goods for the Indian trade, furniture, and supplies for housekeeping.

The Lady was but a bit of a craft, but she was a perfect duck on the water, and fleet before anything like a favorable wind. The Fates, however, if the Fates have anything to do with regulating wedding trips, decreed a long and tempestuous voyage. It was the season when the god of the winds, on the northern lakes, delights to ornament their surface with foam capped waves, and tantalize the impatient mariner with variable breezes and the most disappointing kinds of weather.

The first day, they made the island of St. Helena, where they were compelled to seek the shelter of the harbor. There were a dozen sail or more there, waiting for a favorable change. Several times the Lady ventured out, but was as often compelled to put back. Finally, seizing the most favorable opportunity, she was able to reach Little Traverse. Here she was compelled to remain four days. The newly married couple went on shore, and found comfortable quarters in an Indian house. The woman of the house had been brought up in a white family at Mackinac, and being able to understand the wants of her guests, was in a degree successful in her kind endeavors to make their stay pleasant.

Leaving Little Traverse, the vessel reached the mouth of Grand Traverse bay, when she was again driven back. At the second attempt, she was obliged to heave to, in the mouth of the bay, the captain remaining all night at the helm. As Miller came on deck in the morning, dull, leaden clouds obscured the sky, and the air was filled with snow flakes. He proposed to take the captain's place at the helm, while the latter should turn in for a little rest. The captain gladly consented. Once installed in authority, Miller made sail, and let the captain sleep till the Lady was safely moored in the harbor at Old Mission.

A young bride, coming for the first time to the home of her husband, naturally looks with a great deal of interest at the surroundings. Sometimes there is disappointment. There was probably no serious disappointment in this case, but it is a part of the traditional family history, that as Mrs. Miller came on deck, that gloomy September morning, and looked anxiously out upon the scene, beautiful in its gloominess, and saw only the forest-skirted shore and the smoke curling upward from the log houses of the whites and a few Indian wigwams, the first question she asked her husband was, "Where is the town?"

Mr. Miller's oldest son, Henry L., was the first white child born in the Grand Traverse country.

*Mrs. Dougherty died May 24, 1876. Mr. Dougherty is living at the present time, 1883, in Somers, Wis.

CHAPTER VIII.

The Site of Traverse City as it was—First Purchase of Land—Arrival of Horace Boardman—First House Built—The Lady of the Lake and her Passengers—Women of the Colony—Visited by Indians—Home sickness—Saw-mill Built.

Not far south of the shore of Grand Traverse bay, at the head of its western arm, lies Boardman lake, a sheet of water a square mile or more in extent. From its northwestern angle issues the Boardman river, which flows for some distance in a northwesterly direction, then turns sharply round towards the east, and, after running along nearly parallel with the bay shore, enters the bay at a point nearly opposite that at which it issues from the lake. Its course from the lake to the bay is not unlike the letter V, with its sharp angle turned towards the west. The site of Traverse City lies between the lake and the bay, extending some distance to the south and west, and includes within its limits that part of the river already described.

All accounts agree in the statement that, before the so-called improvements of civilization had marred the adornments of nature, this was a most beautiful spot. The waters of Boardman lake were clear as crystal. The river, without drift-wood or the unsightly obstructions of fallen trees, ran with a swift current through an open forest of pines, which occupied all the space between the lake and the bay. There was no underbrush nor herbage—only a brown carpet of dead pine leaves upon the ground. So open and park like was the forest that one could ride through it in all directions on horseback at a rapid pace.

On the right bank of the river, a few rods below its exit from the lake, just where the land slopes gently down to the water, there was a little open space covered with grass, where the Indians sometimes landed from their canoes. On the higher land above were some Indian graves, of no great age, each with a stake at the head and foot. Not far away were other graves, of a circular, mound-like form, the work, probably, of a more ancient people. On the northeastern shore of the lake were a few bark wigwams, where the women and children of some Indian families usually passed the winter, while the men were absent on their annual hunt. With these exceptions, there was no mark to indicate that the foot of man had ever trod these solitudes, or that his voice had ever been heard above the rippling music of the river or the singing of the north wind in the tops of the pine trees.

However, it was not the beauty of the place, nor its attractive solitudes, so near to nature's heart, but its promised advantages for gain, that brought the first adventurous settler to fix his abode here.

In 1847, Capt. Boardman, a thrifty farmer living near Napierville, Ill., purchased of the United States government a small tract of land at the mouth of the river, and furnished means to his son, Horace Boardman, to build a saw-mill. The latter with two or three men in his employ, arrived at the river in the early part of June of that year, and immediately commenced the construction of a dwelling. The place selected was on the right bank of the stream, a little way below where it issues from Boardman lake, but a few steps from the grass plat and canoe landing above alluded to. The exact location of the building was in what is now East street, between the center of the street and its southern boundary, just east of the eastern boundary of Boardman avenue. It was a house of modest pretensions as to size, being only sixteen feet by twenty-four, and one story high. The material for the walls was pine logs hewn square with the broad-ax. In after years, it was known to the inhabitants of the village as the "old block-house." It was eventually destroyed by fire.

On the 20th of June, a week or more after Mr. Boardman's arrival, the Lady of the Lake, owned by him and sailed by Michael Gay, one of his employes, arrived in the mouth of the river, with supplies. There came with Gay a man by the name of Dunham, who, having been in the bay on a previous occasion, acted as pilot.

The Lady of the Lake,* a craft of only a few tons burthen, had originally been a pleasure yacht. She was sharp built, sloop rigged, and a fast sailer. Having become old and rotten, and therefore undesirable for the purpose for which she was originally intended, Mr. Boardman had been able to purchase her cheaply, as a vessel to answer his present convenience. Her only fault was that, on account of her decayed condition, she was unsafe in a storm.

After assisting for a few days in the building of the house, Gay was dispatched with the little vessel to the Manitou Islands, to bring on a party of employes, who, it had been arranged, should come as far as the islands by steamer. Returning, the Lady entered the river on the 5th of July. There came in her as passengers Mr. Gay's young wife, then only about fifteen or sixteen years of age, and her four-months-old baby, Mr. and Mrs. Duncan, a hired girl named Ann Van Amburg, and several carpenters.

Only the walls of the house had as yet been erected. The building was without roof, floors, doors, or windows. A sort of lean to, or open shed, with a floor of hewn planks, had been built for a temporary kitchen, against one side of the house, in which a cook-stove had been set up. A tent was now constructed of some spare sails, inside the unfinished building, for the accommodation of the two married couples and the girl. The single men shifted for themselves as best they could. The company lived in this manner during the remainder of the summer. The house was not finished till the saw-mill was so far completed as to saw lumber with which to finish it.

It was only a day or two after their arrival that the women, being alone, were alarmed by the sound of the trampling of horses, followed by a confusion of discordant yells, which their excited imaginations magnified into the terrific warwhoop of a multitude of bloodthirsty savages hankering after scalps. Mrs. Duncan and Ann cowered within the tent. Mrs. Gay, though scarcely less frightened, thought it policy to put on a semblance of bravery. She accordingly went out and spoke to the Indians in their own language, a few words of which she had learned, while living near Grand Rapids. To the relief of the women the Indians proved to be friendly. They had seen the Lady of the Lake sailing up the bay, and had come to visit the white man's camp, prompted mainly by curiosity, but had brought for traffic sugar and fish, which they were glad to exchange for such commodities as the whites had to dispose of. They were particularly fond of pork, and were especially glad to give any of their own food in return for it. The trade with the Indians became afterwards an important source of supply, when the failure of provisions threatened the little colony with famine. Mrs. Gay had some acquaintance with the French language, and one of the Indian women spoke it fluently. In future transactions, the two acted as interpreters, Mrs. Gay translating the English into French and the Indian woman the French into Indian, the response being conveyed back in a similiar manner, through a double translation.

How much of homesickness there was in the little colony, we are left in a great measure to conjecture. It may be related on Mrs. Gay's own authority that, as for herself, she time and again sat for hours by the little grass plot at the canoe landing, the only place she could find that had a look of civilization, shedding tears over her separation from the associations of her former home. Mrs. Duncan was fortunate enough to pay a visit to the ladies at Old Mission, the fall succeeding her arrival at the river, but Mrs. Gay was here more than two years before she had the pleasure of looking upon the face of a civilized woman other than the two with whom she came.

It had been Mr. Boardman's intention to throw a dam across the Boardman river, at some point not far below the lake, and build a saw-mill on that stream The convenience of residing near the mill, had been the main consideration that determined the location of the block-house. After a more thorough exploration of the country, however, and an estimate of the probable difficulties in the way of building, he was led to modify his plan. Mill Creek, a small stream that has its sources in the hills to the south and west of the bay, and enters the Boardman at the western angle of its bend, seemed to offer facilities for cheaply building a small mill, that should answer present purposes. He therefore determined to build on that stream, with the intention of erecting afterwards a larger and more permanent structure on the Boardman. By that plan he would have the advantage of the smaller mill for making boards, planks, and timbers for the larger, thus avoiding the difficulty of obtaining from a distance the lumber it would be necessary to have before a large mill could be put in a condition for service. There was no place nearer than Manistee where lumber could be obtained, and the Lady of the Lake was too small and too unsafe to be relied on for bringing any large quantity such a distance. It was not easy, at that time, to induce vessel masters to enter the bay, which to them was an unexplored sea.

Immediately after the arrival of the carpenters, all hands were set to work upon the mill. The Lady of the Lake made a trip to Manistee after plank for the flume. When the frame was ready, all the white men at Old Mission and several Indians came to help raise it. It took three days to get it up. It was finally got into a condition to be set running about the first of October. Then some of the first boards made were used to complete the block-house, which up to that time had remained unfinished.

It was a long walk from the house to the mill. The path from one to the other ran along the southwestern bank of the Boardman. For convenience of reaching it from the house, a foot-bridge of poles was thrown across the river at the canoe landing. This slight structure was afterwardc replaced by a broader and firmer bridge, on which wagons could cross.†

*This vessel should not be mistaken for another of the same name, in which Lewis Miller returned to Old Mission, after his marriage.

†In after years the saw-mill was remodeled and put to a variety of uses. At the present time (1883,) it is still standing, but is unoccupied. It is known among the inhabitants of the village as the "old planing-mill." All vestiges of the bridge have long since disappeared. The remains of the foundations of the block-house may still be seen.

M. L. L.

CHAPTER IX.

The Lady of the Lake Wrecked at the Manitous—Mr. Boardman's Journey Home—Anxiety of the People at the River—A Relief Expedition—Getting Dinner Under Difficulties—Removal from the Block House—Mrs. Gay Turns Shoemaker—Another Woman in the Settlement.

The mill having been completed, and there no longer being suitable employment for the mechanics who had been engaged upon it, it became necessary to provide for their conveyance home. It was arranged that Mr. Boardman should take them in the Lady of the Lake to the Manitous, where they could get passage on one of the steamers that were in the habit of touching there. He would then freight his vessel with supplies, which he expected to find waiting there, and return.

It was about the 10th of October that the Lady of the Lake sailed on this her last voyage. While waiting for the supplies, which had not arrived, after landing her passengers, the little vessel was caught in a storm, driven upon the beach, and totally wrecked. The supplies came, but Mr. Boardman searched in vain for means to transport them to Grand Traverse bay. Convinced at last that he could accomplish nothing by remaining at the islands, he took passage on a steamer for Mackinac. Here he found means to cross to the mainland, and then set out on foot on his toilsome journey home. His route lay for more than a hundred miles along the beach, most of the way without even a semblance of a foot-path, and without a civilized dwelling, except at the missions of Cross Village and Little Traverse, at which he could ask for a night's shelter or a morsel of food.

In the meantime, the people at home became alarmed at his long absence. Then information reached them, through the agency of some fishermen, that the vessel was lost. It was late in the season. Navigation would soon be closed. Something must be done, and done quickly. A consultation was held, the result of which was an agreement that Mr. Gay should go to Old Mission, get a boat there, if possible, and endeavor to reach the Manitous and bring away such supplies as he might be able to find.

Mrs. Duncan accompanied Mr. Gay to Old Mission, for a visit to the ladies there. The day after their departure, Mrs. Gay and Ann, perhaps not having the fear of famine before their eyes, or perhaps expecting to perish with hunger but believing in the maxim "live while you live," resolved to have one more good dinner. An examination of the larder showed on hand a small supply of musty flour, some sour yeast, a little maple sugar, and fish enough for a meal—not a very promising stock, to be sure, out of which to prepare a tempting dinner. Among the men was one named Joe Mead. Joe had a contract with Mr. Boardman to cut logs the next winter. To make sure of provisions for his hands, he had scoured the country—that is, he had been to Old Mission, the only settlement in the region, and brought back all the supplies he could get, the chief item of which was a barrel of hogs' heads. It was known, too, that Joe had some saleratus among his stores. A dinner without meat would be lacking, and sour yeast without an alkali would not raise musty flour. The women applied for a hog's head and a bit of saleratus, but Joe would give them neither, so they were fain to make the best of it. Lye made of ashes, with the sour yeast, served to make the dough light, and some of the sugar was converted into syrup; so they had, after all, a respectable dinner for the time and place—pancakes of musty flour, maple syrup, and fish.

The meal was scarcely ready, when they were agreeably surprised by the arrival of Mr. Boardman, foot-sore and exhausted and glad to be again at home. At table tears of thankfulness ran down his cheeks, as he partook with a keen relish of the homely fare they had unintentionally prepared for him in their efforts to get up a "good dinner."

Mr. Gay was successful in his expedition. At Old Mission he obtained the little schooner Arrow, her owner, H. K. Cowles, with Robert Campbell and several others, volunteering to accompany him to the Manitous. Having loaded with the supplies, at the latter place, he returned in safety, reaching Old Mission on Thanksgiving day and the river on the day following.

It was found that the block-house was too far from the mill for convenience. After Mr. Gay's return from the Manitous, he built a small log house, for the use of his own family, near the mill. Both families, however, and all the hands, were accommodated in it for a short time, till a small plank house could be built for Mr. and Mrs. Duncan and the men.

On examining the stores brought in by the Arrow, it was found that a box of boots and shoes intended for winter use had been left behind. Only one pair of shoes had come, which had been ordered expressly for Mrs. Gay, and these proved to be not a pair, both of them being shaped for one foot. We are not informed how the men managed for the winter, but Mrs. Gay resolved that the women should not go barefoot. Applying to Mr. Boardman, she obtained permission to use some spare belt leather belonging to the machinery of the mill for soles, and some heavy gray cloth found among the stores for vamps and quarters. One of the men made her a last. Then ripping to pieces one of the useless odd shoes to obtain patterns, she made a pair each for Mrs. Duncan, Ann, and herself. Though not remarkable for beauty, they proved serviceable, and much more comfortable than the narrow, high heeled things called shoes, that cramp the feet and deform the limbs of fashionable belles and make graceful motions in walking an impossibility.

And now the little community was shut in for the winter. All connection with the great world outside was severed, except an irregular and uncertain communication by way of Old Mission and Mackinac. Many were the incidents, however, novel, sad, cheerful, and ludicrous, that occurred to break the monotony of their hermit-like existence. The changes of the weather, the peculiarities of the climate, the ever varying phases of the landscape, the wonders of the forest, the strange beasts and birds that visited their dwellings or were captured in the woods, the thousand and one little things attendant on wilderness life in winter, many of them of special interest because of their relations to the character of this new and interesting country, kept the attention engaged and helped to make the time pass lightly. Still they were glad when, at the approach of spring, the snow slowly melted away, and there were indications that the face of nature was about to put on a more cheerful aspect.

In the summer of 1848 a small wharf was commenced at the shore of the bay, and a tram-way built for the purpose of transporting lumber to it from the mill. The next winter a beginning was made towards getting out timber for the construction of the contemplated large mill on the river. Mr. Boardman from time to time varied his business by getting out shingle bolts, and hemlock bark for tanning purposes, for the Chicago market. He cleared three or four acres of land, and was successful in the cultivation of garden vegetables.

The summer of 1849 was marked by several incidents that added interest to the life of the settlement. A man of the name of Freeman came, and got out a considerable quantity of hemlock bark for shipment, employing Indians to perform most of the labor. The bark, of course, was stripped from trees growing upon government land. There was no one in this remote region whose interest it was, or who considered it his duty, to prevent spoliations of the public property.

The government had found it necessary to order a re-survey of the lands in the vicinity of the bay. For some time the surveyors' camps were pitched in the vicinity, the settlement being for them a sort of headquarters and base of supplies.

In the employ of Risdon, one of the surveyors, was Henry Rutherford, afterwards well known in the settlement, having his wife with him. Word was brought to the women at the mill, one evening, that there was a woman in Risdon's camp. The announcement was sufficient to produce a flutter of excitement. Mrs. Duncan had visited the ladies at Old Mission, but Mrs. Gay, since her arrival at the river, had not seen the face of a civilized person of her own sex, except the two who had come with her. Setting out alone the next morning, she found her way to the surveyors' camp, and spent the forenoon with Mrs. Rutherford, remaining to dinner in response to a cordial invitation from the latter. The cloth was spread on the ground, where there was a bit of clean grass, outside the tent, the company sitting round it in oriental fashion. The viands consisted of pork and potatoes, fried, with huckleberries for dessert. The next day Mrs. Rutherford returned the visit, dining with Mrs. Gay. Mrs. Rutherford was partly of Indian descent, nevertheless she was regarded as an important acquisition to the society of the colony.

CHAPTER X.

Hannah, Lay & Co.—Mr. Hannah's Voyage to Grand Traverse Bay—The Vessel Stuck fast on a Rock—Mill Men Playing Old Sledge—Explorations—A Hundred Millions of Pine—Purchase Made—Clearing the Boardman—Steam Saw-Mill Built—Lumber Camps—Running Logs.

In the month of May, 1850, three enterprising young men, in the city of Chicago, entered into partnership, under the firm name of Hannah, Lay & Co., for the purpose of carrying on the lumber trade. The names of the partners were Perry Hannah, Albert Tracy Lay, and James Morgan. The firm opened business on the corner of Jackson and Canal streets, buying their stock by the cargo, in the harbor.

Early in 1851, they conceived the project of having, somewhere, a saw-mill of their own for making lumber, thus saving to themselves the profit they were now paying to the manufacturer. Falling in with a man of the name of Curtis, one of the mechanics who had built Mr. Boardman's mill, they obtained from him their first knowledge of the country on Grand Traverse bay. In the meantime the price of lumber had gone down to a very low figure. Capt. Boardman found that his mill, as managed by his son, was not profitable. Concluding that it would be wise to dispose of the property, he proposed to sell it to the new firm.

In the spring, Mr. Hannah, accompanied by Wm. Morgan and Capt. Boardman, took passage in the little schooner Venus, bound for the bay, for the purpose of viewing the property. The Venus was commanded by Capt. Peter Nelson, a Dane by birth, afterwards well known in the Grand Traverse country, for many years keeper of the light-house near Northport and now a resident of that village.

The voyage was tempestuous. After riding out a gale of three days' duration on Lake Michigan, they finally entered the bay, and made Old Mission harbor in pleasant weather.

The scene before them, as the vessel rounded to in the harbor, appeared to the tempest-tossed voyagers the loveliest ever beheld by mortal eyes. The sun was just sinking behind the western hills, the whitewashed houses of the Indian village gleaming brightly in his parting rays, while the tops of the forest trees seemed bathed in a floating mist of gold. On the bank sat a picturesque group of Indian men, enjoying the fragrant fumes of the pipe. The women were seen engaged in the feminine avocations pertaining to their simple mode of life. The shouting of a company of children in gleeful play, mingled with the sound of tinkling bells from a herd of ponies feeding on the hill-side beyond, made music in harmony with the quiet beauty of the scene. The restless spirit of the white man had not yet brought discontent to these simple children of the forest—the baleful effects of the destroying fire water were yet comparatively unknown.

After remaining two hours at Old Mission, the Venus set sail for her destination, the head of the west arm of the bay. The night was beautiful, with a glorious moon shining brightly in the heavens. When a mile out, with the vessel's prow turned towards the north, and a gentle breeze from the south filling her sails, Capt. Nelson, who had been worn out with labor and watching during the gale, gave directions to the man at the helm, wrapped himself in a blanket, and lay down on the quarter deck, to get a little rest. Fatigued as he was, he seemed to have scarcely more than touched the deck, when a loud snoring indicated that he was in a sound sleep. The instructions given to the man at the helm were to hold a north course till well down past the point of the peninsula, and then call the captain, before tacking to the west. The kind-hearted sailor, knowing how hard a time the captain had had, and desiring to give him all possible opportunity to rest, could see no reason why he should not guide the vessel round the point, as there was but little wind and all looked clear. As he brought her round, at a sufficient distance beyond the point, as he supposed, sailing not more than a mile an hour, the sudden thumping of her bottom on the rocks alarmed all hands, and brought the captain quickly to his feet. Then such a chiding as the poor sailor received for his disobedience of orders, is seldom heard in any dialect of the Scandinavian tongue. The vessel lay quiet, but was stuck fast. Sounding revealed the curious fact that her keel rested on a sunken rock, with not less than twenty feet of water all round. On making further soundings from the boat, which was got out for the purpose, it was found that the rock on which she rested was situated in a pool of clear, deep water, surrounded by rocks on all sides, and that the only way of escape was to draw her back, by means of the kedge anchor, through the narrow and shallow passage by which she had entered. Several hours of tedious labor were required to liberate her from her perilous position. The captain slept no more till his vessel was moored to the slab wharf, at the head of the bay.

The only opening in the forest visible to the party, as they landed, was the narrow clearing which had been made for the tram-road. Following this, Capt. Boardman keeping well in advance, they soon arrived at the mill. The mill was not running. On entering the house, the hands were all found there, amusing themselves with the game of old sledge. After shaking hands all round, Capt. Boardman said to his son, "Horace, how is this, that you are not running the mill?" The reply was, "Father, it was a little rainy to-day; the boys outside couldn't work very well, and they wanted the men in the mill to make up the number for the game; so I concluded to shut down for a time, in order that they might have a little fun." This easy way of doing business, did not suit the energetic old farmer, Capt. Boardman, who was now more fully convinced that the property had best be sold.

After looking over the premises for a day, a party, consisting of Mr. Hannah, Horace Boardman, Mr. Morgan, and a man named Whitcher, with packs of blankets and provisions, set out to explore the country and examine the timber along the Boardman river. At the end of a week, Mr. Hannah estimated that they had seen at least a hundred millions feet of pine, on government land open to sale. This was a sufficient inducement to the firm to accept Capt. Boardman's proposition to sell them his entire interest in the property, consisting of the saw-mill, the cheap buildings that had been erected, and about two hundred acres of land, on which the village plat was afterwards located, for $4,500.

The first work done by the new owners, was to construct a tram-road from the bend of the Boardman to the mill, so that logs floated down the stream could be hauled out at the bend, and transported over land to the mill, whence the lumber, as formerly, could be run down to the slab wharf for shipment.

The next task performed, which proved to be one of no small magnitude, was the clearing of the river, so that logs could be floated down from the immense tracts of pine on the upper waters. It was not merely here and there a fallen tree that had to be removed. In some places the stream was so completely covered and hidden with a mass of fallen trees, and the vegetation which had taken root and was flourishing on their decaying trunks, that no water could be seen. Ten long miles of the channel had to be cleared, before the first pine was reached. With an energy and a steadfastness of purpose that ever after marked the transactions of the firm, the work was pushed on till logs could be run down the stream.

The saw-mill had only a single muley saw. Finding from a few months' experience that it was too small and too slow for their purpose, Hannah, Lay & Co determined to construct a new one, to be run by steam power. A site was selected on the narrow tongue of land lying between the lower part of the river and the bay, where, on one hand, logs could be floated in the stream directly to the mill, and, on the other, the lumber could be loaded on vessels by being conveyed only a short distance on trucks. The project was executed in 1852, and the next year the mill went into successful operation.*

About the first work done in the steam mill, was to saw up the pine timber on the tract of land now occupied by the village. It was cut into bridge timber, for the Illinois Central Railroad Company, who used it for constructing a bridge over the Illinois river, at La Salle.

In those days, the lumber was all carried across the lake in sail craft. The first vessel that carried for the firm, and brought in the boilers for the steam mill, was the Maria Hilliard. No lake surveys had been made in the region of Grand Traverse bay, and the masters of vessels were guided more by guess than by charts. Amusing anecdotes are told of their experiences, one of which we repeat. The Richmond, one very dark night, was beating up the bay against a light head wind. On attempting to tack, for some unaccountable reason she would not come in stays, and, as she seemed to be fast, the captain was forced reluctantly to let her remain. When daylight revealed the situation, what was his surprise to find his vessel lying close to a bold, wooded shore with her bowsprit entangled among the trees.

When the pine in the immediate vicinity of the mill had been worked up, Hannah, Lay & Co. commenced the system of lumbering common on the streams of northern Michigan, which they have successfully pursued up to the present time,† giving employment, both summer and winter, to a large number of men.

The Boardman river had been cleared as far up as the pine forests. At the beginning of winter, gangs of men were sent into the woods, to establish camps.

A gang consisted of twenty men, more or less, a foreman, or boss, a cook, a stable-boss, and perhaps a chore-boy. A number of teams, either horses or oxen, were kept at the camp. A house was built of pine logs, large enough to accommodate the company. A part of the interior, perhaps separated from the rest only by a simple railing, constituted the special domain of the cook, upon which no one was allowed to trespass. Another part was dovoted to the accommodation of the men. Bunks were arranged in tiers, one above another, against the wall, for sleeping places. A huge stove made the apartment comfortable in the coldest weather. Rough benches for seats, and a long table, with the plainest and most durable kinds of dishes, constituted the bulk of the furniture. A large stable, built also of logs, afforded shelter for the animals. Provisions for the men and forage for the animals, were brought to the camp from time to time, during the winter, by teams employed for the purpose.

The first faint gleam of day usually found the men at their work, and, except for dinner, there was no cessation of labor till night had again spread her dark mantle over the scene. Some cut down the pine trees, others divided them with the saw into logs of suitable length, and others again loaded the logs on huge sleds and drew them to the river bank, where they were tumbled into the stream. When the work of the day was done, the teamsters took care of their animals, receiving from the stable boss the rations to which they were entitled. In the house, wet garments were hung up to dry, and every man made himself as comfortable as he might without intruding on his neighbor. When supper was over, various amusements served to while away the time till the hour for retiring. Some read, by the light of a lamp, such books and papers as they could get, some played cards, chess, or checkers, and sometimes a song enlivened the spirits of those who sang, if not of those who heard. Joke, raillery, and repartee passed freely round. If a visitor called, he was made welcome and hospitably entertained. If a minister of the gospel paid them a visit sometime in the course of the winter, all amusement was laid aside to listen to a sermon in the evening, and when he departed the following morning, he was not allowed to go away empty handed.‡

When spring opened, the camp was deserted. The men, except the log-drivers, returned to work in the mill, which was now put in operation for the season, or went to their several homes. It was the business of the log-drivers, or river-drivers, as they were sometimes called, to run the logs down the river to the mill. Not unfrequently, at the place where the logs had been put into the stream, the channel was filled with them from bank to bank to a great height. To break this "jam," or loosen the logs so that they would be carried away by the current, which was usually strong from the melting of the snow at this season, involved no small amount of labor, and was sometimes dangerous. When the logs were all finally afloat in the stream, the drivers followed them down, pushing off those that stranded on the shore, and breaking the temporary "jams" that formed wherever obstructions were met with. Frequently the men rode considerable distances on the floating logs, keeping their position by the aid of sharp spikes in the thick soles of their boots, and by balancing themselves with their long pike poles. At night they slept in temporary camps on the bank of the river, to which supplies were conveyed for their use.

* This mill is now known as the Company's old saw-mill.

† 1883.

‡ This brief description of a lumber camp, has been written up from personal recollections of a visit the writer made to one of Hannah, Lay & Co's camps on the Boardman, by invitation of the foreman, Wm. Rennie, in the winter of 1860-61. That same winter, Rev. J. W. Robinson, the methodist minister at Traverse City, visited Mr. Rennie's camp. The men of two camps came together in the evening to listen to a sermon, and made up a handsome purse for Mr. Robinson, as a token of their appreciation of his interest in their welfare.

CHAPTER XI.

New Partners in the Firm of Hannah, Lay & Co.—Mr. Lay and Mr. Hannah Live at the Bay Alternately—The First Store—Boarding-House Built—Names of Early Settlers—Mill Built at East Bay—First Road Opened—Postoffice Established—How Ann Dakin Carried the Mail—Amusements—Henrietta Baxter's Adventures—First Marriages.

In 1852 a fourth partner, Mr. Wm. Morgan, who had accompanied Mr. Hannah on his prospecting tour, was received into the firm of Hannah, Lay & Co. Afterwards, in 1859, Mr. Smith Barnes, a former resident of Port Huron, was admitted to partnership in the mercantile department, but without any connection with the lumber trade.

Mr. Francis Hannah, a brother of the member of the firm, came to the bay in the fall of 1851, with a view to becoming a partner. After spending the winter in the settlement, he concluded that the financial advantages of a connection with the firm would not be a sufficient compensation for the seclusion of a life in the wilderness, and finally declined the proffered partnership. While there, he had charge of the business of the firm.

After Francis Hannah retired from the employ of the firm, Mr. Lay and Mr. Hannah for several years took turns in the management of the business at the bay and in Chicago, Mr. Lay remaining at the former place during the summer and Mr. Hannah in Chicago, the two changing places for the winter. Finally the oversight of their interests was permanently divided between them, Mr. Hannah residing constantly in Traverse City, and Mr. Lay in Chicago.

From the commencement of their business at the bay, they kept a small stock of goods for supplying the wants of persons in their employ. Their first store was kept in a log building, sixteen feet long and twelve wide, that stood by the side of the old Boardman boarding-house, near the water mill on Mill creek. From that they removed to a small frame building, erected for the purpose, on the north side of the river, just east of what is now the corner of Bay and Union streets. In order to make room for a larger structure, as business increased, the building was afterward moved to the north side of Bay street, opposite the Bay House, and was for many years used as a tin shop. A lady who went shopping to this building in 1853, described the stock as consisting of "a few pieces of calico, and just dry goods enough to supply the little community."

After the erection of the steam saw-mill, it was found convenient to have some place near it, where those employes of the firm who were without families could be accommodated with board and lodging. Accordingly a boarding-house was commenced in the spring of 1854, and by the last of August was so far advanced as to be habitable. The original building with its subsequent additions, occupied a site on the south side of Bay street, a short distance west of the corner of Bay and Union streets, and, at the time of the present writing, is kept as a hotel by Wm. Fowle and known as the Bay House.

A saw-mill in the depths of a wilderness previously unbroken, built only with a view to the profit arising from the manufacture of lumber where land and timber were cheap, has often turned out to be the nucleus around which thriving settlements have grown up. In the case before us, the modest enterprise undertaken by Capt. Boardman and his son, and afterwards greatly enlarged and energetically pushed by Hannah, Lay & Co., proved to be the laying of the foundation for a populous and thrifty community.

The names of all who came to the new settlement in an early day, have not been preserved. Some remained only a short time, and then returned to the places whence they came, or wandered to other parts; others identified themselves with the interests of the community, and became permanent citizens.

At the setting in of winter, in 1851, the following families are known to have been in the settlement: Michael Gay's, John Lake's, Henry Rutherford's, Benjamin Austin's, T. D. Hillery's, Wm. Voice's, Seth Norris's, Robert Potts's, a family named Barnes, a German family whose name has been forgotten, and an old couple of the name of Lowery. The following names of unmarried persons, residents at that time, have been preserved: Henrietta Baxter, who afterwards became Mrs. J. K. Gunton, Catherine Carmichael, sister to Mrs. Hillery and afterwards wife of H. D. Campbell, Dominic Dunn, Wm. Rennie, Cayler Germaine, Dougald Carmichael, brother to Mrs. Hillery and Catherine, James K. Gunton, and Richard Meagher. Francis Hannah was also there, having charge of the business of Hannah, Lay & Co., D. C. Curtis, foreman in the employ of the firm, Thomas Cutler, who had come out as engineer, to take charge of the engine of the steam saw-mill about to be built, and John B. Spencer, who was getting out saw-logs for the mill and timber for building a dock, and who soon afterwards removed to Elk Rapids. Thomas Cutler's family arrived the following year. There arrived also in 1852, John Garland and two men of the name of Evans, with families, and, unmarried, Henry D. Campbell, Thomas A. Hitchcock, R. McLellan, and Hugh McGinnis. Dr. Charles Holton and wife came either in the spring of 1852 or the fall previous. Dr. D. C. Goodale, with his family, arrived in April, 1853.*

Many of the persons named came for the purpose of entering the employ of Hannah, Lay & Co., and most of them were, at one time or another, engaged in some capacity in the service of the firm. Mr. Voice, who had been in the country before, contemplated, in connection with his partner, Luther Scofield, the building of a saw-mill at East Bay, a project which was soon after carried into successful execution.

The population of the settlement was yet small. They were surrounded and shut in by an almost impenetrable wilderness. But few improvements not demanded by the immediate exigencies of the lumber trade, had been attempted. Only one public road—that from the head of the bay to Old Mission—had been opened. This road had been made in fulfillment of an agreement between the inhabitants of the two places, entered into, probably, at the raising of Boardman's saw-mill. The people at Old Mission were pleased to have a mill so conveniently near, and all could see that connection of the settlements by means of a passable road would be a public advantage. The inhabitants of each settlement, by voluntary contributions of labor, built the half of the road nearest themselves.

Up to 1853, the postoffice at Old Mission was the only one in a vast region of country around the bay. In the winter of 1852 and '53, Mr. Lay, while in Washington, was successful in his effort to get one established in the new settlement. The name of the one at Old Mission was Grand Traverse. The new settlement at the head of the bay was beginning to be known as Grand Traverse City. When Mr. Lay proposed the latter name for the new postoffice, the clerk with whom he was transacting the business suggested that "Grand" be dropped, and it be called simply Traverse City, as the name would have less resemblance to that of the office at Old Mission, to which Mr. Lay acceded. Thus originated the name subsequently given to a thriving village.

The mail was carried once a week, coming to Traverse City from Manistee. Mr. Lay was the first contractor, his compensation being $400 per year. At first it was carried by an Indian, called Old Joe, in a pack upon his shoulders. Before the expiration of Mr. Lay's contract, however, the quantity of mail matter had so increased that a horse had to be employed. Hugh McGinnis was then engaged as carrier, who cut out a trail as far as Herring creek, the first move in road-making between Traverse City and the lake shore.

Dr. Goodale was appointed postmaster, who chose H. D. Campbell as assistant. Dr. Goodale continued to hold the office till after Lincoln's election to the presidency, when, in the course of events incident to a change of administration, he was removed.†

Previous to the establishment of the postoffice at Traverse City, whenever any one had occasion to visit Old Mission, he was expected to bring, on his return, whatever mail matter was found waiting in the postoffice there. Ann Dakin, a woman employed in the boarding-house, had relatives at that place, whom she frequently visited. Being strong of frame and a pedestrian of great endurance, she thought nothing of walking to Old Mission at the end of a week's labor, returning in time to enter promptly upon the duties of the following week. On these visits to her friends, she was accustomed to carry a satchel slung over over her shoulder, in which she brought back the mail for the settlement.

The society of the settlement was peculiar. Most of the married people were young. The unmarried men were intelligent, moral, and well disposed, but bent on having their full share of sport. As not unfrequently happens in border settlements, where the male population is apt to greatly outnumber that of the gentler sex, their recreations sometimes assumed a somewhat mischievous character.

On New Year's night, in the winter of 1851 and '52, "the boys" determined to amuse themselves by waking up, in a startling manner, the more sedate citizens. Secretly collecting all the firearms, they found they could muster thirteen guns. With these they went round to several of the houses, firing volleys under the windows, to the utter consternation of the more timid inmates, who, living in constant fear of a hostile visit from the Mormons, thought their dreaded enemy was upon them.

Card-playing and the habits of negligence and idleness to which it leads, had been among the causes that made Mr. Boardman's enterprise unsuccessful. In the boarding house of Hannah, Lay & Co. it was strictly prohibited. Some of the young men, however, were not to be easily deprived of a favorite pastime. At Austin's they found a convenient rendezvous, where card-playing and general hilarity, though the latter was sometimes a little boisterous, were not considered out of order. Michael Gay could play the fiddle, after a fashion. Usually as often as once in two weeks his services were put in requisition, the ladies, married and single, were invited, and music and dancing, neither of them, perhaps, of the most polished kind, served to while away an evening.‡

It is not to be supposed that flirtations, love-makings, and courtships, generally understood to be normal accompaniments of social parties in fashionable life, flourished in a society where the men outnumbered the women three or four to one, and where nearly all of the latter were married, yet the meetings at Austin's were not without their romance. Jim Gunton, as he was familiarly called, seems to have been the sly dog of the pack. Henrietta Baxter lived at Austin's. While his companions, deep in the attractions of euchre or old sledge, were oblivious of all things around them, Jim, fully awake to the main chance, found opportunities to whisper unobserved in the maiden's ear that which sometimes deepened the blush on her cheek. Ere the winter had passed, it became known that there was an engagement of marriage.

Henrietta was the daughter of a Mormon lady, who was a widow. Mrs. Baxter had been inveigled into joining her fortunes with those of the Mormons of Beaver Island, only to find, in a short time, her property held fast in the clutches of the authorities of the Mormon church. The situation on the island for young, unmarried women, not in full sympathy with the peculiar doctrines and practices taught by Strang and his associates, was far from pleasant. Henrietta found employment in the family of James Cable, a "Gentile" living on the island, between whom and the Mormons there existed a strong dislike, if not a bitter hatred. In common with some of the "Gentiles" with whom she was associated, she at length became alarmed for her personal safety. Her fears, in their full extent, may not have been well-founded. Be that as it may, she resolved to take advantage of the first opportunity to escape. One day a vessel touched at the wharf. Though its destination was to her unknown, she determined, if possible, to get on board, and take the chances of reaching a desirable haven. As the vessel was about to sail, she took in her hand a bundle of such personal effects as she conld carry, and started on a run towards it. Before reaching it, however, she was intercepted by some of the Mormons, who took away her bundle, after which she was allowed to proceed, glad to get off the isl and, even with nothing but the garments upon her person. The next port at which the vessel touched was Old Mission, where the fugitive was set on shore. Living in the vicinity of Old Mission was a family of Mormons of the name of Bowers, who, it was understood, had in some way incurred the displeasure of Strang and his associates, and had consequently been compelled to leave the island. In this family Henrietta found a home. From Bowers' she came to the head of the bay, where she found employment in the family of Austin, who also was known as a Mormon exile.

As Henrietta regarded Bowers' house as her home, it was arranged that the marriage rite should be performed there, Rev. Mr. Dougherty to officiate. For a wedding party to get there in the depth of winter, was not easy. The best preparation Mr. Gunton could make, was to procure from the Indians of Old Mission two roughly made pungs, each drawn by a diminutive, shaggy, half-starved Indian pony. One pung was intended for the conveyance of himself and bride; the other for Mr. and Mrs. Austin. It was the intention to return to Austin's at night, but the ponies were slow, the roads in places were almost impassable from drifted snow, and it proved to be all they could do to reach Bowers' in the course of the day, not to think of returning. In the mean time, the "boys" at the head of the bay prepared to give the newly married couple a rousing *charivari* on their return, watching for them in vain till late into the night. When they finally did return, the next day, the issuing of a general invitation to a party at Austin's in the evening turned the contemplated *charivari* into a more civil and more enjoyable infair, the first ever held in what is now Traverse City.

The first marriage in which the ceremony was performed within the limits of the settlement, was that of James Lee and Ann Dakin, which took place, probaby, in 1853. Wm. M. McKellip, a justice of the peace, officiated.§

The first white child born at Traverse City, was Josephine Gay, daughter of Michael Gay, afterwards Mrs. Neil Morrison. The date of her birth was May 15, 1849.

* To some readers the minute personal details in this and preceding chapters, as well as similar ones to follow, will, no doubt, seem dry and uninteresting, but for the old settlers, many of whom still remain, as well as for their descendants and friends, they will possess peculiar attractions, and cannot be omitted. M. L. L.

† Dr. David C. Goodale was born in Waybridge, Vt., Nov. 10, 1809. In June, 1835, he graduated in the medical college at Castleton, which at that time stood in the front rank of the medical schools of the country. Soon after graduating, he married Miss Charlotte Isabella Cheney, and commenced practice in Panton. He was for many years secretary of the Addison county medical society, and took an honorable place in the ranks of the profession. During the political campaign of 1839-40, he published the *Green Mountain Argus*. He came west in the fall of 1852. On removing to the Grand Traverse country, he determined to give up practice, but the needs of the settlement induced him to reconsider his determination. For many years he was the only physician in the vicinity of Traverse City. His death occurred Nov. 13, 1878. M. L. L.

‡ Austin lived in a log house on or near the present site of the Occidental hotel. Unless there was a family living in the block-house, his was the only one on the east side of the river at that time. M. L. L.

§ This was not Hon. James Lee, now living in Traverse City. The Jamee Lee here spoken of left the country with his wife soon after their marriage. M. L. L.

CHAPTER XII

First Deaths—Forgotten Graves—First Religious Services—Rev. D. R. Latham—Methodist Work—First Methodist Class at Old Mission—Class Organized at Traverse City—Privations and Hardships of Early Pioneer Preachers—A Friendly Owl.

There is something peculiarly sad in the contemplation of death occurring in a small and isolated community, cut off from the sympathy of the great, kindly throbbing heart of the world of humanity, and separated, it may be, from the religious consolations that come through the agency of those noble institutions of our christian civilization, the church and the christian ministry.

In the winter of 1852 and '53, a young man was accidentally killed at the camp on the Boardman. Early in the following summer, another young man was taken sick in the boarding house. He was kindly cared for, under the supervision of Mr. Lay, and attended by young Dr. Holton, who, though employed in the store of Hannah, Lay & Co., gave his attention, when called on, to the few cases of sickness occurring in the settlement. Comfortable quarters were provided for the sick man in the old Boardman boarding house, at Mill creek, where, after lingering for a few days, he passed away. A little later in the season, a vessel came into the harbor, having on board a family, in destitute circumstances, of the name of Churchill. Mrs. Churchill was taken ashore dangerously sick, and, though everything that kindness could suggest was done by the women as nurses and Dr. Goodale as physician, she lived only a few days. The three early victims of death were buried on the sandy plain, not far from the margin of the bay. A thriving village has extended its streets and buildings above their forgotten graves, all traces of which have long since disappeared. Unconscious of the daily tread of the busy throng above their humble resting place, they await, we may hope in peace, the summons that shall bid them, like Lazarus, come forth to a new and a higher life.

At the burial of the unfortunate young man accidentally killed, there was no funeral service. At the burial of the one who died of disease, religious services were conducted by Rev. H. C. Scofield, a young baptist minister, who was residing for a time at East Bay, in charge of the business in which his brother, Mr. Luther Scofield, was a partner. At the funeral of Mrs. Churchill, Mr. Lay read the episcopal burial service at the grave. There is a tradition, not well authenticated, that Mr. Whitcher, who was early in the employ of Mr. Boardman, sometimes conducted religious services for the benefit of the men, but the funeral of the young man at the old boarding-house, is the earliest occasion, so far as we have reliable proof, on which such services were ever had in Traverse City.

The several deaths occurring so near together, produced, perhaps, a feeling of solemnity in the community, and a desire on the part of some at least for regular religious services. Mr. Scofield consented to preach. An appointment was made for a certain Sunday, at the log house which had been fitted up for a school house. Mrs. Goodale, who took an active interest in the matter, went round and gave notice to the people.

To some of the residents a religious meeting was a novelty. The children who attended went to it with something of the feeling of expectant curiosity with which they would have visited a traveling show An amusing incident, preserved in memory by some who were present, illustrates this fact. While Mr. Scofield was offering an earnest opening prayer, two boys watched him very attentively As he pronounced the amen, one of them, with a comical look, gave his companion a punch, and said, so loud that all in the house could hear, "There didn't I tell you amen would be the last word he would say?"

Mr Scofield preached a few times during the summer of 1853 After that, there was no stated religious service at any point in the Grand Traverse region till June, 1857, except at the several Indian mission stations

A letter, written by some person in the vicinity of Old Mission to a friend in northern New York, saying that there was no clergyman in northern Michigan and asking where one could be obtained, attracted the attention of Rev. D R. Latham, a young local preacher recently licensed by the M E. Church Mr. Latham had just determined to go to Kansas Thinking that now was perhaps the last opportunity he might have of seeing the great lakes, he resolved to go by the lake route, and visit on his way the destitute communities referred to in the letter Finding encouragement at Old Mission, he resolved to remain there, and accordingly sent for Mrs Latham, who joined her husband early in October

Mr Latham began to preach regularly at Old Mission on the 21st of June, 1857. The services were held in the mission church, which had been occupied by Mr Dougherty previous to his removal to the west side of the bay The first class meeting was held on the 19th of July, and the first class was organized on the following Sunday This first church organization for white people on Grand Traverse bay, consisted of the following persons Roxana Pratt, Eliza Merrill, Mary A. Wait, Jane Chandler, Myron Chandler, Peter Stewart and Joanna Stewart. The next Sunday two others were added—Charles Avery and Catherine McCluskey The same day on which the class was formed, a Sunday school was organized, of which Jerome M. Pratt was superintendent The teachers were Miss Louisa Colburn, (who was afterward Mrs. S E Wait,) and Mr Latham

The congregation sometimes presented the scene of a curious mixture of races and classes of people, and of an assortment of costumes that to one having a keen sense of the ludicrous might have been sufficient to banish all thoughts of devotion. The U S. revenue cutter Michigan sometimes anchored in the harbor and remained over Sunday, when some of the sailors and marines would attend service in the church. Old Mission still had a considerable Indian population. One Indian used to attend, wearing a large silver ornament suspended from the cartilage of the nose. Another, Asa-buo, who was credited with having been seen eating a human heart torn from one of the victims who fell in the unfortunate attempt of the Americans to recapture Mackinac, in the war of 1812, was sometimes present. Another, the chief Aish qua gwona ba, who was supposed to have a number of white scalps safely hidden away in a certain old trunk, used to come, in warm weather, clad in only a shirt and breech-cloth, and sit through the service as stiff and sober as an old time deacon

In the course of the summer, Rev. W H Brockway, on some sort of an expedition, found his way from the southern part of the state up through the woods to Old Mission, and falling in with Mr Latham persuaded him to join the Michigan conference As there was no quarterly conference at Old Mission to give the necessary recommendation, Mr. Brockway took his church letter to some Indian mission farther south, probably the one in Isabella county, where he was formally recommended to the annual conference. As he had not been examined, however, he could not be admitted The next year, 1858, he attended in person, and passing the preliminary examination, was received into the conference on trial

At the annual conference of 1857, two circuits were formed on Grand Traverse bay—Old Mission and Elk Rapids, and Northport and Traverse City. Mr. Latham was to supply the former, and Rev. L J. Griffin was appointed to the latter On learning the relative situations of Northport and Traverse City—forty miles apart—Mr Griffin wrote Mr Latham, asking him to take Traverse City off his hands, which he consented to do. Mr Griffin labored at Northport and Carp River, forming classes at those places, and Mr Latham at Old Mission, Traverse City, and Elk Rapids.

The first quarterly meeting of the circuit of which Mr. Latham was now the regularly appointed pastor, was held at Old Mission, the presiding elder, Rev. H. Penfield, being present. J M Pratt had been appointed class leader, and was the only official member on the circuit; the quarterly conference therefore consisted of only three—the presiding elder, the pastor, and the class leader It is said that in making out the official list Mr Latham made the nominations, Mr Pratt did the voting, and the presiding elder declared the result.

The first methodist class in Traverse City was organized by Mr Latham on the 11th day of April, 1858, consisting of Wm Fowle, Mrs. Goodale, and five others. The meetings were held in the district schoolhouse, which had recently been built.

At that time Mr. Latham taught school at Old Mission during the week, preached there on Sunday morning, walked to Traverse City and preached in the evening, and then walked back to Old Mission in the night. A circumstantial account of one of those night journeys will illustrate the hardships and dangers that attended the labors of the pioneer preachers of those early days

On the evening of the 14th of March, 1858, Mr Latham preached at Traverse City as usual, going home with Mr. Hannah, at the close of the service, for refreshments After partaking of a lunch, he started for Old Mission As a considerable distance could be saved by going diagonally across the bay on the ice to Bowers' Harbor, he determined to take that route. Mr Hannah walked with him to the beach, and at parting cautioned him to keep away from the shore, as the ice near it was becoming rotten and dangerous. When about two miles on his way, a dense fog came on, hiding the shore from view. Some Indians were having a dance, near the mouth of the river, in Traverse City, and the sound of their drum could be distinctly heard Taking it for a guide, he went forward, walking in the direction opposite the sound. In due time he reached the island. Finding himself near the shore, he recollected Mr. Hannah's caution, and kept away, hoping that by taking a circuitous route through the harbor he could strike the shore at Mr. Bowers' house In making the attempt he became completely bewildered, and, to make matters worse, the density of the fog increased till all objects were hidden from view. He knew that there were several dangerous fissures in the ice in that part of the bay, and that farther down, in the vicinity of New Mission, there was open water It is not a cause of wonder that his anxiety to get on shore rapidly increased After traveling a long time, he heard what he took to be the barking of a dog, and turned his steps in the direction of the sound As he came nearer the place whence the sound proceeded, the barking of the dog gradually changed to the hooting of an owl. But even the hooting of an owl had a cheering influence. He knew that the owl must be on land, and, anxious to get on shore anywhere, he took him for a guide, and pressed forward. It now began to rain, but there was this relief—as the rain began to fall, the fog began to clear away. In a little while, he could discern the faint outline of the shore. Fatigued with his toilsome walk, he stopped to rest a moment and survey the situation, when, glancing over his shoulder, he discovered a light in the distance. Thanking God, he moved with new courage towards the light. But now a new danger presented itself. Suddenly, while still a quarter of a mile from the shore, he came into water two feet deep, on the surface of the ice. Shouting loudly for help, he was cheered by answering shouts and the firing of guns from an Indian camp on the shore, some distance from the light, while the faithful owl, as if cognizant of the situation and desirous of rendering assistance, kept up his hooting. With the Indians, the owl, and the light for guides, and with the dim and shadowy outline of the shore in view, he moved slowly and cautiously forward, carefully feeling his way, till he found himself on solid ground, and was received within the hospital walls of a human habitation.

CHAPTER XIII.

The First Sunday School In Traverse City—The Children After Huckleberries—Further Sunday School History—The First Schoolhouse and the First Schoolma'am—Later Schools—A School on Board a Vessel.

The first Sunday-school in Traverse City, was begun in June, 1853, in the little log schoolhouse to be hereafter described. It was under the supervision of Mr. Scofield, assisted by Mrs. Goodale. Mr. Lay encouraged the enterprise by his presence and approval, and Miss Scofield, afterwards Mrs. John Black, usually came with her brother, though all the teaching was done by Mr. Scofield and Mrs. Goodale. There was no necessity, however, for a numerous corps of teachers, as there were only eight pupils in the school. Only two of these had ever been in Sunday-school before. There were no Sunday-school books or papers or singing-books—nothing but the bible. It is related that on one occasion, the four persons assembled at the schoolhouse, and waited in vain for the children, who failed to appear. At length, Mrs. Goodale, perhaps having a correct suspicion of the cause of their absence, proposed that her companions should wait, while she should go out and look for them. She found them not far off, picking and eating huckleberries, their hands and faces all stained with the purple juice, in which condition she managed to gather them into the schoolhouse. On questioning the children as to what the parents knew concerning their doings, it came out that the latter had all gone out for a boat ride.

At the approach of cold weather in the fall, the Sunday school was closed. The next summer it was reopened, but lacking the support of Mr. Lay and Mr. Scofield, neither of whom was in the settlement, it was soon abandoned. Sometime afterwards, Mr. Lay's mother sent eighty volumes of Sunday-school books to Traverse City.

The next attempt at Sunday-school work was made in the fall of 1858, and proved successful. The sessions of the school were held in the new district schoolhouse. It does not appear that there was a regular superintendent, but Rev. W. W. Johnson, successor of Rev. D. R. Latham as pastor of the M. E. church at Old Mission and Traverse City, and presiding elder of the newly formed Grand Traverse district, who preached in the schoolhouse every alternate Sunday morning, took charge of the school when present. The teachers were Mrs. Oscar Stevens, Mrs. Jacob Barns, Mrs. Hathaway, Mrs. Goodale, and, later, Miss Belle Hannah. At the opening session, Mr. Johnson prayed, "Lord, send some one to help the women." To these engaged in the work, it was a pleasing circumstance that among the children gathered into the school were all of the eight pupils who had constituted the classes in the log schoolhouse, five years before.

In 1859 the school was prosperous. Mr. E. L. Sprague was superintendent. In the spring Mrs. Goodale and Miss Hannah collected, in four hours time, partly from the men employed in the mill, about $30, for the purchase of books. That year the school took four Sunday-school papers, published by four different denominations. Three were paid for by the school, and Mr. Sprague donated the fourth. As at that time the postage on papers had to be paid at the office of delivery, Dr. Goodale relieved the school of that item of expense by assuming it himself.

This Sunday-school seems to have been truly non-sectarian and undenominational, members of several churches and persons not members of any church working harmoniously together. It was the parent of the several denominational Sunday-schools that have since graced Traverse City.

Dr. Goodale, recently from Vermont, whose arrival at Traverse City in the spring of 1853 has already been noticed, had come to keep the boarding-house of Hannah, Lay & Co. It was a part of the contract between the doctor and the firm, that his elder daughter, Helen, then in the fifteenth year of her age, should teach school. Her compensation was to be a dollar a week and board, and the firm promised that if the people failed to pay the full amount, they would make up the deficiency.

As yet there had been no legal organization of a school district. There was no vacant house suitable for the accommodation of a school. The best that could be done, was to put in order an abandoned and dilapidated log building, which had been constructed by Mr. Spencer and used by him for a stable, while getting out logs and timber, in the winter of 1851 and '52. It stood in a wild locality, some distance from the main part of the settlement, in what is now the eastern part of the village. The exact location is lot 3, of block 12, on the south side of Front street, a short distance east of Boardman avenue. Under the supervision of Mr. Lay, who manifested much personal interest in the enterprise, the house was repaired, and furnished with such appliances as circumstances would admit of, at the expense of the firm. The door was in the west side. There was a small window near the door, and another at the east side of the room. A stove stood in the middle. The teacher's desk was near the west window. A blackboard hung against the wall. The desks were neatly made, but not painted. The floor was loose and open, and on one occasion teacher and girls suddenly gathered their skirts closely about them and sprang upon the seats for safety, as a snake, with threatening looks but harmless intent, was seen leisurely coming up through one of the chinks. The books were such as the pupils happened to have. Reading, spelling, writing, arithmetic, and geography were taught, in the old-fashioned way.

While teaching, Miss Helen lived with her father's family, in the boarding-house, the expense of her board being defrayed by the patrons of the school or assumed by Hannah, Lay & Co., according to the contract. It was something of a walk to the schoolhouse. On the direct route, there was no bridge over the river, except the timbers of the boom, near the saw mill, which served as a narrow foot-bridge, not very safe or pleasant for a timid woman to cross, but we are told that the men in the mill, with respectful gallantry, were always on the alert to lead the schoolma'am over.

The following list comprises the names of the pupils who attended this first school: George, John, Thomas and Elizabeth Cutler; Almond and Ellen Rutherford; Augusta, Clarissa and Lucius Smith; Elizabeth Whitney; an adopted son of the Mrs. Churchill who had recently been buried; Albert Norris. The next summer, the school was increased by the addition of James, William, John and Richard Garland; Mellissa, Emma and Anna Rice, and a girl whose name has been forgotten. Elizabeth Cutler was the youngest pupil; Albert Norris was the oldest, being about a year older than the teacher.*

After the close of her first term of school, in the fall, Miss Helen went to Chicago, where she spent the winter in study. Returning the following spring, she was again employed to teach, in the log schoolhouse, at an advance of fifty cents per week on the former wages.

At this point, we take leave of Miss Helen Goodale, the first schoolma'am of Traverse City, with the statement that she afterwards became Mrs. T. A. Hitchcock, and, respected by a large circle of acquaintances, has lived to see her humble school-house swept away by the onward march of improvement, and a populous and thriving town occupying the locality of the scene of her youthful labors.

During Miss Goodale's absence in Chicago, in the winter of 1853 and '54, Miss Helen Gamon, an experienced teacher, who was visiting her sister, Mrs. Holton, taught the school. It was kept that winter in the old Boardman boarding-house, it being more easily reached by the children than the log schoolhouse, when the snows were deep. In the winter of 1854 and '55, the teacher was Farwell Campbell, the old boarding-house being again occupied by the school. A school district had been organized, and Mr. Campbell was employed by the legal authorities. It does not appear who was the teacher in the summer of 1855. The following winter the school was taught by a Mr. Enos, in a building which, at the time of the present writing, constitutes a part of the hotel known as the Front Street House. In the winter of 1856 and '57, the school was kept in a new district schoolhouse, which had been built, Theron Bostwick being the teacher.

Before dismissing the subject of the early schools in the vicinity of the head of the bay, it is proper to mention one other, so unique in its inception and execution as to stand as a curiosity in the history of educational institutions.

In November, 1851, five young men arrived at Old Mission, in the schooner Madeline, with the intention of wintering in the vicinity. Three of them were brothers, named Fitzgerald. A fourth was called Wm. Bryce. The name of the fifth, who was employed by the others as cook, has been forgotten. The five were all good sailors, and three of them had been masters of vessels during the past season, but all were deficient in education. None of them were even tolerable readers, and one of the number was unable to write his name. An eager desire to learn was the occasion of their coming. Here in the wilderness they would be removed from the allurements that might distract the attention in a populous port. It is probable, also, that diffidence arising from a consciousness of their own deficiencies made them unwilling to enter a public school, where their limited attainments would be displayed in painful contrast with those of younger pupils.

At Old Mission, the man who had been engaged as teacher failing to meet the contract, Mr. S. E. Wait, then only nineteen years of age, was employed, at $20 per month and board. Bryce and the Fitzgeralds were to pay the bill, the cook receiving his tuition in compensation for his services. The Madeline was brought round to Bowers' Harbor, and securely anchored for the winter. The after-hold was converted into a kitchen and dining-room, and the cabin used for a school room. Regular hours of study were observed, and the men voluntarily submitted to strict school discipline. Out of school hours, they had a plenty of exercise in cutting wood and bringing it on board, to say nothing of the recreation of snowballing, in which they sometimes engaged with the delight of genuine school-boys. The bay that year did not freeze over till March. Previous to the freezing, the wood was brought on board in the yawl; afterwards it was conveyed over the ice. Except by way of Old Mission, to which occasional visits were made, the party was entirely cut off from communication with the outside world.

The progress of Mr. Wait's pupils in their studies, was a credit to themselves and their youthful teacher. Their after history is not known, except that four of them were captains of vessels the following season.

* Undoubtedly this was the first school ever taught in the lower peninsula north of Manistee, except those connected with the Indian missions, and Mr. Wait's on board the schooner Madeline. M. L. L.

CHAPTER XIV.

First Settlement of Leelanau County.—John Lerue—Rev. George N. Smith—The Colony at Northport—First Fourth of July Celebration—How to Make a Flag—Scant Supplies—Glen Arbor—Leland—Going to Mill.

While the events narrated in the preceding chapters were occurring in the vicinity of Old Mission and Traverse City, men were beginning to penetrate the wilderness and establish homes at other points in the Grand Traverse country.

In 1847, John Lerue came from Chicago to the Manitou Islands, in search of health. At that time there was a pier, or wharf, on each of the two islands, where passing steamers used to call for wood, the one on the north island being owned by Mr. Pickard, that on the south by Mr. Barton. On the north Manitou were two fishermen, without families. The lighthouse was kept by a man named Clark.

There were no white men at that time in Leelanau county. Farther south, at the mouth of the Betsey River, there was living a white man named Joseph Oliver, with an Indian wife, who supported his family by trapping and fishing. There were no Indians living on the Manitous, but they frequently came there to trade.

Finding the climate favorable to his health, Mr. Lerue commenced trading with the Indians, and the next year moved his establishment over to the main-land, locating at what was then called Sleeping Bear Bay, but now Glen Arbor, thus becoming the first white inhabitant of Leelanau county.

Rev. George N. Smith, a minister of the congregational church, had spent ten years in missionary work among the Indians of Black river, in Ottawa county. A colony of Hollanders had recently settled in the vicinity of the mission. What was the real nature of the trouble, does not appear, but the proximity of the new-comers made it in some way unpleasant for Mr. Smith and the Indians. Perhaps the action of the government with regard to the Indians also had an influence in determining Mr. Smith's future course. At all events, he made arrangements to remove the mission to the Grand Traverse country. Visiting the bay in the summer of 1848, in company with some of the mission Indians, he selected a location on the shore, some distance north of the site of the present village of Northport.

In the mean time, the government gave orders to James McLaughlin, Indian farmer for the Waukazoo band of Ottawas, at Old Wing, Allegan county, to remove to Grand Traverse bay. In obedience to these orders, Mr. McLaughlin left the mouth of the Kalamazoo river on the 27th day of May, 1849, in the schooner H. Merrill, of which he was owner. There were on board his own family, consisting of six persons counting himself, and that of his brother-in-law, Wm. H. Case, consisting of three persons. Entering Black lake, the vessel proceeded up to the place where the village of Holland is now situated, and received on board Mr. Smith and family, increasing the number of passengers to fifteen. After a tempestuous voyage, the vessel passed Cat Head Point on the morning of the 11th of June, and entered the bay.

Mr. Smith and family were landed, in a drenching rain, at the place previously selected. The prospect was gloomy enough to dismay the stoutest heart. There were no whites in the vicinity, and only a few Indians. A little way back from the beach rose a barrier of interlaced cedars and hemlocks, apparently impenetrable, and they knew that beyond it there stretched away an unbroken forest to the lake shore on the west, and to the distant settlements of the lumbermen at the mouth of the Manistee and on the Muskegon in the south. Both Mr. Smith and his wife were much depressed by the influence of their unpropitious surroundings, even doubting for a while whether they had really been acting under divine guidance. But the die was cast. There was no opportunity for retreat.

Mr. McLaughlin, not liking the location chosen by Mr. Smith, sailed along the shore to the mouth of the little creek that runs through the village of Northport. Here the vessel was anchored, and preparations were made for building a house. It was a common log house, nineteen feet square on the outside. The logs were hauled to their place and hoisted to their positions in the building by the aid of a tackle brought on shore from the vessel. This first house in what is now the village of Northport, stood on the bank of the creek, about six rods back from the beach. At a later period, it was used for several years as a store by White and Burbeck.

After a little time spent in exploring, Mr. Smith concluded to change his location. Accordingly a tent was erected, on the spot which, from that time, became the permanent home of the family, within the present village limits, in which they lived while Mr. Smith was building a log house. Mr. Case built a log house, east of the creek, also within the village limits.

A considerable number of Indians, some say forty or fifty families, followed their missionary to the Grand Traverse bay. A log school house was built, and an Indian village, called Waukazooville in honor of a noted chief, was established on the present site of Northport. During the first years of his residence here, Mr. Smith gave his time and talents to mission work among the Indians. Afterwards he organized a congregational church among the whites, of which for many years he was the pastor. His death occurred on the 5th day of April, 1881, after a brief illness caused by long continued physical exposure. His remains lie buried near the home he hewed out of the forest, on the shore of the beautiful Grand Traverse bay.

The little colony at Northport were scarcely settled in their new home, when they were reminded that the anniversary of the nation's birthday was close at hand. They determined to celebrate it in a becoming manner. They had no cannon or flag. An old sailor on board the vessel undertook to supply the latter. Cutting up a red flannel shirt and a white cotton sheet, he manufactured of the two a flag that was deemed respectable for the occasion. The morning of the Fourth was ushered in with a salute from all the guns that could be mustered. Then all the party, young and old, repaired to the little island in the bay, where the day was passed pleasantly. We may well believe, what we are told by one who was present, that this first Fourth of July celebration in the Grand Traverse country was as full of patriotism and love of country as any that has ever been held since.

Early in autumn the settlers began to make preparations for a long and tedious winter. They were agreeably disappointed, however, as the fall months passed away, to find the weather remaining pleasant. The winter proved to be exceptionally mild. There was no snow till the 12th of December. Very little ice formed in the bay. By the first of April, every vestige of snow and ice had disappeared, and the ground was in good condition for tillage.

At the setting in of the second winter, (1850-'51,) the prospect was not cheering. The vessel that was expected to bring supplies, was wrecked on the voyage. A son of Mr. McLaughlin has put on record a description of the provisions on hand for his father's family of six persons. The supply consisted of half a barrel of damaged flour, fifty pounds of pork, a barrel of white-fish, a little tea, potatoes enough to last through the winter, and a small quantity of corn, of home production, which they ground in a hand mill. It is not probable that the other families were better supplied.

In the summer of 1851, a second settler, John Dorsey, located at Glen Arbor. In the fall of that year, Mr. Lerue brought his family into the country, spending the following winter at Northport. Soon after Mr. Lerue's arrival, Mr. McLaughlin, who had previously been engaged in building A. S. Wadsworth's saw-mill at Elk Rapids, removed from Northport to that place, leaving the original number of three families at Northport—Smith's, Case's, and Lerue's. In the spring of 1852, Mr. Lerue returned to his former location, at Glen Arbor.

In 1853, Mr. A. Manseau, still a resident of Leelanau county, settled at Carp river, where the village of Leland is now situated. He was followed, in 1854, by J. L. Miller, John Porter, H. S. Buckman, John Bryant, Sr., and Frederick Cook. Plans were laid by some of the new comers looking towards the building of a pier at the mouth of the river, and a saw-mill.

In the spring of 1854, John E. Fisher came to Glen Arbor, looking for a location. Having made a selection, he brought his brother-in-law Cogshell's family from the state of New York, and, later in the season, his own, from Fond du Lac, Wis. The next year was marked by the arrival of Dr. W. H. Walker, of Fond du Lac, George Ray, and a man from Ohio named Nutt. The three last named built a pier, where the one owned by Charles Rossman is now standing.

Soon after the removal of Messrs. McLaughlin and Lerue from Northport, other settlers began to arrive at that place. Deacon Dame, having removed thither from Old Mission, was the first to open business. He commenced the construction of a wharf, in 1853 or '54, which was afterwards completed by H. O. Rose. At the opening of navigation in 1855, it was still in an unfinished condition, a part of it, for want of planks, being covered with poles. A list of residents of the settlement for 1855 and '56, contains the following names: Joseph Dame, H. O. Rose, Amos Fox, Wm. Voice, Capt. Peter Nelson, A. B. Page, S. W. Wilson, Thomas Retford, J. M. Burbeck, O. L. White, Henry Boyes, A. O. Stevens, Theodore Woodruff, Hiram Beckwith, Jesse Morgan, Wm. Gill, and Wm. Thomas. Of these the greater number were heads of families, but a few were unmarried men. In 1855 there was not a frame house in the place—only a part of one, a structure in size about fourteen feet by twenty, which now constitutes a part of the dwelling occupied by W. F. Steele. The first one complete, was built by Mr. Thomas for Mr. Woodruff, in 1856. Mr. Voice commenced in 1855 the construction of a saw-mill, which was got to running in the summer of the following year. In 1855 no roads had been opened, except one leading to the Indian settlement called Cat Head Village, some three miles distant. There was not a horse team in the settlement, and only two or three yoke of oxen. During that year, only one propeller, running between Grand Haven and Buffalo, made calls at the half-built wharf.

For a few years, many of the settlers in Leelanau county endured great privations. An authentic incident will illustrate the extremity to which they were sometimes pushed, and the shifts they were obliged to make for the purpose of securing the necessaries of life.

On one occasion, in winter, Mr. Timblin, having left of his supplies a bushel and a half of corn and a dollar and a half in money, proposed to divide with his needy neighbor, Mr. Cook, on condition that the latter should go to Traverse City, get the corn ground, and invest the money in groceries. Mr. Cook was only too glad to accept the proposition. A single ox, which Mr. Timblin had taught to work alone, was the only team the two men could muster. Placing the bag of corn on the ox's back, Mr. Cook drove him across the country by an Indian trail, from the vicinty of Leland to Peshawbatown, the scattered Indian settlement on the shore south of Omena. Procuring a pony and sled of the Indians, he left the ox in their care, and proceeded up the bay on the ice to Traverse City. Having got the corn ground, and the money invested in groceries, he started on the homeward journey. Before he reached Peshawbatown, a snowstorm came on, which completely hid the shores of the bay from view. Coming to a crack in the ice so wide as to be difficult to cross, he was at a loss which way to follow it, but after some hesitation took the direction which seemed to lead down the bay. Some Indians whom he fell in with advised him by signs to go in another direction, but having little confidence in their ability to direct, he continued his course some distance farther. Finally concluding that the Indians were probably right, he decided to change his course. He thought it would perhaps save travel, if he could get on the other side of the crack. It may or may not have been a foolish attempt, but it resulted in a disheartening failure. The pony jumped just far enough to get his fore feet on the solid ice of the farther side, but, failing to get his hind feet on a firm foundation, both pony and sled went into the water. To prevent the pony from sinking, Mr. Cook seized him by the ears. As he did so, his own feet slipped, and he came down in a sitting posture, in the shallow water that covered the edge of the ice. Holding on still to the pony's ears, he called loudly for help. Fortunately the Indians he had met were yet within hearing, and promptly came to his assistance. When relieved, Mr. Cook was so thoroughly chilled as to be almost helpless. Some of the Indians drew him on a hand sled to Peshawbatown, while others cared for the half dead pony. The meal and the groceries had gone to the bottom of the bay. There was a scene of sorrow when Mr. Cook reached home. Mrs. Cook wept freely for the loss of the little that had seemed to promise a short respite from starvation.

The early business interests of Northport were developed mainly by the enterprise of Messrs. Fox & Rose. Mr. H. O. Rose came to the place in June, 1854, and, as already intimated, purchased the wharf privilege owned by Deacon Dame, pushing to completion the wharf already commenced. In September, 1855, he sold a half interest in the property to Mr. Amos Fox, the two entering into partnership under the firm name above mentioned, their principal business being dealing in wood. At that time, the steamers running on the lakes depended almost wholly on wood for fuel. The wharf built by Mr. Rose, and afterwards twice enlarged by the firm, was the first in Grand Traverse bay at which a propeller could stop. It was easy of access, and not far off the route of steamers plying between the ports on the lower lakes and those on the western shore of Lake Michigan. In 1856, the firm supplied by contract the Northern Transportation Company's line of boats plying between Ogdensburgh and Chicago, handling that season about 5,000 cords of wood. Afterwards contracts were made with other lines of steamers. In 1858 the firm handled from 13,000 to 15,000 cords, and for several years after the amount of wood annually sold did not materially diminish.

In the winter of 1856 and '57, Messrs. White & Burbeck built a wharf three miles north of the present village of Northport, and engaged in selling wood and shipping hemlock bark and cedar posts.

Mr. Rose was the first treasurer of Leland township, which at that time embraced the whole of Leelanau and Benzie counties. He relates having traveled over nearly the whole of it, going as far as Glen Arbor, to collect the annual tax, the amount of which did not exceed six hundred dollars.

CHAPTER XV.

The Pioneer Family of Elk Rapids—Mill Built—More Settlers—Hard Times—A Trip on the Ice—About to Freeze to Death—Old Joe's Remedy—Relief—The Village of Elk Rapids Laid Out—Driving in Cattle—The First Funeral—Changes—James Rankin & Son—M. Crow & Co.—Dexter & Noble.

Mr. A. S. Wadsworth, the pioneer of Elk Rapids, first visited Grand Traverse bay in 1846, stopping a few days at Old Mission. On that occasion he came from his home in Portland, Ionia county, in a small boat, passing down Grand river to its mouth, and then coasting along the eastern shore of Lake Michigan. The next year, in August, accompanied by his brother-in-law, Samuel K. Northam, he took his family to Detroit, where the party embarked on a propeller for Mackinac. From the latter place they found passage on a schooner as far as Cross Village. There, after camping for several days on the beach, waiting for a storm to subside, they embarked in a small boat for Old Mission.

At Middle Village they again went into camp, and waited two days on account of rain. The next stop was made at Little Traverse, where they hoped to obtain provisions of the Indians. They only succeeded, however, in getting a few potatoes and a single loaf of bread. The party had lived on fish till that food had ceased to tempt the appetite. The children, especially, were suffering for want of their accustomed diet. After leaving Little Traverse, they were favored with pleasant weather and got on rapidly. The last day, the bay was rough, and they had some fears about crossing to Old Mission from the eastern shore, along which they had been coasting. Seeing a smoke on the shore near Elk river, they ran to it. Fortunately they found there some Indians, with an excellent sea boat, who were about to cross. As a matter of precaution, Mrs. Wadsworth and the children were put into the Indians' boat, which was navigated by Mr. Wadsworth and one of the Indians, while Mr. Northam and the remaining Indians occupied Mr. Wadsworth's boat. In a short time the party landed at Old Mission in safety. They had been nearly two weeks coming from Mackinac.

Mr. Wadsworth remained about two years at Old Mission. In the mean time, he conceived the project of improving the excellent water power at Elk river, which seemed to promise generous returns for investment. Accordingly, in the spring of 1849, he commenced building a house at what is now Elk Rapids. With the exception of the log house built by Mr. Dougherty during his temporary residence on the east side of the bay, the material of which had already been removed to Old Mission, this was the first building erected by a white man in Antrim county.* In October the family moved into it, while it was yet in an unfinished state. Mr. Wadsworth soon after commenced building a mill for the manufacture of pickets and laths, which was got to running in the spring of 1851. The following winter it was rebuilt as a saw-mill. Both house and mill have disappeared before later improvements, not a vestige of either remaining to mark the place where it stood.

Until 1851, Mr. Wadsworth's family, including his hired help, all of which lived in his own house, was the only one in Elk Rapids. In July of that year, Mrs. Wadsworth and the children went east to spend the winter, Mr. Wadsworth remaining at home. The fall was marked by the arrival of four families—those of Amos Wood, Alexander McVicar, James McLaughlin, and a Mormon family named Barnes. The Mormons remained but a short time. McVicar removed to a lumber camp on Round Lake, leaving only two families—Wood's and McLaughlin's—in the settlement during the winter. Mr. McLaughlin, as we have already seen, had come from Northport, to be near his work on the new saw-mill.

The winter of 1851 and '52 set in early and proved to be severe. The ice on the bay formed nearly three feet thick, and the snow was three feet deep in the woods. By the middle of January the two families found themselves nearly out of provisions. Twice some of their number went across the bay with hand sleds, to Hannah, Lay & Co's establishment, after flour. Towards spring the supply of flour gave out, no more being obtainable at that place. Hulled corn was used for a while as a substitute for bread, but at last the store of corn was exhausted. Some fisherman had left a quantity of white-fish in his shanty, near where the village of Torch Lake now stands. Two trips were made to that place, after some of the fish.

On one of these trips to the fisherman's shanty, James J. McLaughlin, then but a youth, came near losing his life. His companion was the Indian, Old Joe. Having opened a half barrel to pour off the brine, in order to make their load lighter, they took out one of the salt fish and roasted it by the fire while resting. James ate heartily of it, notwithstanding the caution of his more prudent companion. Starting on their return, they found that drawing their loaded hand sled against a head wind, with two or three inches of snow on the ice, was no child's play. James soon began to suffer with a terrible thirst, which could be only partially allayed by drinking at every crevice in the ice. The day was bitterly cold. The fatigue, the extreme severity of the weather, and the large quantity of cold water taken into the stomach, all, perhaps, had their influence in producing that condition of somnolency which often precedes death by freezing. Only by the watchfulness of the Indian was he prevented from deliberately lying down to sleep. Old Joe had finally to relieve him from the load, drawing it himself. Darkness came on while they were yet several miles from home. James could no longer control himself. Lying down upon the ice, he was asleep in a moment. In a moment more he was roused to wakefulness by a tingling sensation on the less protected parts of the body, that reminded him of the schoolmaster and the birch of his early school days. Old Joe had detached from the sled the leather strap used for drawing it, and was laying it on to his companion with a will. Not satisfied with making him regain his feet in a lively manner, he left the sled, and drove him in advance all the way home. The next day Old Joe went back alone after the load of fish.

By the 16th of April their seed corn and seed beans, intended for planting the following season, had been consumed. For some time the ice in the bay had been so rotten as to make traveling upon it unsafe, and they had been anxiously waiting for it to break up, so as to permit them to cross in boats to Old Mission, where they hoped to get a little corn and a few potatoes of the Indians. About three o'clock in the afternoon of that day, the ice began to move. With the dawn of the 17th, all were astir. Looking out upon the bay, a belt of open water was seen, and, to their great joy, not far off was a vessel working her way up through it. She proved to be the schooner Liberty, of Racine, Wis., Captain Miller, loaded with provisions. She was soon boarded by the men. Hearing their story, Capt. Miller at once hoisted out a barrel of flour and another of pork, with which they returned to their half famished but now happy families.

In the spring of 1852, Mr. Wadsworth laid out the village of Elk Rapids. Lots were sold for twenty-five dollars each. The employment furnished by the mill was an inducement for new-comers to settle in the vicinity. Among those who came that season were Michael Gay, John Lake, Jared Stocking, John B. Spencer, and their families. Messrs. Gay and Spencer, it will be remembered, have already been mentioned as among the early settlers at Traverse City.

Up to 1852 there were no cattle in the vicinity of Elk Rapids, except a yoke of oxen at the lumber camp on Round Lake. In July Mr. McLaughlin went to the south part of the State, and returning brought with him a yoke of oxen and a cow. At Grand Rapids he was joined by Wm. Slawson and Perry Stocking, each with a cow. From Grand Rapids the party struck north, their route from the Muskegon River to Traverse City being through an unbroken wilderness, with only the section lines for guides. The first day out from Grand Rapids, Mr. Slawson's cow broke away and was lost. The party were thirteen days in accomplishing the distance to Elk Rapids. Not a little excitement was caused in the settlement by the sound of a cow bell worn by one of the animals, as the party approached, it being the first ever heard there. Soon afterwards Mr. McVicar moved his father's family in from Canada, bringing two cows, making altogether a herd of eight head of cattle in the settlement.

About the first of November, 1852, a cloud settled over the community, caused by the death of Charlie, youngest son of James McLaughlin, a bright boy of thirteen. It was the first death. There was no clergyman on the east side of the bay, but appropriate funeral services were conducted by a layman, Mr. John McDonald. The grave was made in a grove of pines, in a beautiful spot, on the first terrace above the bay. For several years afterwards the place was used as a burying-ground by the inhabitants. The remains of the first occupant were removed at a later date to Maple Grove cemetery.

The year 1853 brought many changes. Large additions of immigrants were made to the population. Among those who became residents of the village or settled in the vicinity, were John Denahy, E. L. Sprague, J. W. Arnold, David F. Parks, Alexander Campbell, and Hiram Robinson. The clearings of farmers began to dot the shores of Elk lake.

Within the next few years the settlements spread in all directions. A. T. Allen, Orrin Page, and Edwin Pulcipher located near the shore of the bay, south of Elk Rapids, and were followed a little later by Joseph Sours, Riel Johnson, and others. Wm. Copeland, Wm. Merrill, Almon Young, and several others, attracted by the choice lands on Round lake, founded what has since been favorably known in the history of Grand Traverse agriculture as the Round lake settlement.

In 1853 Mr. Wadsworth sold his mill to James Rankin & Sons, who built a store and brought in a stock of goods. Jared Stocking opened a hotel. In the fall and following winter Mr. Wadsworth built another saw-mill, on the site of the mill since owned by Dexter & Noble, Mr. Northam having charge of the business. The mill was scarcely completed, when he sold it to M. Craw & Co., of which firm Mr. Wirt Dexter was the principal partner.

In September, 1855, Mr. Henry H. Noble came to Elk Rapids, as an employe of M. Craw & Co. In the fall of the following year,* (1856,) that firm was dissolved, and a new one was organized, under the name of Dexter & Noble, Wirt Dexter and Henry H Noble being the only partners The stock of goods and the saw-mill of the former firm passed into the hands of the latter In the course of the winter the saw-mill was rebuilt, and in the spring the new firm commenced the manufacture of lumber with facilities for making three millions of feet annually The business was continued on this very moderate scale till 1861, when a gang saw mill was built, with a capacity of ten millions.

To the enterprise and energy and the far-seeing and wisely conducted liberal business policy of Dexter & Noble, the prosperity of Elk Rapids and the surrounding country is largely due The only change ever made in the *personnel* of the firm, was the admission of Mr. E S Noble as a partner, in 1869 Of the immense business enterprises of later years, successfully built on the modest foundation of their first little saw mill and small store, it would be out of place to speak at this stage of our narrative

To return to earlier dates A notable event of the year 1853, was the opening of the first school. The house in which it was kept is still standing, not far from the brick school house that has since been built The young teacher, George W. Ladd, of the peninsula, has long since passed to his reward, having fallen a victim to that dread disease consumption. Several of his pupils are still living in the country, looking back, no doubt, with fond remembrance to their association with that school as a pleasing and important event in the history of their lives.

*Rev J J McLaughlin writes me that in 1854 he discovered the remains of a log house on the shore of Elk lake, about four rods south of the county line, between Grand Traverse and Antrim counties It had been built of cedar logs Mr McLaughlin thinks from appearances that the logs had not been removed, but that the building had settled down where it stood There was nothing to show of what materials the roof had been constructed The door way was in the south end, and there had been a stone chimney, or fireplace, in the northeast corner That it had been inhabited was evident from the ashes and coals found in the fireplace

That this structure was not the work of Indians, is evident from the fact that the fireplace was built of stones and was in the corner of the building If built by white men, and if, as Mr McLaughlin thinks, time enough had elapsed for it to rot down previous to 1854 there must have been white men on Elk lake a generation or two earlier than Mr Dougherty's arrival at Old Mission, for cedar timber does not rot readily Who they were and why they were here, is a mystery that perhaps will never be solved M L L

CHAPTER XVI

Early Church Work at Elk Rapids—A Minister Builds a Raft—What Happened to the Raft and the Minister—Rev J W Miller—Potatoes and Salt—Scolding the Lord—A Friend in Need—"The Lord is my Shepherd"

Until 1857 there had been no stated religious service anywhere on the east side of the bay On the second day of August in that year, Rev D R. Latham crossed from Old Mission, and preached at Elk Rapids. He attempted to include that point in his round of regular appointments, but often found it difficult to cross the bay. When, in the fall of 1858, the Michigan conference detached Elk Rapids from Old Mission and Traverse City, and erected it, with the adjacent territory, into what was known as Whitewater circuit, Mr Latham was assigned to it as preacher in charge, and removed from Old Mission to his new work.

It seems to have been Mr Latham's fortune to meet with many of those adventures and mishaps, some dangerous, some ludicrous, that fall to the lot of the pioneer, especially if the pioneer, like the subject of our sketch, is courageous, confident, careless of the cost, and inexperienced in the wild life of a new country. We have given one to the reader; another may not be out of place

On one occasion, when going to fill an appointment to preach in Mr Allen's house, in Whitewater, he resolved to save time and distance by following the beach instead of the usual route by the road Between Elk Rapids and Whitewater there is a little lake, called by the Indians Petobego, separated from Grand Traverse bay by only a narrow sand bar Sometimes the outlet of Petobego is a shallow brook, that one can easily wade through. Sometimes it is entirely filled up with the shifting sand, so that one may walk across it dry shod Sometimes, again, a large part of the bar is washed away, and the channel between the little lake and the bay is broad and deep Of the uncertain character of the bar, however, Mr. Latham was ignorant. On arriving at Petobego, he found the outlet about ten rods wide and several feet deep, and, what to him was a mystery, instead of Petobego running into the bay there was a strong current from the bay into Petobego The mystery would have been no mystery to one familiar with the phenomena of the lake shore—there was a strong west wind blowing, driving the waters of the bay into the little lake Here was a dilemma. He must either go back by way of Elk Rapids or cross the stream. There was not time for the former, besides he was now more than half way to his appointment. There was plenty of drift-wood on the beach. He resolved to build a raft. Laying off his overcoat and gloves, he brought it together, till he supposed he had collected material sufficient for a raft large enough to carry him over. Putting into the water a layer of poles and slabs, arranged side by side, he covered them with a second layer, placed crosswise Then putting on his overcoat, he took a long piece of edging for a setting pole, and pushed off The current was stronger than he had supposed In pushing off, he stood on one edge of the raft The poles of the opposite edge being left loose, were washed away by the current, and he soon saw a row of them chasing each other into Petobego. Next he discovered that he was drifting out of his course. To regain it, he gave an extra push with all his might The edge of the raft on which he stood settled down into the water, while the poles of the portion opposite floated away in a body. At the same time, the setting pole snapped in two, leaving a piece only three or four feet long in his hands There followed a moment of anxiety He could not swim. He knew that the remaining fragment of the raft would not hold together a minute longer He was standing on two slabs, which lay side by side, with their flat surfaces uppermost. A thought came like a flash of inspiration Stooping down, he turned one of them over, placing it atop of the other with their flat surfaces together, and quickly jumped astride of them. The water was unpleasantly cold, for it was in November, but he felt safe and happy. With the fragment of edging he paddled ashore, climbed up the bank, emptied the water out of his boots, and went on to Mr. Allen's But Mr Latham's troubles were not over. The congregation was waiting There was a good fire in the stove, and the big family bible had been placed on a stand near it. He was not proud of his adventure, and did not desire to have it known. It was fortunate, he thought, that the stand and bible were so near the stove He would quietly dry himself while conducting the services, and nobody should be the wiser As he knelt down to pray, he purposely pushed his feet under the stove. The action disturbed an overgrown puppy that was sleeping there, which came out, and, after smelling at him till satisfied of his friendly character, began to lick his face. Mr. Latham shut his eyes tightly, and tried to endure it while he went on with his prayer, but the performances of the puppy at length became too much for the patience of one of the men. Seizing the poor dog by the skin of the neck, he hurled him across the room to the door, where a boy caught him by the feet and threw him yelping outside. In after years Mr. Latham asserted that he could not remember how he preached or what was the subject of his sermon on that occasion.

It is understood that at the conference in the fall of 1859, Mr. Latham was assigned to Whitewater circuit for another year. He had labored faithfully, enduring hardships and battling with difficulties such as the ministers of more favored localities know nothing of by experience. He had been literally starved out. Seeing an opportunity to get an appointment as teacher in a government Indian school, he thought it his duty to take advantage of it, and accordingly, in November, left the Grand Traverse country for his new field of labor.

The Whitewater circuit was without a pastor till April of the following year, when Rev. J. W. Miller arrived and took charge of the work.

Mr. Miller had been converted about a year previously. He was a young lawyer, just admitted to the bar, and had been appointed by Judge Littlejohn as circuit court commissioner. He was in love with his profession and his worldly prospects were bright, but the call to the ministry was imperative. He promised the Lord of the harvest that if he would open a door for him, he would enter in, regardless of consequences. Soon afterwards, Rev. S. Steele, who had succeeded Rev. W. W. Johnson as presiding elder of the Grand Traverse district, called on him and proposed that he should take the abandoned field at Whitewater. The proposal was promptly accepted, and Mr. Steele, with the approval of the quarterly conference, gave him a local preacher's license.

Mr. Miller had no great amount of funds. It cost between forty and fifty dollars to move, besides the misfortune of breaking and spoiling a large proportion of his furniture. For some time he and his young wife lived on their own means, but they were at length exhausted, and then many a meal was made on only potatoes and salt. No wonder if they became discouraged, and if their faith in God's care of his servants began to waver.

One day, before going to his appointment, Mr. Miller went out into the woods in front of his house, as he has since related, "to give the Lord a scolding for getting them into such a fix," after they had trusted to his guidance and relied on his aid. He could not understand or appreciate the situation, but while talking with God—"praying and scolding by turns"—the good Father was pleased to open his eyes. He saw his own unworthiness as never before, and the goodness of God in even giving them potatoes. He was conscious of receiving a wonderful blessing. Then and there he promised God that if he would furnish potatoes, he would remain in the ministry, and never murmur again. Returning to the house, he put the saddle on old Jack, his Indian pony, and started for his appointment at Elk lake. On his way, he called on Mr. Hill, an unconverted man, and talked and prayed with the family. As he left the house, Mr. Hill walked with him across the fields to the road. The latter seemed nervous, evidently having something on his mind that caused him much distress. Finally he burst into tears, as he said, "Elder, I suppose you will be offended and say it is none of my business, but for over a week I have been thinking about you; not only in the daytime, but I wake in the night and wonder if you have anything to eat, and there is such a pressure on me I must out with it, regardless of consequences." Mr. Miller told him all, and Mr. Hill insisted on dividing with him what he had, and then went round to the neighbors and collected what they could give. "Thus," says Mr. Miller, "while I was fretting and complaining, the good Lord was working and caring for us. It is a lesson I have never forgotten and never wish to forget. From that day to the present, I have never murmured at the work of the ministry or for a single moment wished myself out of it. Another thing—from that day to the present, I have never asked, either as pastor or presiding elder, for a single dollar. After twenty-five years, I can still say with the Psalmist, 'the Lord is my shepherd.' My only regret is that I have not been more faithful and efficient in the great work."

Mr. Miller remained on Whitewater circuit till the fall of 1861, when by the action of the annual conference he was transferred to Northport. He usually preached three times on Sunday and once during the week, the appointments being Elk Rapids, Elk Lake, Round Lake, Williamsburg, Acme, and Yuba.

CHAPTER XVII.

Richard Cooper—Little Traverse—Fishing and Fishermen—Captain Kirtland—Mission at Bear Creek—Helpfulness of the Indians—An Indian Mother and her Boy—Progress of the Pupils—Indian Farming.

The first white settler at Little Traverse, now called Harbor Springs, except those connected with the Catholic mission, was Richard Cooper.

Mr. Cooper came from Genesee county, N. Y., to the Beaver Islands in 1848, to engage in fishing. In the fall of 1850 he returned home. In the spring of 1851 he came back on the trading schooner Eliza Caroline, owned and commanded by Capt. Kirtland. Touching at Pine River, now Charlevoix, the Caroline landed several fishermen and a quantity of salt. Stopping next at Old Mission and then at Northport, she sailed for Gull Island, where Mr. Cooper remained during the summer, buying fish for Kirtland. In the fall he removed to Little Traverse, where he opened a store for Kirtland, in whose employ he still remained.

At the time of Mr. Cooper's settlement at Little Traverse, the fishermen had already established themselves at several points on the northern part of Lake Michigan, but there were none at that place. That same fall, however, was marked by the arrival of Charles R. Wright, Albert Cable, James Moore, Harrison Miller, Thomas Smith, and Patrick Sullivan. Wright and Cable at first stopped on the point; the others in the village. All of them were in some way connected with the fishing interest.

Fishing at that time was perhaps more profitable than it has been during a later period; at all events, the testimony of those of the early fishermen who still remain agrees as to the fact that fish were much more plentiful then than now. Pound nets were not used. After they came into common use, there was a sensible and rapid diminution in the quantity of fish.

Some who came to the country in those early days to fish, remained as permanent citizens; but generally the fisherman was a transient person, establishing himself anywhere on the shore where there was a promise of success in his pursuit, and readily changing his location as immediate interest seemed to dictate. Associated with the fishermen, wherever they were numerous, were always a number of coopers, who found employment in making barrels for the fish. Sometimes the cooper's shop was in the immediate vicinity of the fish shanties; sometimes, for the convenience of obtaining material, it was located at a distance. The material for barrels was derived from timber growing on the public lands, which was looked upon as lawful plunder. Small trading establishments, like that of Capt. Kirtland under the management of Mr. Cooper at Little Traverse, sprung up at various points, drawing their custom from both the fishermen and the Indians. A few small vessels, or "hookers," found a lucrative business in trading from place to place, selling supplies and purchasing fish. Not unfrequently whisky was a principal article of trade. It is remembered to the credit of Capt. Kirtland that he never sold whisky to the Indians or took advantage of them in business transactions.

At the time referred to, the Indians were much more numerous in the vicinity of Little Traverse than at a later date, and that place remained for many years to all intents and purposes an Indian village, the only white inhabitants being a few fishermen and traders. In the meantime, an enterprise grew up on the opposite side of the bay, almost within the present limits of the village of Petoskey, that is worthy of an extended notice.

When Mr. Dougherty's flock began to scatter from Old Mission, some Indian families from that place removed to the vicinity of Bear Creek, where a band of Ottawas and Chippewas were already living. It was perhaps through the influence of the new comers that a request was made to Mr. Dougherty by the Indians that a school might be established among them. By order of the Presbyterian board, under whose authority he was acting, Mr. Dougherty visited them in the winter of 1851 and 52, and made so favorable a report that the board determined to accede to their request, and Mr. Andrew Porter, who had previously spent some time as teacher at Old Mission, was appointed for the work.

Mr. Porter, with his family, left his home in Pennsylvania early in May, 1852 arriving at his destination the first of June. From Mackinac he came in Capt. Kirtland's vessel, the Eliza Caroline, the captain bringing him for a very small sum. Mr. Dougherty had previously sent a vessel with a cargo of lumber for the construction of the necessary buildings. The pile of lumber on the beach, served to guide Capt. Kirtland to the proper landing. On leaving the vessel, the party were kindly received by the head man, Daniel Wells, or Mwake we nah, whom the band afterwards elected chief, and who, a few years later, laid down his life for the country in the war of the rebellion. He placed his best room at the disposal of Mr. Porter, till the Mission house could be built.

The place selected for the Mission was on the high land west of Bear Creek, half a mile back from the bay. How to get the lumber to the spot, was a problem that caused some anxiety. The only domestic animal in the settlement that could be put to such work was a single pony, and the only vehicle was a cart, and then the new road which had recently been cut through the forest by the Indians was too rough and uneven for a wheel carriage of any kind. The anxiety, however, was soon removed by the announcement that the Indians of Little Traverse were offering their assistance. Soon after, on a set day, about seventy men, and seven ponies with "sled cars," were found to have come together on the beach, ready for work. The ponies did very well, but more than half the lumber was carried up the hill to the site of the proposed buildings on the shoulders of the men.

Mr. Porter found the Indians uniformly kind. He never failed to secure their services, when the services of a friend were needed. On first coming among them, he and his family threw themselves upon their honor and honesty, never turning a key to prevent them from stealing, and, though they were then poor and often hungry, the confidence reposed in them was not betrayed.

The mission board adopted the plan of giving to the pupils in the school a generous lunch every day at noon. There seemed to be a necessity for this, as the corn soup, (min-dah min-ah-boo,) which was the principal food of the Indians, could not be conveniently carried with them; and then it was found by experience that if they were allowed to go home for dinner, which was not generally practicable, as most of them lived too far away, they were not likely to return the same day.

For a long time the Indians took a deep interest in the school. This statement is illustrated by a touching incident, related by Mr. Porter. Joseph Na-bah-na-yah-sung, or, as he named himself, Gibson, a boy about ten years old, while the school was suspended for sugar making one spring, had the misfortune to break both bones of the leg between the ankle and the knee. When the school opened again, he was still unable to walk. With a womanly devotion that stands as a living argument against the doctrine of the total depravity of human nature even in those we call savages, his mother and sister alternately carried him three-quarters of a mile to school every day on their shoulders. If inquiry be made as to the life and fate of the boy thus highly favored, it only remains to write—and let it be written among the records of the honorable dead—that he died, as many other noble men died, by cruel starvation in Andersonville prison.

There were many hindrances to success which it seemed impossible to remove or entirely overcome. Some of these were incident to the Indian mode of life. There was of necessity a long vacation in the season of sugar-making, during which the village was deserted. In planting time the school was small, though never entirely closed. At the proper season for peeling cedar bark, collecting rushes for mats, or picking strawberries, raspberries, or huckleberries, the Indians would leave by boat loads, taking their children with them. Notwithstanding these drawbacks, the children made commendable progress, considering that they had to learn a new language, the teaching being done in English. Many learned to read and write very well, and some made more or less advancement in arithmetic and geography. The success, however, was scarcely what the parents had anticipated, and some degree of discouragement was the result. Add to this the fact that influences adverse to the education of the masses, emanating from the Catholic missions at Little Traverse and Cross Village, at length began to be felt by the whole Indian population of the vicinity, and it is no wonder that the interest in the school fell to a lower degree of interest than that manifested at the beginning.

A church was organized at the mission. Mr. Porter was a layman. On the occasions of Mr. Dougherty's visits, there was preaching and the communion service. At one time Rev. H. W. Guthrie, a young minister, resided for two years at the mission, preaching there and at Middle Village. Except when Mr. Dougherty or Mr. Guthrie was present, the Sabbath services, in which some of the Indians always took part, consisted of singing, prayer, and the reading of the scriptures with remarks on the portion read.

During the continuance of the mission, the Indians made steady improvement in the art and practice of farming. In 1852 there was only one pony and one plow among them. The surface of the ground in their small fields was strewn with the trunks of fallen trees, among which cultivation was carried on with no implement but the hoe. Afterwards, when they had to some extent been provided with teams and farming utensils by the government, according to treaty stipulations, their fields were cleared and plowed. Oats, wheat, corn, and potatoes were the principal crops. Of the last two, enough was usually raised to supply their own wants and leave a surplus for sale. Unfortunately the men sent to that locality by the agents of the government as Indian farmers, whose duty it was to instruct them in the art and practice of farming, were frequently too shiftless to do anything but draw their own salaries. A well remembered case will illustrate the statement. The Indians had become dissatisfied with one of this kind, and resolved, if possible, to get rid of him. Accordingly an old chief was delegated to present a complaint to the agent, which he did in the following brief terms: "For the first year or two, he would sometimes come out to the field where we were plowing, take hold of the plow handles and go half across the field, and then would say 'I am hungry,' and return to the village and remain there the rest of the day; but now he never comes near us at all." As the so-called farmer, who was sitting by and heard the complaint, had no defense to make, he was promptly discharged.

For the first two or three years the expense of the mission was borne wholly by the presbyterian board. After the establishment of Indian schools by the government, the one at the mission was adopted by the agent as a government school, and the usual salary was paid to Mr. Porter as teacher. About 1871, the government funds set apart by treaty for the benefit of the Indians being exhausted, and the board finding itself straitened for means, the mission was discontinued. The landed property of the establishment passed into other hands, and Mr. Porter returned to his Pennsylvania home. The place is now occupied by Mr. N. Jarmin, and is still known among the older residents of Petoskey as the mission farm.

CHAPTER XVIII.

The Mormons—Settlement on Beaver Island—Strang is Prophet, Priest and King—Several Kinds of Subjects—Polygamy—"Consecration"—Religion and Robbery—Destroying Angels—Forts—Society of the Illuminati—The Covenant—Mormon Worship.

After the death of Joseph Smith, the founder of the sect of Mormons, at Nauvoo, in 1844, several aspirants for the honor of being his successor as head of the Mormon church sprang up among his followers. The most successful of these was Brigham Young, whose history is familiar to all readers of current literature. Only one other seems to have been successful in getting and retaining any considerable number of adherents. That one was James J. Strang, whose adventurous project of establishing an independent kingdom in northern Michigan is so closely interwoven with the history of the Grand Traverse country as to require a somewhat extended notice.

In February, 1844, Strang went from his home in Voree, Wisconsin, to Nauvoo, for the purpose, it is said, of hearing Smith preach. Within a week after his arrival, he professed to be converted to the Mormon faith, and was received into the church. There was already a considerable number of Mormons at Voree. Strang returned home a zealous advocate of the doctrines he had espoused.

On the 24th of May, in the same year, he wrote to Smith, "proposing the planting of a stake in Zion in Wisconsin, and the gathering of the saints there." Smith replied on the 18th of June following, saying that at first he had disapproved Strang's scheme, but Brother Hyrum thought otherwise, and also that God had since made a revelation in favor of it. The letter contained what purported to be the revelation alluded to, which clearly authorized Strang to proceed with his scheme, and promised that the flock should find rest with him, and that God would reveal to him his will concerning them. The letter closed with an intimation that Strang's duty was made plain, and that, if evil should befall Smith, Strang should lead the flock to pleasant pastures.

Smith was killed on the 27th of June, nine days after the letter was written. Strang claimed to have had a vision at the very hour of Smith's death, in which the angel of the Lord informed him that God had annointed him and set him above his fellows, and, in substance, that he should be their teacher, prophet, ruler and protector, but there is no evidence, except his own subsequent statement, that he mentioned this vision to any of his followers till after the news of Smith's death had been received at Voree. On Smith's letter and his own pretended vision, Strang rested his claim to the leadership of the Mormon church.

After the death of Smith, the Mormon community at Nauvoo was broken up. A large body of the people, under the leadership of Brigham Young, eventually found their way to Utah. Smaller parties sought refuge in other places. Some who started for Utah, becoming dissatisfied with their leaders or discouraged, returned, wandering from place to place for several years, literally seeking rest and finding none. Gradually a considerable number collected at Voree, who acknowledged Strang to be the legitimate successor of Joseph Smith and the divinely appointed head of the Mormon church.

Whatever may have been at this time Strang's ultimate aim and object, he was shrewd enough to see that his plans could be carried out to better advantage, if his community were farther removed from the influence of those Mormons who disputed his authority, and from the interference of the "Gentiles," as all were called who were living outside the pale of the Mormon church. It was for this reason, probably, that he determined to remove to some locality better situated in this respect. The Beaver islands, in the northern part of Lake Michigan, seemed well suited to his purpose, and he resolved to remove thither. The harbor at the north end of the largest island, was selected as the central point for the colony, and the future village named St. James.

We are not informed at what time the first Mormons were transferred to their new home. A lady, whose father was a Mormon preacher and afterwards became one of the Twelve Apostles under Strang, who came to the island with her father's family in June, 1849, gives it as her opinion that there were not more than fifteen families there at that time. Another, who had been brought up a Mormon, and who came with her mother in the fall of 1850, estimates the number of families at that time at twenty five or thirty. From the founding of the colony till the breaking up of the settlement and dispersion of the Mormons, in 1856, there seems to have been a gradual and steady increase of population. It is not probable that there were more than 1,300 persons on the island at any one time, including several "Gentile" fishermen, nor that more than 370 of them were legal voters. Strang was publicly crowned king on the 8th of July, 1850.

It might be interesting to inquire whether Strang was sincere in his profession of conversion to the Mormon faith, in 1844, or whether dim visions of future self aggrandizement did not at that time influence his conduct. Be that as it may, his course of action, from the time of Smith's death up to his own assassination, at Beaver Island, twelve years afterward, reveals a settled purpose to make himself the absolute ruler of the faction of Mormons over whom he had gained an influence. To accomplish this, he appealed to both the best and worst instincts of human nature.

His subjects consisted of several classes. The most numerous class, but not the most influential in the affairs of the church or the commonwealth, were the sincere believers in the original and fundamental doctrines of Mormonism, and in his divine mission and office as the successor of Joseph Smith. To them he was really prophet, priest, and king. His advice was sought and followed in all matters, temporal and spiritual. His word was law. No sacrifice was too great to be made, if the prophet advised it; no crime too revolting to be committed, if the king commanded it. In their view it was no crime. Not only could the king do no wrong, but an act in obedience to his authority could not be wrong, no matter how cruel or unjust it might be to a "Gentile," or how wicked, judged by "Gentile" standards of morality.

Another class, comparatively small in numbers but in influence more , about than the former, consisted of unprincipled men, whose adherence to Mormonism arose, not from conviction of its truth as a religious system, but from the opportunities it afforded for unbridled license under the pretended sanction of religion. These men were the willing tools of Strang. Without being themselves deceived by his profession of having a divine commission, they helped to fasten the deception upon others. The most important trusts were sometimes committed to persons of this sort, and they were usually chosen for leaders in the execution of projects likely to be distasteful to persons of tender conscience and large philanthropy.

A third class, neither numerous nor influential, consisted of those who were at first sincere believers in Mormonism, but whose faith had been shaken or wholly destroyed by the doctrines and practices taught by Strang and his minions, and who remained upon the island from inability to get away. An apostatizing or dissatisfied Mormon might leave, but he was not allowed to take away his property. That was "consecrated," that is, confiscated for the benefit of the church.

That polygamy is right, was a doctrine of the Mormon church. It was an object of ambition to be the father of many children. In eternity a man would be crowned king over all his descendants. Marriage by the civil law was not held to be binding, but only the marriage ordained by the church. In the ceremony of the marriage of the first wife, the officiating church officer said to each of the parties, "You take this woman (or man) to be your lawful wife (or husband) in this life, and in the life to come, and in life everlasting, so help you God." The parties having signified their assent, he then added, "By virtue of authority vested in me by the Father, Son, and Holy Ghost, I seal you husband and wife in the indissoluble bonds of matrimony." The marriage of the first wife was public; that of a succeeding wife was not. If there was any ceremony connected with the latter, its nature is known only to the initiated. The marriage bond could be broken only by the crime of adultery.

Lawful concubinage was this: If a man died leaving no children, his brother should take his wife, according to the Mosaic law. If a man died leaving children, the widow might choose the man with whom she preferred to cohabit, and the offspring of the union were to be the children of her deceased husband and his subjects in eternity. If a woman loved her departed husband, and desired to honor his memory, she could do so in no more effective way than to raise up children to his name.

Strang himself was the first to set the example of polygamous practices. In the early period of the settlement of the island, many conscientious Mormons were assured, at Voree, that he did not approve of polygamy or the "consecrating" of property, but on arriving at the island found him preaching both. His lawful wife came with him to St. James, but returned to Voree when his open association with other women made her position no longer endurable. His second wife was openly acknowledged as such only after the birth of her first child. After that, three others were openly taken. Of the number of concubines falling to his share by the voluntary choice of dutiful widows, we have no authentic record, but it is reasonable to conclude that, from the regard in which he was held by all good Mormons, male and female, he enjoyed a monopoly of that luxury.

The number of practical polygamists was not large, owing to the fact that the supply of available women was limited. Young girls, averse to taking the place of second or third wife, found themselves continually harrassed with urgent offers of polygamous marriages, sometimes seconded by the authority of their parents. So unendurable did this sort of persecution become, in some cases, that desperate but unsuccessful efforts were made to escape from the island. In one instance, a girl managed to get on board a steamboat that called at the wharf, and was locked in a state room, but the boat was detained by the Mormons till she was given up. A young, unmarried woman did not really have her liberty.

The "consecrating" of "Gentile" property, or, in other words, the robbing of those who were not Mormons, was a recognized and established practice, from the earliest settlement of the island till the time of Strang's death. It was the natural and legitimate sequence of the doctrine that the Mormons were God's peculiar people, who alone had a right to the earth and were eventually to possess it, and that the "Gentiles" were to be "stricken with a continual stroke." The plundering operations were conducted with the utmost system. They were under the control of a class of officers, called in the church destroying angels, but known to the outside world by the harmless name of deacons. Brothers were generally chosen for destroying angels, as being more likely to stand by each other in times of danger. Every Mormon was under obligation to go on a thieving or marauding expedition, when ordered to do so by a destroying angel. The destroying angels were under the immediate direction of Strang himself, and the expeditions were always organized under his supervision. When any party or individual discovered a good opportunity for obtaining plunder, it was reported to him, but nothing was done without his approval. When booty was brought in, it was usually taken to the residence of some one participating in the expedition, where a division was made, one-tenth being set apart for the use of the church. The remaining nine-tenths became the property of the plunderers. It was the usual practice, however, to sell it, so that those in whose possession it should be found, if accused of theft, could claim the immunity from punishment accorded to innocent purchasers. In some cases, the greater part of the booty was given to the church. In order that the practice of plundering the "Gentiles" might be carried on with ease and safety, stations, called "forts," were established in many of the towns, both large and small, on the borders of the lakes. A "fort" was usually the home of a family who professed to have renounced Mormonism, and to have been driven from the island by the incensed Mormons in consequence of forsaking the faith. Having secured the sympathy and confidence of the people among whom they seemed to have found refuge, their house became a safe retreat for the spies and emissaries of the deacons, when engaged in their work, and especially in times of danger. At one time, there were not less than a dozen of these "forts" in the city of Chicago.

There was an organization called the Society of the Illuminati, which regulated all the affairs of the church, in which were discussed such matters as it was not thought prudent to bring before the people. Women were not admitted to membership, and only such men as could be trusted. It was a truly secret society, bound together by the most terrible oaths. Of its internal working we know but little—its secrets have been faithfully kept by the initiated.

There was another society, called the Covenant, to which all good Mormons, men and women, were expected to belong. The initiatory ceremony was conducted in an evening meeting, called a conference. The candidate for membership laid his hand upon a cross, which rested on the bible, and swore to stand by the king and all the rulers, viz, the apostles, high priest, elders, teachers and deacons, and to stand by all the ordinances of the church, even to the shedding of his blood. In case he should divulge the secrets of the Covenant to any one who had not taken the oath, or to any person outside of the church, he should suffer the penalty known only to the Illuminati. The Covenant had a system of grips, used for the recognition of members, and for giving warning of the presence of traitors or unsafe persons.

A school was opened, in a log schoolhouse, at St. James, while there were only a few families in the settlement. Education was encouraged. A house of worship, called the tabernacle, was commenced at an early day, but was never finished. A room in the basement was completed, in which religious services were held. Saturday was the Mormon Sabbath. The manner of conducting religious services was similar to that prevailing in orthodox churches. The Mormons took pride in the excellence of their singing. Their hymns were all such as had been composed by Mormons. The Book of Mormon was generally used, instead of the bible, though sometimes the preacher selected his text from the latter. Strang generally preached when at home, though he had around him and under his direction a number of other preachers, many of whom were young men, corresponding in position and office to the Twelve Apostles and the Seventy. He always appeared at church plainly dressed, sometimes even going there barefooted.

CHAPTER XIX.

Pretended Loyalty to the State—Mormon Depredations—Horses and Cattle Stolen—Tannery Robbed and Burned—Piracy—Men Robbed on the Island and set Adrift in a Boat—Gentile Fishermen—Strang and Gen. Miller on an Expedition—Fishermen and Refugees at Pine River—A Battle.

While it was understood by all good Mormons that allegiance was due only to the king, an outward appearance of loyalty to the state of Michigan was carefully maintained. County and township officers were elected according to the state constitution, courts were held, and the forms of state law observed. But even the machinery of legal government was converted into an instrument for the aggrandizement of Strang, the protection of Mormons in their villainies, and the harrassing of the "Gentiles." Strang was elected a member of the state legislature by fraudulent votes. Care was taken that courts, juries, and civil officers should always be under Mormon influence. Vexatious lawsuits were a favorite means of making troublesome "Gentiles" and pseudo-Mormons feel the displeasure of the king and the church. The destroying angels and their emissaries, if arrested abroad might be in some danger of having justice meted out to them; within Mormon jurisdiction they were safe.

So complete and perfect were the arrangements for carrying on an extensive system of thieving and robbery, that immense quantities of "consecrated" goods were, from time to time, brought to the island, and converted to Mormon use. On this point, the concurrent testimony of persons who lived there from the early days of the colony up to the time of Strang's death, and who were in positions to know the facts, is conclusive. The plunder seen by them, and portions of which some of them used, consisted of dry goods, leather, fishing nets, horses, cattle—anything, in short, of practical value, that could be purloined with comparative safety.

Horses were stolen at a distance, and brought home on the steamboats which sometimes touched at St. James. At one time, several head of cattle were stolen from lumbermen on the mainland, and conveyed to the island. A tannery, near Grand Haven, was robbed of its stock of leather, a part of which was in a half tanned condition, and the building burned to hide the theft. The newspapers reported the fire as a case of supposed incendiarism, but the Mormons were not suspected at the time. A small vessel, or "hooker," loaded with whitefish, was robbed, scuttled, and sunk. The fate of the vessel was for a long time a matter of conjecture to the outside world. As she never returned to port, she was supposed to have been lost. The fate of the unfortunate crew has remained a secret with those who authorized and executed the robbery. Those immediately concerned in the act, on returning to St. James, with their own boat loaded with as much of the booty as it could carry, reported that they had set them on shore. The wives of the robbers believed they had murdered them.

It is not probable that the Mormons were guilty of every case of wrong charged to them. On the other hand, it is not probable that their worst deeds, in all their enormity, have been brought to light. To what extent piracy was carried on, is not known. "Dead men tell no tales." During a considerable period previous to Strang's death, several vessels were lost, none of the crews ever returning to tell their fate. It was generally believed that they had been plundered by the Mormons, the crews murdered, and the vessels sunk. Some captains were so certain of the piratical character of the Mormons that they feared to become becalmed in the vicinity of the islands, and would lie to and wait for a good sailing breeze, before approaching them.

Persons visiting the island against the wishes of the Mormon authorities, were not sure of coming off unharmed. The following incident, related by an old gentleman still living on the island, illustrates the point. It is proper to mention that our informant went to St. James a true Mormon, in an early day. At Voree, Strang had said to him that polygamy and the "consecrating" of property were of the devil, but on arriving at St. James he was astonished to find him teaching the legality of both. He lost faith in him immediately, but could see no way to get off. A Mormon might leave, but his property could not be taken away; that must remain, to be "consecrated." He had a large family, and could not afford to lose all his means of support, so he remained. He continued to pass for a Mormon, and was recognized by them as one of themselves. He thinks, however, that they had little confidence in him. We give the account nearly in his own words.

"Some men by the name of Martin, were compelled by stress of weather to land on the island. A watch was always kept, to report the approach of strangers. The arrival of the Martins being reported, Strang, with a party of men, went to interview them. Chris Scott, who was a secret friend of mine, was one of the party, and gave me an account of what was done. On arriving at the place where the Martins were, some of the party proposed putting them to death, but the measure was strongly opposed by Strang. It was finally decided by vote that they should be robbed of everything and set adrift. Accordingly everything valuable was taken out of the boat, the men were forced into it, and it was shoved off. As it was shoved off, Chris threw into it a pair of oars."

The "Gentile" fishermen, of whom there were a considerable number on the islands and the adjacent shores, suffered more or less from the depredations of the Mormons. Not being strong enough to resist successfully, they were often compelled to submit to such exactions as were put upon them. A characteristic incident, related by the gentleman quoted above, will illustrate the relation that existed between the "Gentile" residents of the Mormon kingdom and the Mormons. It may also serve to show how those Mormons, or those who passed for Mormons, whose sense of right would not permit them to engage in the current unlawful practices enjoined by the church, were compelled to perform the parts assigned them. As before, we give the narrative nearly in his own words.

"A man named Martin, (not one of the Martins mentioned in a preceding paragraph,) was fishing at the head of the island. At the beginning of winter, he packed up his property, hauled his boats out on the beach, and left all in the care of one of his men. One Saturday, Strang preached a very able sermon, advocating the right and duty of "consecrating," and declaring he would not ask others to do what he would not do himself. The next day Silas Miller, who was a 'Gentile,' and myself went to Sand Bay, after hay. There we found one of Martin's boats, loaded with his own property, stuck in the ice, near the shore, and Strang and old Gen. Miller drying themselves by a fire, in a shanty. They appeared to have been in the water. On returning to the village, Strang and Gen. Miller sent out teams to bring in the goods, but boat and goods were missing. The man in whose care they had been left, discovering the theft, had followed to Sand Bay, and, arriving after the departure of Strang and Miller, had taken the property back home. The next day, a party was organized under Gen. Miller, to go to Martin's and recover salvage on the goods, Strang and Miller pretending that they had found the boat abandoned in the ice. I was ordered to accompany the party with my team, to bring home the goods. I made excuses, but was given to understand I must go. Thinking to get rid of it, I hid my harness, and started with my horses for the interior of the island. A party of ten or twelve men pursued me. Finding that I should be overtaken, and concluding that final escape was impossible, I turned back and met them, saying if they would not force me, I would go. They replied that that was all they wanted. A strong party went to Martin's. We found there ten or twelve fishermen, some of whom seemed to be putting their guns in order. Our party was received in a friendly manner. After a little time, Gen. Miller announced our business—to get salvage on the goods. The man in whose charge Martin had left them, but whose name I have forgotten, asked how much. Miller said they would look over the goods and see. The goods were accordingly looked over, and Miller took what he pleased, which we carried back to the village. The fishermen were well aware that resistance, must, in the end, result disastrously to themselves."

In the difficulties between the fishermen and the Mormons, the latter, though numerically much the stronger and generally successful, did not in every case get the best of it. At Pine River, on one occasion, they met with a serious repulse.

Pine River seems to have been a favorite resort for the fishermen, and a community respectable for numbers had collected there. Capt. T. D. Smith had an establishment in the bay, southwest of the mouth of the river, between it and Pine River Point. There were four more west of Smith, between him and the point, three at the mouth of the river, and one half a mile farther north. These were not simply bachelors' homes, but contained families of women and children. There were also two other families, who had been Mormons, but had renounced Mormonism and escaped from the island. Their names were Hull and Savage. They had made their escape by pretending to embark, with Strang's approval, for Drummond's island, where he proposed to plant a colony. Once on the lake, they had laid their course for Pine River, and asked the protection of the fishermen. The fishermen had promised protection, provided the fugitives would help to protect themselves.

One of the fishermen, named Moon, had had a serious difficulty with the Mormons. To get Hull, Savage, and Moon into their power, seems to have been thought important by the Mormon leaders. Knowing that either stratagem or force would have to be employed, they still thought it prudent to proceed under color of law. The time of the sitting of the circuit court at St. James was chosen for the execution of the project. An armed party, accompanied by an officer with a subpœna for the three men, embarked for Pine River.

There was a quilting at the house of a fisherman named Morrison, at the mouth of the river, on the south side, at which all the women of the settlement were assembled. Some of the men had gone up Pine lake. Nearly all the others were in the "other end of the town," as the westernmost houses in the settlement were called. Two boats were seen approaching, heading for the mouth of the river. It was noticed that they seemed careful to keep close together. One of the fishermen had a spy-glass, by the aid of which he was able to count the strangers. There were nine men in each boat. The circumstances looked suspicious, and the fishermen determined to ascertain at once the object of the visit.

Between them and the river there was a stretch of beach where it was difficult to pass between the water and the bank. Launching a boat, ten or twelve men, seizing their weapons, sprang into it, and rowed past the difficult place. Then they landed, and proceeded on foot, following the beach till they reached the sand hillocks, when they turned into the woods, where they struck a path that led over the bluff and down to Morrison's house. The Mormons had arrived before them, and had been blustering about, declaring they would have what they came after or they would wade in blood. The women were terribly frightened. On the arrival of the fishermen, the Mormons ceased their threats, and said they had not come to make any trouble, but insisted on having the three men for whom they claimed to have subpœnas. They were at once distinctly told they could not have them. This was followed, as the fishermen learned from the women the purport of the Mormons' threats, by an intimation that the best thing they could do was to leave immediately, and that if they did not go voluntarily, they would be made to go. The Mormons prudently consented to leave, and went to their boats. Among the fishermen was a young man, named Louis Geboo, who had lived a year or two on the island, and now recognized some of his former acquaintances in the Mormon party. Thinking the danger of a collision was over, young Geboo started for the beach, where the Mormons were embarking, for the purpose of speaking to those he had formerly known. When half way to the beach, it occurred to him that, as a matter of precaution, he ought to know that his gun was ready for effective use. Stopping a moment to examine it, he heard the sound of a gun, and felt the bullet strike his leg. He learned afterwards, from his acquaintances in the Mormon party, that the shot was fired from a horse pistol by Jonathan Pierce, one of Strang's "hard-fisted men," who accompanied the act with the exclamation, "We are running away, like a set of d—d cowards; I'll let them know that I'm not afraid." As Geboo started to limp back to his own party, the latter opened fire on the Mormons, who got away with the utmost haste, and were soon beyond gunshot. There is no evidence that they returned the fire. Three of their number were severely wounded. The fishermen manned a boat, and went in pursuit. As they again got within rifle range, seven or eight miles out on the lake, the Mormons took refuge on board a vessel, which, fortunately, was lying there becalmed.

A few days afterward, a rumor reached the fishermen that an expedition of a hundred men was fitting out at the island, to come over and punish them. There could be no hope of successfully resisting such a force. There was no other way than to fly. Fortunately the little steamer Columbia came in. The fishermen put on board their families and effects, and left, only Alvah Cable remaining a short time longer. When he went away, the Pine River region was left without a white inhabitant. Most of the fishermen went to Washington island, at the mouth of Green bay, but some of them to other places.

CHAPTER XX.

Mr. Dixon and family at Pine River—The Mormons Already There—Reorganization of Emmet County—The First Township Meeting—County Election Controlled by Mormons From Beaver Island—Property Stolen—Mormon Picnic on Holy Island—Intimidation—Mr. and Mrs. Sterling—The Women Left Alone—A Mormon Plundering Party—Preparation for Defense—A Night of Watching.

Mr. John S. Dixon, with his family, arrived at the mouth of Pine river, where the village of Charlevoix is now situated, on the 11th day of May, 1855, in the little schooner Emeline, which had been chartered to bring him from Old Mission. The party consisted of Mr. and Mrs. Dixon and their three children, Mr. Wolcott, who had come with a view to a business partnership with Mr. Dixon, and Frank May, a young man who had been hired at Northport.

Mr. Dixon's purchase of a considerable tract of land, lying on Pine river and Round and Pine lakes, had been consummated a year before, and he had left Lansing with the intention of occupying it; but receiving at Mackinac information, which he deemed reliable, of the depredations of the Mormons and the danger he would incur by attempting to settle in the territory over which they claimed jurisdiction, he had been induced to defer his project, and had passed the year at old Mission. Within that time, he had visited Lansing, while the legislature was in session, and procured the passage of an act for the reorganization of Emmet county. By the terms of the act, the islands in Lake Michigan which had been a part of Emmet were detached from it, and organized into a new county, called Manitou. The object of the move was to prevent all legal interference with the affairs of Emmet by Strang and his followers.

No sooner were Mr. Dixon's party and effects landed on the beach, than the captain of the Emeline, who was in bad odor with the Mormons, fearing an attack, set sail, and the schooner soon disappeared in the distance. Mr. Dixon had brought with him a considerable amount of supplies, including a small boat and a quantity of lumber. Of the latter a temporary residence was built on the beach, in which the family remained for the next three days. The current of the river was so rapid that the boat, when loaded, could not be propelled against it, and the banks were so obstructed by overhanging trees, brushwood, and fallen timber as to make towing impossible. The three days were spent in clearing a path along the south margin of the stream. Then, by towing, the family and goods were transported up the river, and landed on the north shore, just where the stream leaves Round lake.

On his arrival at Pine river, Mr. Dixon found five Mormon families living in the vicinity, who had settled there since the place was abandoned by the fishermen. If any of them were not Mormons, they were at least under Mormon influence. On landing, he was met by some of the young men with the question, "What have you come here for," accompanied by plain indications that he was not welcome. There had been several fisherman's shanties on his premises. One of them was still standing and in a good state of preservation, when he landed from the Emeline, and he had hoped to occupy it, but before he succeeded in getting up the river with his goods, the Mormons had torn it down. However, he soon had it so far rebuilt as to be able to occupy it as a temporary dwelling.

The act of the legislature reorganizing the county of Emmet, divided it into several townships, and provided for holding the first township meetings and the first election of county officers. The township meetings in all the townships except Charlevoix, were to be held on the first Tuesday in May; that in Charlevoix on the last Tuesday in May. The county election was to be held on the first Tuesday in June. Neither the township meeting nor the county election was observed in any township except Charlevoix. Mr. Dixon served as clerk of election at the township meeting in that township. There were eight legal voters present, five of whom belonged to the five Mormon families in the vicinity; the other three were Mr. Dixon, Mr. Wolcott, and Frank May. Several Mormons from the island were present, but did not think it necessary to vote, as the legal vote stood five Mormons to three "Gentiles." Of course a Mormon township board was elected. At the time of the county election, which occurred one week afterward, about fifty Mormons came over to Charlevoix from Beaver Island, and were allowed by the recently elected township board to vote.

As there was no township meeting held in any township but Charlevoix, of course the supervisor elected in that township was the only one in the county. According to the view the Mormons chose to take of it, he constituted the board of supervisors. In the following autumn, this board of one man, doubtless acting under instructions from Mormon headquarters, proceeded to construct several new townships in the county. The record, which looks innocent on the face of it, is found in the appendix to the session laws of 1857, where Galen B. Cole, as chairman of the board, and George T. Preston, as county clerk, certify that the several acts for the organization of the new townships were passed by a majority of votes of all the members elected to the board of supervisors, upon due notice and application according to law, at an adjourned sitting of the annual meeting of the board of supervisors, the 22d day of October, 1855. What ulterior measures the Mormon leaders had in view in this proceeding, can only be surmised. If it was a preparation for carrying out in the future a far-reaching scheme for keeping the county under the complete political control of their own party, which seems probable, the death of Strang and the breaking up of the Mormon kingdom, the following year, put an end to it. Of the townships organized in this questionable manner, two, Evangeline and Eveline, retain their names, and one of them, Eveline, its original boundaries, at the present day.

Mr. Wolcott, seeing there was likely to be continual trouble with the Mormons, threw up the project of a business partnership, and left the place.

For a few weeks, the current of events seemed to run smoothly, no ripple on the surface being caused by anything of greater importance than the loss of a new lumber wagon and three sugar kettles, stolen by the Mormons. The wagon had come on board a vessel, by way of Mackinac. It was not immediately put together for use, but, with the kettles, was stowed away in an old shanty used for an outhouse. Two weeks afterward, having occasion to use it, the theft was discovered. On mentioning the loss to some of the Mormons, they denied, with a calmness and self-control that was almost convincing, having any knowledge of it. Two of the women, however, when the subject was spoken of in their presence, by their visible agitation convinced Mr. Dixon that they were in the secret. Careful inquiries and the course of subsequent events, seemed to make it certain that nearly all the men in the vicinity we e privy to the theft. Some of the women, particularly the two alluded to above, had strenuously opposed and denounced the proceeding. Mr. Dixon eventually recovered the wagon and two of the ket-ties, which were found on Beaver island, after the breaking up of the Mormon settlement.

The eighth of July was observed by the Mormons as their principal holiday, it being the anniversary of Strang's coronation. The present summer, a day or two after the general celebration at Beaver island, about fifty men and women, with Strang among them, came over to Pine River, on a sort of picnic excursion. The real object of the expedition, probably, as would seem to appear from their proceedings, was to make an impression upon, and intimidate, the new "Gentile" settlers, who had had the temerity to locate within what they claimed as Mormon territory. Mr. Dixon had received from a friendly Mormon a hint that his oxen were to be "sacrificed," that is, they were to be slaughtered, to contribute to the dinner of the picnic party. Profiting by the hint, he had taken the precaution to send them to Mr. Porter, at Bear Creek, for safety.

The party passed with their boats up Pine lake, entered the south arm, and spent the night on the little island, two miles beyond the entrance, to which they gave the name it has since borne of Holy Island. When they returned, the next day, Mrs. Dixon noticed that some of the boats were towing long timbers. Mr. Dixon was absent. As the boats, with the timbers in tow, passed down the river in front of the house, in charge of a few of the men, the other members of the party filed along the path, back of the house, towards the mouth of the river, having landed from the boats at the residence of one of the Mormon families, on the shore of Pine lake. Suspecting mischief and being somewhat alarmed, Mrs. Dixon resolved to ascertain what was going forward. A Mormon neighbor to whom she applied, declined to give her any information, but said if she wished to go and ascertain for herself, she would not be harmed. Following the party down towards the mouth of the river, she found that they had crossed to the south side, and were standing in a group, on an elevation, with Strang in their midst. Some of the men were busying themselves with drawing the timbers out of the water, and one was bringing a spade. Asking what they were going to do, she received for reply that they were about to erect a gallows, on which should be hanged all who violated their laws. Frightened at what seemed impending danger, Mrs. Dixon returned to the house.

After the Mormons had gone, the gallows was found standing, with four roughly carved wooden images of men hanging by the neck, and another standing erect on top of the frame. On one of them was the figure of a coffin, drawn with red chalk, and three men walking away from it, with this inscription: "Dixon, successor to the Pine River murderers, in his dying hours abandoned by his friends." On another was the inscription, "May his days be few, and his name be lost and blasted from among men. God hear our prayers, and those of our wives and children, for vengeance."

In the course of the summer, Mr. Wm. Sterling, his wife and infant child, arrived from Elk Rapids, and were received into the house occupied by the Dixons. There was also an addition of four families to the Mormon population, two of which settled at the mouth of the stream since called Porter's creek, where Advance is now situated, and the others on the opposite side of the lake, at Bay Springs.

Messrs. Dixon and Sterling conceived the project of building a saw-mill on Pine river. It was proposed to build a dam on the lower river, at some point between Round lake and Lake Michigan. It was thought advisable that the margin of the stream and of Round lake should first be cleared of driftwood and fallen timber, which could be conveniently accomplished only by the aid of a scow. Accordingly, a quantity of clear stuff pine plank, for building a scow, was brought from Elk Rapids, and piled up on the bank of the river, ready for use.

Soon after the lumber was received, it happened that both men were absent on business, Mr. Dixon at the mission at Bear creek and Mr. Sterling at Mackinac. Frank May had left Mr. Dixon's employ some time before, so the women and children were alone. On a Saturday, the Mormons held religious service, at the house of one of their number, at which their preacher dilated upon and defended the practice of "consecrating" the property of "Gentiles." It does not appear that either Mrs. Dixon or Mrs. Sterling was present at the meeting, or that they knew till afterward of the preacher's discourse. They were, however, in the absence of their husbands, sufficiently afraid of violence to provide for defense.

At a late hour on Saturday night, they had barred the door and retired to bed, Mrs. Sterling in the garret and Mrs. Dixon below. Suddenly the latter was startled by the sound of what seemed to be the splashing of a paddle in the water. Springing from bed and peering cautiously out of the window, she saw three men landing from a canoe. They wore tall, pointed hats, such as she had seen worn by the men of the Mormon families that had gone up Pine lake. Believing they were bent on mischief, she called Mrs. Sterling, and the two made such preparations as they could for defense. Mrs. Dixon had already learned to load and discharge a gun. Gathering up all the weapons at hand, they found themselves in possession of a double-barreled gun, a pistol, a carving knife, and two or three axes. Armed with these, they stationed themselves by the door, determined to give the invaders a warm reception, should they attempt to force an entrance. But the enemy had business elsewhere than at the house that night. It was the pile of valuable pine plank on the shore that was the object of their expedition. Watching stealthily from the window, the women saw them commence loading it into Mr. Dixon's boat. When they were seen taking the boat, Mrs. Dixon asked, not in the coolest manner imaginable, "Shall I shoot?" Mrs. Sterling advised her not to shoot, unless they came near the house, saying that if they were only after property and did not intend personal violence, it was better to let them go.

Mrs. Sterling was a spiritualist. While the danger seemed to be imminent, she held bravely to carnal weapons, but when it became evident that there was to be no immediate attack upon the house, she bethought herself of other means of defense than the ax and carving knife. Laying down the latter, she knelt by a chair, placing the tips of her fingers on the front edge of the seat, and called on God and the spirits for protection. In answer to the question asked of the latter whether she and her companion were safe from violence, the chair repeatedly tipped an affirmative response. Though Mrs. Dixon had no faith in the intervention of spirits, Mrs. Sterling's earnestness and the favorable responses indicated by the movements of the chair, as she many years afterwards confessed, went far towards reassuring her.

Finally, the men having loaded the boat with all it could carry, threw the remainder of the plank into the river, and withdrew up the lake.

The women watched all night. Mrs. Sterling repeatedly declared that as soon as daylight appeared, she would take her baby, and endeavor to make her way to Bear creek, by following the beach. It was evident that both women could not go—with all the children they would never be able to get through. Mrs. Dixon, being a rapid and enduring pedestrian, proposed that Mrs. Sterling should remain with the children, while she should undertake the hazardous journey, promising that, if the Lord would let her go through, she would send help that should reach Mrs Sterling by nine o'clock in the evening Mrs. Sterling had the good sense to see the wisdom of the plan, and finally consented to the arrangement

CHAPTER XXI.

Mrs Dixon's. Journey—Difficulties of the Way—Surprise at Bear Creek—Return to Pine River—A Courageous Woman's Stratagem—A Part of the Stolen Property Found—The Mormons Commence a Lawsuit—Sterling Leaves—Arrival of Pratt—A Consultation—Women and Children Sent Away—Arrival of Friends—Watching for Thieves—Pine River Abandoned By the "Gentiles."

In the morning, as soon as it was light enough to see to travel, Mrs Dixon, armed with the pistol, set out on her journey to Bear Creek It is fully eighteen miles from the point of starting, now Charlevoix village, to the mission farm at Bear Creek, near the present site of Petoskey, by the nearest wagon road of modern times. At the time of which we write, there was no road—not even an Indian trail that a woman could follow. Mrs Dixon's only way was to go down to the mouth of the river, and then follow the beach, through all its sinuosities, to her destination.

Those who, in the primitive days of northern Michigan, performed long foot journeys on the beach, could tell, if they were to speak, how the bendings of the shore in and out add to the distance They could tell, too, of difficulties attending that mode of travel, of which their descendants, never having been driven to it by necessity, have no just conception Sometimes the traveler strikes a stretch of smooth sand, packed by the receding waves to the solidity of a pavement, that answers to his tread with a sharp, ringing, metalic sound, as he moves easily and rapidly forward Then, for miles, loose sand, drifted about by the wind, in which his feet sink at every step, makes even the slowest progress toilsome Piles of driftwood, fallen timber, and overhanging trees, gnarled and twisted into fantastic forms by the fury of the elements, obstruct his way Jutting crags block up the passage. Perpendicular precipices rise from the very margin of the lake, leaving no room for even the narrowest path Often he must take to the water or, if it is above his depth, leave the beach and face his way through thickets almost impenetrable, on the land. The beach as a highway, however, has one excellence in advance of ordinary new-country roads—on it the traveler can not lose his way

Once on the beach, Mrs Dixon pressed rapidly forward, wading round obstructions, where the water was shallow, in preference to climbing over them It seemd to take less time, and time was precious The prints of her husband's feet were seen in the sand, where he had passed along a day or two before Finding the tracks was like meeting company on that lonely shore. At Kah-gah-che-wing there had formerly been an Indian settlement It was now deserted Here she lost her husband's tracks Thinking he might have left the beach for a trail, she sought for them in vain in the intricate net work of the grass-grown and almost obliterated paths of the village Returning, she pursued her way along the beach, feeling more lonely than before Beyond Kah-gah-che-wing a vessel had been lost. It was known that a company of men had been for some time at work there, trying to raise the wreck She had hoped to find them, but their camp was deserted. Farther on, where perpendicular cliffs rise from the very margin of the water, she could no longer follow the beach. Ascending to the top of the bluff, she found the country covered with a dense, tangled swamp, which it seemed almost impossible to penetrate No path could be found, but go through she must. For full three hours, as she estimated the time, she struggled onward, being careful to keep within hearing of the sound of the waves dashing against the foot of the cliff When, finally, she emerged into more open ground, her pistol was lost, her shoes were nearly torn off her feet, and her clothing hung in shreds about her person. When within three miles of Bear Creek, she came upon an inhabited wigwam Making the old Indian, Pa-ma-saw, understand that she wished to go to Mr Porter's, he kindly sent with her a little boy as guide. Path there was none, but only a blind trail, such as none but an Indian or an experienced backwoodsman could follow.

It was communion day at the Mission, Rev Peter Dougherty being present to officiate The congregation were just collecting at the chapel for afternoon service, when Mrs. Dixon arrived It was, perhaps, one or two o'clock p m The interest excited by her appearance and her story of the doings at Pine River, broke up the meeting for the time Mrs. Dixon was quickly provided with refreshments by the ladies of Mr. Porter's family Mr. Porter held a consultation with the Indians as to what it was proper to do The result was a decision that three Indians, well armed, should man one of their boats, and return with Mr. and Mrs. Dixon immediately The party were not long in getting off. The wind was fair, and they arrived at Pine River a little before nine o'clock in the evening

During Mrs. Dixon's absence, Mrs. Sterling, with an ingenuity and courage which, if she had been a man, might, under favorable circumstances, have made her a leader in the devices and intrigues of war, had adopted an artifice to deceive the enemy with a false show of force. Disguising herself in her husband's clothes, she walked about, where she would be likely to be seen by some of the Mormons, changing the suit several times in the course of the day, to give the impression that there were several men stopping at the house.

The plank stolen or thrown into the river by the Mormons on Saturday night, had been piled up on the south side of the river There was another pile on the north side, nearly in front of the house Thinking that the marauders would return for it under cover of night, Mr. Dixon and his Indian allies organized a watch. In the middle of the night a sound was heard, such as might have been made by carelessly moving the lumber The Indians immediately gave the alarm On going out, Mr Dixon saw several men near the pile of plank. Hailing them, he was answered in a voice which he recognized as Mr Sterling's, notwithstanding the effort of the speaker to disguise it Mr Sterling, returning from Mackinac, had reached Bear creek a few hours after the departure of Mr Dixon's party. Learning the state of affairs at home, and fearing, as Mr Dixon had done, a return of the marauders, he had hired some Indians with a boat to bring him through. On landing, presuming that somebody would be on guard, he had ventured to indulge in the somewhat dangerous amusement of causing an alarm by pretending to move the lumber

The next morning, Messrs Dixon and Sterling resolved to make an effort to recover the stolen property One of the Indians was induced to accompany them with his boat in the proposed expedition up Pine lake. The others returned to Bear creek The three men were well armed On their way up the lake, they met two Mormons coming down. On being questioned, they denied all knowledge of the missing property At the mouth of Porter's creek, the lumber was found on the beach, and near it the oars and one of the thwarts of the missing boat. The boat could not be found. Two Mormons who were present, like the two met on the lake, denied all knowledge of the theft, and asserted that the lumber was their own, brought by themselves from Beaver island The boat in which the party had come, was too small to carry away all the lumber. Taking a part of it, they prepared to return. When all was ready, Mr. Sterling still lingered on the shore. In response to Mr. Dixon's earnest request to come on board, he proposed that Mr. Dixon and the Indian should proceed homeward in the boat, while he should walk along the shore. However, Mr. Dixon's earnest entreaties at last induced him to enter the boat. He then confessed that his object in remaining was to kill the Mormons and recover the stolen boat. The plan he had contemplated was to shoot one of them, then threaten the other with death, to make him reveal the place where the boat was concealed, and finally kill him also.

During Mr. Sterling's stay at Pine River, he was inclined to resort to sanguinary measures in the contest with the Mormons, but was overruled by the milder counsels of Mr. Dixon. The latter insisted that personal violence should not be resorted to, except in case of necessary self-defense. Finally, convinced that the project of building th mill could not be carried out in peace, and his wife being unwilling to remain longer, Mr. Sterling dissolved his connection with Mr. Dixon, and left the place.

In the mean time, the Mormons at Porter's Creek commenced a suit against Dixon and Sterling, before a Mormon justice of the peace at Pine River, for the value of the lumber they had seized and brought home from the former place. The defendants knowing the plaintiffs would have everything their own way in the trial of the suit, thought it better to settle the claim by paying for their own property than to risk the result. The matter was accordingly arranged to the satisfaction of the Mormons.

While the project of building the mill was still entertained, a correspondence had been opened with Mrs. Dixon's brother, Mr. Charles Pratt, of Ashtabula, Ohio, who had some interest in the original purchase of the land, with a view to his becoming a partner in the undertaking. After Mr. Sterling's departure, and before Mr. Pratt's arrival, Mr. Dixon, having become thoroughly discouraged by the constant annoyance of the Mormons, and feeling his inability to successfully oppose force to force, or otherwise protect his property against their thieving depredations, reluctantly came to the determination to abandon the settlement. He accordingly wrote to Mr. Lewis Miller, at Old Mission, to send a vessel to carry him away.

One morning the family were awakened at an early hour by the shrill whistle of a steamboat. It came from the little steamer Stockman, which had arrived at the mouth of the river, having on board Mr. Pratt, his sister, and two hired men he had brought with him. Soon after the landing of Mr. Pratt's party, a small sloop appeared, commanded by Capt. Sheppard, and having on board Mr. Schetterly, (a son of Dr. Schetterly,) and one or two more, sent by Mr. Miller to Mr. Dixon's relief. In view of the additional strength brought by Mr. Pratt's party, the questson now arose whether it would be better to go or stay. The day was spent in consultation. The conclusion arrived at was that Mr. and Miss Pratt, with Mrs. Dixon, the children, and one of the hired men, should embark for Northport at once, while Mr. Dixon and the other man should remain, at least for the present. The plan was immediately put in execution. As much of the property as could be carried by the little sloop, was placed on board, leaving little with Mr. Dixon except some growing crops and a valuable cow. Mrs. Dixon's silver spoons had already been sent to Mr. Porter's for safe-keeping. It was a part of the Mormons' policy to keep on good terms with the Indians. To accomplish that, it was necessary to keep on good terms with the missionaries; consequently Mr. Porter was never molested, and property in his hands was considered safe.

About two weeks after the departure of the party for Northport, Capt. T. D. Smith and his brother Thomas arrived at Pine River from Middle Village, having come for the purpose of rendering any assistance Mr. Dixon might need in his conflict with the Mormons. Some months before, the Mormons had burned a cooper shop at Middle Village, belonging to the Smiths; they were therefore prepared to take advantage of any opportunity to avenge their own wrongs, while assisting others.

Before the settlement of the lawsuit mentioned above, an adjournment to a future day had been had. The arrival of the Smiths occurred just before the time that had been set for the trial. The Mormons of Beaver Island, not knowing that the suit had been settled, sent over a force of eight or ten men, for the double purpose of securing a result of the suit in accordance with Mormon policy, and robbing Mr. Dixon of such remaining property as might pay for the trouble of carrying it away. The cow was particularly an object of their rapacity. Mr. Dixon's party, suspecting their designs, and possibly having received a hint from a friendly source, laid on their arms all night, keeping a sharp lookout. At least three of the party, Mr. Dixon and the two Smiths, were somewhat desirous that the Mormons should attempt to steal the cow, thus affording a plausible pretext for paying off old scores. There were now no women and children present, and it seemed a good time for a bloody and decisive battle. But the Mormons were wary. They had noted the number of their opponents, and perhaps also the thoroughness of their preparations and their apparent willingness to fight. At all events, they returned to Beaver Island the next day, without any attempt at robbery. Fearing that the cow would be stolen at some future time, Mr. Dixon, assisted by his hired man, drove her to Bear Creek, where he sold her to Mr. Porter.

The hired man did not return to Pine River, but went from Bear Creek to Ohio, by way of Mackinac. When Mr. Dixon got back to Pine River, the Smiths had gone. There was no longer any necessity for them to stay. Ever since Mr. Dixon's determination to leave the place had been made known, the Mormons in the vicinity had been more friendly. There was no longer any property remaining to tempt the marauders of Beaver Island. Mr. Dixon remained alone for a few weeks, in tolerable security, till his crop of potatoes was dug and disposed of, when he joined his family at Northport.

CHAPTER XXII.

The Wheat and the Tares—Bitter Indignation Against the Mormons—The Conspirators—How to Enforce a Dress Reform—Strang Makes Enemies at Home—"Forty Stripes Save One"—Plans of the Conspirators—Assassination of Strang—The Assassins at Mackinac—General Rejoicing Among the "Gentiles."

No human being is so depraved that there are not in him some germs of good. No one has attained to such a degree of purity that the roots of evil within him, though apparently dead, may not be nursed into life. The actions of the bad are not all bad. The life work of the good has its beauty marred by stains of wrong. In societies and organizations we find the wheat and the tares growing together. Ethical systems are made up of truth and error.

The historian has to do with facts. It is not his province to discuss the truth or falsehood of systems of philosophy or religion, but simply to present them in a clear light, in their relations to the events of history.

The Mormons, (we speak of the Beaver island branch of the Mormon sect,) believed that Strang was the annointed of God—that he was really prophet, priest, and king. Strang taught that the spoiling of the "Gentiles" was right.

The thefts, robberies, and persecutions described in the preceding pages, were the natural and legitimate product of the people's belief and Strang's teaching. Those who deny the acts, in order to give the denial even a semblance of plausibility, must go down to the root of the matter, and deny Strang's teaching of the doctrine of "consecration," a denial that, as far as the writer is informed, has not, since the death of Strang, been put forward in Mormon defense.

What of good there was in the Beaver island community, is so overshadowed by these acts of lawlessness as to be easily lost sight of by the student of Mormon history. Aside from the doctrines of polygamy and "consecration," and the practices to which they naturally led, little can be said against the morality of the more numerous class of the residents of the island. Even these practices, unlawful when judged by the accepted standard of christian ethics, but lawful as seen from the Mormon stand point, were confined to a minority of the people. The practice of polygamy, as already stated, was limited by the scarcity of available women. The plundering of the "Gentiles" and other questionable work, was usually committed to those whose natural aptitude for crime made them willing instruments in the hands of the Mormon leaders. Doubtless there were many persons on the island, true believers in the Mormon faith, whose hands were never soiled by the touch of goods dishonestly obtained.

In the administration of the internal affairs of his kingdom, Strang sometimes exhibited a regard for the welfare of his subjects worthy of commendation. Intellectual culture was encouraged. A newspaper, published at St. James, under his immediate control, was ably conducted. Industry was enjoined as a cardinal virtue. Temperance was taught by precept and example, and enforced by the execution of stringent laws. The use of intoxicating drinks was prohibited. In the early years of the colony, a few "Gentiles" settled at a place called Whisky Point, at the northeast extremity of the island, where a store was opened for the sale of fishermen's supplies. Here a great deal of whisky was sold, not only to the fishermen, but to the Indians inhabiting the government reservation on Garden Island. Sometimes Mormons visiting Whisky Point, came home drunk. Strang determined to break up the traffic, and so harrassed the sellers that they were glad to leave the island. It was a good thing done for the Indians, who from that time showed evidence of improvement in dress and manner of living. After Strang's death, however, the liquor-sellers returned, and the Indians soon fell into their old habits of drunkenness and squalor.

The depredations of the Mormons at last became so wide-spread and annoying as to arouse a general feeling of indignation throughout the region bordering on the northern part of Lake Michigan and the Straits of Mackinac. To punish the marauders at all hazards, was fast becoming the settled purpose of the "Gentiles." A gentleman who visited Mackinac in the fall of 1855, and who, on his return home, published a short account of the state of affairs, says: "So frequent and so extensive have been these robberies, that the people at many points on the lake shore have become highly excited, so highly, indeed, that we should not be surprised to hear of serious conflicts and bloodshed. At Mackinac and Grand Traverse, particularly, nothing but the cautious and constant absence of the suspected will prevent severe and fatal chastisement. Stopping recently for a few days at Mackinac, we had ample opportunity to feel the public pulse, and we must say that we were really surprised at the deep and determined feeling which has taken hold of every person in that community. We met several gentlemen from Grand Traverse and other places in that portion of the state, from whom we ascertained that the same spirit pervades that entire region of country."

While the storm of "Gentile" wrath was gathering without, rebellious elements were developing within the Mormon kingdom that eventually hastened its overthrow.

Among Strang's subjects were some who were not earnestly Mormons, if at heart they were really Mormons at all. Such were Thomas Bedford, Dr. McCullough, and Alec. Wentworth. Perhaps Bedford should not be called a Mormon, though they evidently counted him as one of themselves, to which he seems to have given his tacit consent. His principal business was fishing. Dr. McCullough, a person of some talent and a good education, was a Mormon outwardly. In addition to doing a limited professional business, he kept a store in the village of St. James. Wentworth was at first a Mormon, and was a ready and willing tool for Strang. He had no standing or influence. It was reported on the island that he had been in some rough scrapes before coming there. He married a woman who was not a Mormon, apostatized, and became one of the bitterest enemies of the Mormon church. It is not known that he had any personal grievances to redress.

A bitter antagonism seems to have grown up between Bedford and Strang. The former was a rebellious subject, outspoken, and doing as he pleased without regard to the wishes of the king. He was an unsafe person to be entrusted with the keeping of secrets that could not be hidden from him. Strang was persistent in the attempt to procure obedience by wily maneuvering and the system of harrassing persecutions by which recusant Mormons were usually brought to see the wisdom of submission.

In the summer of 1855, repeated efforts were made to induce Bedford to assist in stealing the nets of "Gentile" fishermen, the object being, as he believed, to get him entangled with the Mormons in the crime of "consecrating," and so close his mouth as a witness. Failing in this, they endeavored to get him to commit himself by purchasing of them stolen nets, but he was too honest or two wary to be caught in that snare. Finding they could do nothing with him by persuasion, they stole a part of his own goods, and then commenced a series of vexatious lawsuits, on claims for debt, real or pretended, attaching his fishing nets and other property. It was not their policy, however, to let the suits come to trial, and adjournments were had from time to time, to vex and worry him, the attached property, meanwhile, remaining in their possession.

In the meantime, a formidable rebellion sprang up among Strang's female subjects, which, as most of the witnesses agree in saying, had much to do with bringing about his overthrow. He had promulgated a law against the wearing of long dresses, and requiring the universal adoption of the Bloomer style. Most of the women readily complied, but some, regarding it as an unwarranted interference with feminine affairs, indignantly refused acquiesence, among whom were Mrs. McCullough, Mrs. Bedford, Mrs. Johnson, Mrs. Wentworh, and Mrs. Orson Campbell. It was understood that those Mormons whose wives would not obey, were to be treated as "Gentiles." After it became apparent that some of the women were not disposed to yield, Strang declared in public that the law should be obeyed, if he had to wade ankle deep in blood. The leaders of the revolt threw defiance in his face. Eventually, however, most of them were compelled to submit. In the course of the vexatious lawsuits against Bedford, he had commenced a counter suit. On the morning of the day set for trial, the justice of the peace, one Whipple, came into Bedford's house. Mrs. Bedford was wearing a long dress and sewing on another. When the case was called for trial, Whipple informed Bedford that he could not have the benefit of law, as he (Whipple) had that morning seen Mrs. Bedford wearing a long dress, and refused to allow the trial to proceed.

Mrs. McCullough being one of the leaders of the dress rebellion, in keeping with the policy of reducing them to submission by harrassing their husbands, a lawsuit was commenced by Strang against McCullough. When a constable was sent to levy on the goods of the latter, McCullough is reported to have said to Strang, "Now it is you and I for it; you will destroy me or I shall destroy you." Strang burst into a laugh, and said he had heard men talk before. From that time forward, McCullough seems to have entertained a settled determination to work the overthrow of the Mormon power.

At what time Bedford, McCullough, and Wentworth came to an understanding is uncertain. It was probably in the latter part of the winter of 1855-6, or early the following spring, when, after the whipping of Bedford, the latter had determined on Strang's death.

The losses and annoyances to which Bedford was subjected, instead of subduing him, roused his indignation, and he became more outspoken regarding the acts of the Mormons than before.

The Mormons had stolen a boat, for the recovery of which the owner had offered a reward of fifty dollars. On one occasion, Bedford remarked to a young man, whom he met in McCullough's store, that if he wanted to make fifty dollars, he would go to Mackinac, and give information of the whereabouts of the stolen boat. Bedford's friends were frightened at his temerity. Several persons were present, and the remark was no doubt reported to Strang. It is supposed that this was the immediate cause of the whipping that followed.

At eight or nine o'clock in the evening, a man called at Bedford's house, and induced him to go down to the printing office, on the pretext that some one wished to see him there. When near the place indicated, he was met by several men, armed with whips—a rawhide, the teamster's whip popularly called a "black snake," and several beech switches, toughened by heating and twisted. Bedford was terribly whipped. The Mormon limit for whipping was "forty stripes save one." In this instance four more than the lawful number were given by some over zealous administrator of the law, but the excess was objected to as a grave wrong by the more scrupulous of the party, and, it is said, when the fact was reported to Strang he expressed his decided disapproval.*

Bedford returned home, took down his gun, without telling his wife what had happened, and started to go out. Mrs. Bedford, fearing that he had finally been persuaded or driven to undertake some of Strang's unlawful work, said interrogatively, "You are not going to do anything for Strang?" He replied, "I'll do for Strang, if I get hold of him." He watched that and the two following nights for Strang, leaning on a fence, where he could see a light in his window, for the purpose of shooting him, but without getting an opportunity. For some time after the whipping, Strang was constantly attended by a guard. An interview between the parties ended with mutual expressions of defiance, Strang bidding Bedford do his worst. The latter, however, prudently replied that he should not do his worst. He well knew that an open attempt to punish the king would result in immediate destruction to himself. By the advice of McCullough, the project of shooting Strang was finally deferred till after navigation should open in the spring, as there was no means of escape from the island.

In the spring, McCullough, intent on carrying out his resolution to do what was possible to be done to overthrow the Mormon power, took passage on the first steamboat that touched at the island, proceeding by way of Chicago to Lansing. There he laid before governor Bingham a full statement of the condition of affairs on the island, exposing the false census reports, fraudulent voting, false election returns, and false school reports, and solicited the aid of the executive in suppressing the Mormon power. The governor had already had a secret agent for some time on the island. In consequence of the information furnished by this agent, seconded by the representations of McCullough, fifteen hundred dollars of primary school money, that had been apportioned to Manitou county, was withheld. The governor was not averse to doing what he lawfully could, but the matter was surrounded with difficulties. McCullough found in the motion of the State authorities, as he himself expressed it, a practical illustration of the saying that heavy bodies move slowly. He returned to Beaver Island, fully resolved to bring about the overthrow of the Mormon kingdom without State aid.

In the mean time, Bedford and Wentworth had gone to Mackinac, and procured a boat, with which they returned to the island, in order to have means of escape at hand. For five days after their return, both the boat and themselves were kept concealed, during which time they watched for Strang at night, but without getting a suitable opportunity to execute their purpose. Fearing the boat would be discovered and suspicion excited, they concluded to appear openly. Accordingly taking the boat out some distance upon the lake, they sailed into the harbor, as if just returned from Mackinac. In the next number of the *Northern Islander*, Strang advertised the boat as one supposed to have been stolen by Tom Bedford and Alec. Wentworth. Soon afterward the boat was seized by the Mormons at night, filled with stones, and sunk in the harbor.

The vexatious lawsuits against Bedford still remained unsettled. It happened that on the day set for the trial of one of them, the United States revenue cutter Michigan was in the harbor. Some of the officers, willing to give Bedford the moral support of their presence, went with him to the place of trial. The Mormon party refused to proceed, and the case was again postponed. On the next adjourned day, the Michigan came in again, and some of the officers, as on the former occasion, accompanied Bedford to the place of trial. As on the previous occasion, the prosecution refused to proceed, and the case was again adjourned.

Soon after the officers returned on board, the commander of the vessel sent a messenger to Strang, requesting him to come on board, for the transaction of some business. Strang excused himself on the plea that it was not safe for him to appear in public. However, on receiving a second and more pressing request, he started for the vessel. He was obliged to pass for some distance along a narrow road, having continuous piles of cordwood on each side. When near the vessel, he was fired upon by both Bedford and Wentworth, who had previously concealed themselves behind the piles of wood. Strang fell in the path. Bedford and Wentworth started on the run for the vessel. As the former stepped over the body of his victim, Strang seized him by the leg, and released his hold only on receiving a stunning blow from the butt of a pistol. Some men who were standing around the printing office and McCullough's store, hearing the firing, ran to the spot, and carried Strang into a building not far away, when McCullough and the surgeon of the Michigan examined his wounds and pronounced them mortal.

After Bedford and Wentworth went on board, claiming the protection of the vessel, the sheriff made repeated efforts to induce the commander to give them up, but he refused, assigning as a reason that there was no jail on the island, and the prisoners would not be safe, therefore he would take them to Mackinac. The shooting occurred in the afternoon, but the families of Bedford and

Wentworth knew nothing of it till nine o'clock in the evening, when an officer and some men from the Michigan came to assist them to carry their property on board, preparatory to leaving the island. The next morning, six families—those of Bedford, Wentworth, McCullough, Johnson, who was a business partner of McCullough, Fred Longfield, and a German whose name has been forgotten—who did not think it safe to remain after the departure of the Michigan, were received on board, and carried to Mackinac.

On the arrival of the party at Mackinac, there was great excitement and universal rejoicing. Bedford and Wentworth were received as heroes and public benefactors. The formality of surrendering them to the sheriff of Mackinac county was observed, and they were conducted by that functionary to the jail, accompanied by several officers of the Michigan. At the jail a spontaneous ovation awaited them. Citizens flocked in with congratulations and offers of assistance. Everything necessary for comfort was placed at their disposal, and the luxury of cigars and whisky was not forgotten. The doors of the jail were not allowed to be locked, and before night the prisoners informally walked out, and became the guests of their friends.

After it appeared that Strang was not killed outright, the Mormons, fearing that a further attempt would be made upon his life, organized a guard for his protection. After a few days, he was removed to his former home in Voree, where he shortly afterward died of his wounds. During his last days, he was tenderly nursed by his first and lawful wife.

*The statement has been widely circulated that Bedford was whipped as a punishment for unlawful intimacy with another man's wife. A careful investigation of the facts has convinced me that there is not a shadow of truth in it. M. L. L.

CHAPTER XXIII.

Fishermen's Expedition—Retribution—The Innocent Suffer with the Guilty—Narrative of a Mormon Witness—The Mormon Settlement Broken up—The Mormons Driven From Pine River.

McCullough and his accomplices immediately set about organizing an expedition, for the purpose of driving the Mormons out of the country. St. Helena Island was chosen as a rendezvous. Here a party of sixty or seventy men was quickly assembled, all eager to lend a hand in punishing the common enemy. Nominally the party was under the leadership of Archie Newton; practically it was an irresponsible mob. A schooner was chartered to convey them to Beaver Island.

In the mean time, the Mormons were warned of the approach of the hostile party. Strang had for years advised that every man should keep ready for defense such arms as he had, but now, being himself helpless, and probably fearing that a conflict would result disastrously to his people, he recommended that the leading men—probably those who were most obnoxious to the Gentiles—should leave the island. In accordance with this advice, a large number left, some taking their families with them, and others, lacking means of transportation, leaving their women and children to the tender mercies of their foes.

The invading force landed on the west side of the island, and cautiously advanced towards St. James, expecting sharp resistance. When it was found that no resistance was to be offered, the island was patrolled by armed parties, who notified the Mormons to collect at the harbor by a certain time, with all their effects, that they might be sent away on the steamer Keystone State, which was expected in at that time. The direst vengeance was threatened upon all who should fail to obey. The only chance for personal safety was in uncomplaining submission. Remonstrance was answered with curses, threats, and blows.

When the Keystone State arrived, the unfortunate people were driven on board, like so many sheep destined for the shambles. But it was no part of the policy of the invaders to allow them to carry their property with them. That was seized as lawful booty. More than a hundred head of choice cattle, horses, and mules were taken, as well as boats, nets, fish and fishermen's supplies, and large quantities of provisions, furniture, and household goods. Three stores and the printing office were rifled, and their contents added to the plunder. The unfinished house of worship—the tabernacle—was burned.

The property was divided among the invaders, as they could agree, ostensibly to reimburse them for losses sustained by Mormon robberies. Practically, a considerable number got more than they had lost. It is said, no doubt with truth, that some, who have since figured as men of property, got their first start with the goods that somehow fell to their share on this occasion.

Had only those Mormons been robbed and sent away who had themselves been concerned in the robberies previously committed under the pretended sanction of religion, it would have been but retributive justice, even though administered by a mob; but, as frequently happens in the administations of mob law, the innocent were made to suffer equally with the guilty. Only a few families, designated by McCullough, escaped pillage, or were permitted to remain upon the island. Those whom the Keystone State could not carry away, were taken off by other boats, a few days later.

The scenes attending the assembly of the Mormons at the harbor and the embarkation, are graphically described in the personal narrative of Mr. W., a Mormon gentleman of probity and candor, still living. Mr. W. is still a firm adherent of the Mormon faith. The narative is given verbatim, as furnished to the author in writing, except that only initials are given instead of full names.

"Between the coming of the mob and our departure upon the Keystone State, I had occasion to go down from my home, in about the center of the island, to Beaver Harbor, a few times, to see how things were going, and to get some necessaries. On the last occasion, I was met, about a half a mile from the harbor going home, by two mobocrats, each armed with rifle, pistols, and 'bowie knives flashing' in their belts. They had just come, or were coming, through a little gate, from a Mr. M. M. A's, where they had been threatenig and ordering his wife and family to leave. They had been on like business to various other houses that afternoon.

'Where are you going?' says one of them, as I was passing along on the other side of the road.

'I am going home,' said I.

'Where do you live?'

'I live,' said I, 'about six miles up on the island.'

'Well, G—d d—n ye, get your things down here to the harbor by one o'clock to-morrow, or your house will be burned over your head.'

My wife had been about two days confined of our second eldest daughter, at that time, and I told him of the circumstance, saying that I could not well leave on that account.

'That's a G—d d—n pretty fix you've got into now. G—d d—n ye, get yer things down,' etc., etc., as before.

I merely remarked, 'Gentlemen, that's pretty hard.' Then they G—d d—d me again and said, if I called that hard again, 'we will lash you to that tree,' a small cherry tree by the roadside, 'and we will whip you while we can stand over you.' I saw by the flush of their faces that they were both well armed with whisky, as well as with weapons of war, and concluded that I had better move on. Two persons, a young man and his sister, of the name of B., had started up the island before me, and by these the mob sent word to all on the road, to get their things down by such an hour, etc. They had called to my house before me, and delivered the words of the mob. My wife remarked that if the mob wanted her to go, they would have to carry her, for she was not able to go herself. The B's passed on, the young woman remarking '*I am glad.*' I soon after got to the house, and both feeling that we would have to go, my wife concluded that, by taking it very slowly, she might possibly be able to walk down next day. Next morning I went to the harbor again, to see, and hire a team to bring our few things, or such of them as we could not do without. It seemed as if I could get no one to move our things, and was again on the road homeward, expecting to leave all behind, and come away with just what we had on our backs; but after I had started home, my brother-in-law, J. S., procured an ox team for me, and sent a young man with it up that evening, and he was on hand with it the next morning at nine o'clock. To get to my house, he had to go some nine or ten miles of a round, for the straight road for several miles was not passable for teams, except in winter, it being very rough and swampy.

Putting our stove and a few boxes and bedding aboard the wagon, I took the little babe in my arms, and walking very slowly, we managed to get down to the harbor about one o'clock in the afternoon. This was on the 3d day of July. The beach around the west side of the harbor, seemed here and there like an open fair, or market place, with cattle, tents, fires, smokes, furniture, and household goods of every description; all waiting, according to the dictates of the mob, to be off on the boat's arrival, chartered or hired for the business.

'The Book of the Law of the Lord,' an octavo of some 336 pages with explanatory notes, had been printed and folded and awaiting the binder, before Mr. Strang's assassination. This work some of the elders boxed up and took away before the mob came on. This Law, let me say in passing, was, according to its claim, translated by Mr. Strang from ancient records mentioned in the Book of Mormon. The testimony of six other men, who claimed to have seen and hefted and examined the engravings upon those plates, accompanied this work.

Soon after the mob came on, they took possession of the type and printing office of the *Northern Islander*, the weekly paper of the Mormons, and set up and printed a manifesto of their grievances, so called, and circulated it around among the Mormons and Gentiles. A copy of it fell into my hands, and I aimed to preserve it, but it has long since been lost, and I know not whether there is another whole copy of it on earth. It was scarcely readable, and was gotten up after the style of the one set forth in Jackson county, Missouri, by the mob who drove the Mormons there. There were several bound works in pamphlet form left in the office; some in proof and vindication of Mr. Strang's claims as against Brigham Young and others; one called the 'Diamond,' containing the letter of appointment sent by Joseph Smith to Mr. Strang, a little before Mr. Smith's death; and another, entitled 'The Prophetic Controversy,' a very able work; and still another work entitled 'Oliver Cowdery's Letters to W. W. Phelps, on the Bringing in of the New Dispensation.' These, with some others, were all hurled into the street, and lay fluttering in the wind, all about the printing office door, in the eyes of all passing that way.

A very extensive library, containing many volumes of rare works, collected with great pains and no small outlay by Mr. Strang, stood in the printing office, and of course fell into the hands of the mob. In all probability they were sacrificed for a trifle, to whosoever would buy; for surely such a set of ruffians cared nothing for books upon science, history, and moral culture and progress themselves.

I overlooked in the proper time of it, that two stores of general merchandise—one belonging to a man of the name of J. W. W., and another to the Mr. M. M. A., before mentioned—became the prey of the mob. Indeed, I don't know but the greater part of the merchandise of two other stores—for there were four in all—became a part of the general spoil.

In the year 1851, an escaped felon from Ireland, had been killed in the act of resisting the arrest of a couple of noted criminals of the name of O'D. and H. and was buried on the beach, on the west side of the harbor. The Mormons, according to a principle of their faith, piled rough stones upon his grave, and taught their children to add a stone to the pile as they passed by. These stones the mob compelled some timid Mormons to remove, at the gun's muzzle. The felon's name was T. B.

In fact it seemed the pleasure and delight of the mob to be as directly opposite to the Mormons as they knew well how to be, in almost everything.

A day or so before the boat arrived, while stopping at my brother-in-law S's house, Dr. H. D. McCullough came to the house, and had a chat with this S. They were reckoning on who could stay and who not. While in an adjoining room, I heard McCullough say that 'W. was too good a Mormon,' he guessed, 'to stay.' One would think then that McCullough—the chief leader in the assassination of Mr. Strang—was in high esteem among the mob. We little thought that a few days after we left we should find him, and some others who were piloting the mob around on the island, as we did, in Milwaukee, driven off with the rest of us, his beautiful Gothic mansion, store, and dock confiscated to the mob. Possibly he got a trifle of their cost, for I have never heard just how it was. One thing, he desired, and thought he could stay; but he did not remain more than three days behind the rest of us.

The Keystone State, whether steamer or propeller I don't now remember, came in finally on the evening of the sixth day of July, and then a general bustle and flurry commenced among the people, with here and there a 'G—d d—n ye, get yer things aboard,' from the mob.

My brother-in-law had made calculations to move off on the Iowa, Capt. Alexander, and, not expecting him for a day or two, he had only a few of his things packed up. McCullough, moreover, told him he could stay till then; but N. and one of the two mobocrats who met me a few days before and threatened me, came in, as we were thinking of sitting down to supper, and greeted Mr. S. with a 'G—d d—n ye, why an't ye gettin' yer things aboard?' 'Why,' says S. 'I was waiting for the Iowa to come in.' 'G—d d—n ye, get yer things aboard,' says N. giving him at the same time a tremendous slam with his open hand on the side of his face, that fairly whirled S. half around, following him up with a revolver, and jamming it against his breast, repeating 'G—d d—n ye, get yer things aboard.' 'Why,' says S., 'McCullough told me that I could stay till the Iowa came in.' 'G—d d—n McCullough,' said N., 'we'll play hell with him pretty soon.' The other mobocrat commenced slamming water in the stove and pulling things about, and, pulling the bed-clothes off one of the beds, he was within a very little of pulling our little six days old infant off on to the floor. Its mother cried out in time to save it.

By the accommodation of a Mr. W. E. W., who had a one-horse spring wagon, I got what few things I brought down off the island aboard; but poor brother-in-law S. got next to nothing of his large property. The industry of 30 years with him was mainly swept away in an hour. He had, with his brother-in-law, S. R., come on to the island, from Pittsburg, Pa., and built a large saw-mill, bringing machinery of various kinds with him, with blacksmith's shop, turning lathe, and belting, so that there was scarcely anything in a common way that needed doing in such a place but what could be done, from the making of a small screw to the boring of a cannon, etc., yet all was possessed by the mob, innocent, as he was, and without a charge of any kind being laid against him. Plead as he might and did, he never got a penny of the thousands he had invested there. 'He was a damn Mormon,' you know.

The Keystone State lay at Mr. Aldrich's dock, at the west side of Beaver Harbor, and when all living and camped thereabouts were hustled on board, the boat was steamed up to the head of the bay, where McCullough's dock stood. My wife, I think, was the last to get aboard at Aldrich's dock. Walking before her with the little babe in my arms, she rather feebly and slowly walked along towards the boat. A mobocratic ruffian and companion of N., was walking, still armed, behind her. She was not moving quickly enough to suit him, 'G—d d—n ye,' said he 'move on.'

When the lines were made fast at McCullough's dock, the same hurry and bustle commenced among the Mormons camped around there, and soon [they] were hustled aboard. But all the Mormons, it seems, were not taken on this boat; there were several other boats called there afterward, upon which various families came away.

It was now about 7 o'clock in the evening, and the boat having taken in as many of the people, with the few things they were permitted to take, as could well be stowed together, the lines were cast off, and the Keystone State headed for Chicago."

It is not necessary to pursue farther the present narrative quoted above. Of the Mormons carried away on the Keystone State, a part landed at Milwaukee and the rest at Chicago. From those points they scattered in various directions.

While these events were occurring on Beaver Island, a party of "Gentiles," remembering the Mormon settlement at Pine River, paid it a hostile visit. The Mormons had been notified of the danger, and those who thought it unwise to fall into the power of their enemies had prudently left the place. Not finding some particular individuals, whom they wished to punish, and suspecting that they had recently been entertained by the widow King, the invaders revenged themselves by burning her dwelling. The settlement, like the principal one on Beaver Island, was broken up, only two or three of the least obnoxious families being allowed to remain.

The history of the rise and fall of the Mormon kingdom of Beaver Island, affords a striking example of systematic, organized, and wide-spread lawlessness, lawlessly punished.

CHAPTER XXIV.

The Pine River Country after the Expulsion of the Mormons—Arrival of Immigrants—The Rover and her Passengers—Mr. Dixon's Return—Mr. and Mrs. John Miller—A Dream and its Fulfillment—A Mormon Demand for Rent—Early Settlers on Pine Lake—Lost in the Woods.

The driving out of the Mormons left Medad Thompson and his family the only inhabitants at Pine River. However, they were not long alone. About the first of August, 1856, a sail might have been seen coming round the point from the direction of Little Traverse, and heading for the mouth of the river, with a number of persons on board. It proved to be the Rover, carrying as crew and passengers Samuel Horton and his family, and two young men—John Newman and Archie Buttars.

Mr. Horton had left Toledo in the Rover with the intention of coasting round the lower peninsula of Michigan and up Grand river, to Grand Rapids, where two of his sons were living. Getting short of provisions, he put into Pine River in the hope of obtaining a supply. Here adverse winds induced him to remain for several days. It is said that, getting weary of the delay, he finally determined to start on a certain day, if the wind was fair; if not, he would take it as an indication that Providence had ordered that his home should be beside the bright waters of Pine lake. On the day appointed, the wind was unfavorable for proceeding on the voyage, and accordingly the prow of the Rover was turned towards the head of the lake. He selected a location at the head of the charming sheet of water that has since been named in his honor Horton's bay, where he found an improvement, which had been made by the Mormons previous to being driven off. Newman and Buttars, who seem to have been for some time drifting aimlessly about the world, became permanent residents of the country, the latter taking up his abode at Pine River, and the former remaining for some time at Horton's bay.

The Rover was for many years the largest craft on Pine lake. On account of her peculiar build and somewhat dilapidated condition, she was the object of many witticisms, but however unseaworthy she may have been, judged by accepted nautical standards, she carried many a load of staves and hoops from Pine River to the Beaver islands, and, in return, brought provisions in safety to those who would have been left in destitute circumstances, had she been cast away.

After the Mormons were driven off, Mr. Dixon, who, since his expulsion from Pine River, had remained at Northport, resolved to return. He first visited Beaver island, where he was successful in recovering the greater part of his stolen property. This he conveyed to Pine River, and then returned to Northport for his family. At the latter place, he fell in with Mr. John Miller, afterwards familiarly known as "Uncle" John Miller, who, with his wife and two sons, had come from Oswegatchie, St. Lawrence county, N. Y., in search of a home in the west. It was arranged that Mr. Miller should take passage in Mr. Dixon's boat, and the two families sailed for Pine River in company.

After stopping a short time at Pine River, Mr. Miller and his family were conveyed to their new home by Mr. Dixon in his boat, arriving at eleven o'clock at night. The location which had been selected, was on the north shore of Pine lake, near its head, in the vicinity of the present site of Bay Springs. The place had been occupied by the Mormons, who had made a clearing, built a log house, and planted some crops.

Mrs. Miller relates a curious dream she had before leaving Oswegatchie, the fulfillment of which she recognized in the circumstances of their arrival at their new home. She saw in her dream the log house, as it actually was, with a roof made of troughs, as the settlers sometimes made them where boards were scarce, with a trough inverted on the ridge in place of weather-boards. In front of the house was what appeared to be a swamp. She thought they built a fire on the floor, in the house. Then the man who brought them there took the end board out of his wagon box to close an open window, and said to her that she would never want while she remained there. The features of the man were indelibly fixed in her memory. When, at Northport, she first caught sight of Mr. Dixon on the wharf, she recognized him at once as the person she had seen in her dream, and pointed him out to her husband as such. Arriving at their destination, everything appeared as she had seen it. What she had taken to be a swamp, however, was the lake, hidden by a row of evergreen trees along the beach. They did build a fire on the floor, or, rather, on the charred remains of the floor, which had already been partly consumed by accident or design. Then Mr. Dixon brought, not the end board of a wagon box, but the center board of his boat, and with it closed a window, to keep out the night air. We are not informed whether Mr. Dixon then actually spoke the words attributed to him or not, but his prophecy as heard in the dream made such a deep and lasting impression on Mrs. Miller that, many years after, when, by the building up of the villages of Boyne City and Bay Springs, their land was made valuable and tempting prices were offered for it, she steadfastly refused to sell.

The place selected by Mr. Miller had been occupied by a Mormon whose wife claimed to hold it under a pretended grant from Strang. It is said that, assuming to have supreme authority over the country, he gave it to her as a bribe, to induce her to second, by her influence and example, his attempt to establish by authority the exclusive use of the bloomer costume among his female subjects. It is a curious illustration of the sincerity of a class of honest but misguided Mormons, and of their implicit faith in the divine authority of their leader as prophet, priest, and king, that, many years after, the woman, still believing herself to be the rightful owner, demanded the payment of rent from Mr. Miller. The latter, however, having obtained a patent under the seal of the United States, was unable to see any justice in the demand.

At the closing in of the winter of 1856-7, there were four families in the Pine River region—those of Medad Thompson, J. S. Dixon, Samuel Horton, and John Miller—and, probably, the two young men, Newman and Buttars. The following spring the settlement was re-inforced by the arrival of S. F. Mason, Frank May, and a man named Hyde. They were followed in the course of the summer by J. R. Dean and A. A. Corwin, sons-in-law of Mr. Horton, and in the fall by M. J. Stockman. In the spring of 1858 came Hugh Miller, J. Beebe, and a man named Cross, and in the fall of the same year Richard Williams and two men named Cochran and Childs. D. H. Pierce came in 1857 or 1858.

Of this number only five—Mason, Stockman, Miller, Pierce, and Williams—became permanent residents. May and Hyde stopped at Advance during the summer of 1857, but in the fall left for some other locality. The former, who had been in Mr. Dixon's employ during his first season at Pine River, had since married. A daughter, born to him while at Advance, was the first white child born in the vicinity of the head of Pine lake. Dean and Corwin settled near Horton's bay, but left the country in 1859. Williams, Cochran, and Childs settled at Advance. Williams soon left, but afterwards returned to Pine River. The other two, after remaining about a year, removed to Northport. Beebe and Cross retired from the settlement in 1859. The former, as he was leaving, met with a terrible affliction, in the loss of his wife and two children, by the capsizing of a sail boat, on the reef at Pine River point. Mason and Stockman took up their residence at Pine River. Miller and Pierce located farms—the former a short distance south of Pine River; the latter on the north shore of Pine lake, some six miles distant.

Wm. H. Porter was the first permanent settler at Advance. He first came to the place in 1859, selected his land, which he purchased of the U. S. government, and then went to Bear creek, where he remained till 1865. In the latter year he returned to Advance, and built a saw-mill, and afterwards a grist-mill, where the village now stands, on the stream named in his honor Porter's creek.

The site of the present village of Boyne City remained an unbroken wilderness till a somewhat later date. The first settler at that point was Andrew J. Hall.

Amos Williams was the first settler at the head of the south arm of Pine lake. The exact date of his arrival is not known, but he was already there in 1862. At first he "squatted" on what he supposed to be government land, but which proved to be the property of a railroad company. He afterwards took a government homestead.

Williams is remembered as the owner of a large canoe, or dug-out, made from the trunk of a pine tree, which he christened the Old Ship Zion. At the same time, Hugh Miller owned a craft of the same sort, named the Leviathan, and an old gentleman of the name of Holland a sail boat known as the Bucephalus. These three vessels, with the Rover, brought in by Mr. Horton, seem to have bequeathed their names to history as among the most famous of the earliest fleet traversing the waters of Pine lake.

A volume might doubtless be written about the hardships, strange experiences, and curious adventures of the early settlers of the Pine River region, were the facts, in all their interesting particulars, at command. In addition to those already given, one or two must suffice.

Mrs. John Miller relates that, in 1858, her oldest son, Hugh, being absent in the employ of Mr. Porter at Bear Creek, Mr. Miller and the younger son, James, went away with a boat to obtain supplies. Stress of weather compelled them to remain away longer than had been anticipated, and for fourteen days she did not see the face of a human being.

In June of the same year, she got lost in the woods, and laid out two nights. She had gone out in the morning after her cows. Usually, when the cows were started, they would go directly home, and Mrs. Miller had fallen into the habit of depending on them for guidance. On this occasion, for some unaccountable reason, they took a wrong direction, and she sooon became aware that she was lost. She kept with the cows, living upon milk. When they laid down at night, she too laid down, with her back against one of them, assuming that position for the sake of warmth, and for the purpose of being awakened, if the cows should again start on their wanderings. She had learned from observation that at the time of the longest days in June, when shadows are shortest, she could step exactly the length of her own shadow at twelve o'clock. On the second day, while measuring her shadow in this manner to see if it was noon, she discovered a glittering object among the dead leaves on the ground. It proved to be a shirt button, and further search revealed the remains of an old flannel shirt. Then she remembered that two land-lookers, who had been entertained at her house sometime before, had mentioned throwing away their flannel shirts in the woods, several miles up the Boyne. Concluding that she must be several miles east of home, she took the sun for a guide, and drove her cows in a westerly direction till sunset. Then the cows laid down to rest, and she with them, for a few hours. After the moon had got up high enough to be a convenient guide, she traveled awhile by moonlight, and then laid down for another rest. In the morning, she was cheered by the distant blowing of horns and firing of guns. Understanding the sounds to be the welcome signals of a searching party, she seized the bell carried by one of the cows and rang it with all her might in response, but was unable to make it heard. Soon afterwards, she came upon and recognized the survey marks of the original line of the Grand Rapids and Indiana railroad, which she knew was only two miles or a little more from home. Pushing on as well as she might, she was cheered and encouraged by a repetition of the signals of the searching party. This time, by a vigorous ringing of the bell, she was able to attract their attention. They proved to be a party of Indians from Bear Creek. Mr. Miller had gone over to the Mission for help. The party had crossed Bear Lake in their canoes, firing guns and blowing horns as they landed on the south shore. Not hearing any response, they had proceeded to the house, where Mr. Miller provided a breakfast. Then two of them had started up the Boyne in a canoe, while the others proceeded eastwardly by land. Mrs. Miller would, no doubt, have finally reached home without assistance, but the dusky faces of her friendly rescuers were none the less welcome, after a lonely sojourn of two days in the forest.

CHAPTER XXV.

Village Platted—Fox & Rose—Wharf Built—The Wood Trade—Steam Tug on Pine Lake—First Sunday-School—Sunday-School in a Fish Shanty—A Minister Arrives—Parsonage Built—The Women Resolve to Build a School House—How They Did it—Letter to Mrs. Fox.

To one having an eye to either business or beauty, the banks of Pine river early presented attractions as an eligible site for a town. A mile back from the shore of Lake Michigan lies Pine lake, its two arms stretching away to the southeast long distances into the interior. Between it and Lake Michigan lies Round lake, covering an area of a hundred acres or more. Pine river, the outlet of Pine lake, in its course to Lake Michigan runs directly through it. The river in its natural state was a narrow, crooked, swiftly flowing stream, full of snags and overhung with frees, as unlike the broad, deep, and almost straight channel through which large steamers now go up into Pine lake as one can well imagine.

At an early day Mr. Dixon surveyed and platted a part of what is now the village of Charlevoix, in the sheltered basin lying south of the lower river and west of Round lake. At that time, furnishing wood for the steam craft navigating the great lakes was a profitable business, where wood was easily accessible. Charlevoix was only a few miles off the usual route of passing steamers. Messrs. Fox & Rose, who were engaged in the wood trade at Northport, saw the advantages of the situation, where was an almost unlimited tract of hardwood forest, from which Pine lake and the river afforded means of cheap transportation to the shore. In 1863 an arrangement was entered into between them and Mr. Dixon, mutually advantageous to the contracting parties. In consideration of their building a wharf and establishing business, Mr. Dixon conveyed to them a narrow strip of land along the shore of Lake Michigan, which gave them the control of the lake front for some distance both sides of the river. Mr. Fox soon after took up his residence in Charlevoix, a store was opened, and the construction of a wharf commenced in 1864.

Charlevoix soon became an important wooding station for steamers, and the cutting of wood, here as well as at the Manitous and in the vicinity of Northport, furnished employment for a large number of men. From the first it was seen that the supply must come largely from the shores of Pine lake. To facilitate transportation, a tug was necessary. Messrs. Fox & Rose accordingly had one built—a diminutive craft called the Commodore Nutt—which arrived in June, 1867, and, after the exercise of considerable engineering skill, the deepening of the channel of the river in some of its shallower parts by the aid of teams and road-scrapers, and the expenditure of a large amount of muscular force in towing, was finally got into Pine lake on the morning of the fourth of July.

Not the least important feature of the history we are tracing, is that of the development of the religious and educational interests of the various localities passing under observation. Some interesting facts connected with the early church work in Charlevoix, have been preserved. Some reminiscences also of the early efforts to give the children educational advantages equal to those afforded by the common school in other places, are worthy of being put on record.

The first religious work of which we have any account, was a Sunday-school, conducted by Mrs. Dixon in her own house. It was commenced in the fall of 1859, and closed in the summer of 1860, having been kept up, with some irregular intermissions, between these two dates. Four families were represented—those of S. F. Mason, Medad Thompson, Hugh Miller, and J. S. Dixon. The pupils were Oscar Mason, Albert Mason, Melvin Thompson, Wm. Miller, John Miller, Mary Ann Miller, Ellen Miller, Frances P. Dixon, Joseph R. Dixon, and Charlie Dixon. There was no formal organization, and the exercises were of the simplest kind. Desiring some Sunday-school books for the children, Mrs. Dixon wrote to Mr. T. Marvin, publisher of the *Missionary Herald*. Her letter was referred by him to the Young People's Missionary Society of Park street church, Boston, which promptly responded by the donation of a ten-dollar library. Mr. Dixon's residence was situated near the beach of Pine lake. As the homes of the other families were similarly situated, the easiest way for the children to reach the school in winter was to go on skates. It was quite natural that, returning, the attractions of skating should prove too strong for their regard for the Sabbath, and that they should while away a considerable part of the afternoon on the ice. At one time it became a serious question with Mrs. Dixon whether her school, indirectly, was not doing more harm than good.

After the close of this Sunday-school, in the summer of 1860, brought about indirectly by severe domestic affliction in the family of Mr. and Mrs. Dixon in the loss by death of a little daughter, nothing more was attempted in that line of work till 1865. In the summer of that year, for a short time, Mrs. Dixon again conducted a Sunday-school, in the little log school house that had been built on a terrace overlooking Pine lake, on the grounds now occupied by the Charlevoix summer resort.

In the spring of 1867, the writer found himself in Charlevoix, with the prospect before him of spending the summer and autumn there. At the earnest solicitation of the young people, he consented to undertake the organization and management of a Sunday-school. Within a radius of two miles, there were, all told, about sixteen young persons of both sexes of suitable age for a bible class, and about the same number of children old enough to attend the school. They were all gathered in, almost without an effort. There was no minister of the gospel at Charlevoix. Rev. Leroy Warren, engaged in home missionary work, preached there when his duties, at long intervals, called him into that region, and Rev. A. J. Sensabaugh, the methodist minister on Antrim circuit, held meetings there occasionally, but during the greater part of that season the Sunday-school was the only Sunday service.

Some difficulty was encountered in finding a suitable place for meeting. There was a fisherman's shanty on the south side of the river, on or very near the site now occupied by the block owned by L. D. Bartholomew, in which the odd fellows' hall is situated. All around it the forest yet remained in its pristine beauty. The shanty was without windows, and was filled with a heterogeneous collection of barrels, nets, and other implements of the fisherman's art. Permission was obtained of the owner, and the young men of the neighborhood undertook to put it in order. Openings were cut in the wall and windows inserted, to obtain which it was necessary to send to Traverse City. A strong scaffold of poles was built overhead, on which was stowed away everything of value. The useless trash was carried outside. Seats were made by placing logs of wood on the floor, across which boards were laid.

The whole number of names on the roll of the school was thirty six, including almost all the children and youth of the settlement. Sixteen of the older ones constituted the bible class, taught by the superintendent. The following is a list of the officers and teachers: Superintendent, M. L. Leach; secretary, Miss Frances P. Dixon; treasurer, Mrs. Nelson Ainslie; librarian, Joseph R. Dixon; teachers, Mrs. Ainslie, Mrs. Wm. Chamberlain, Miss Lottie Ainslie.

This Sunday school was, to say the least, unique. Organized at the earnest solicitation of the young people themselves, gathering in all the young ladies and gentlemen of the settlement, taking the place of the ordinary religious services of older communities, held in a shanty of the roughest and most primitive construction, with the nets and other fishing gear of the owner in plain sight overhead, enveloped in the shade of the primitive forest, with the crystal waters of the little lake, the swiftly flowing river, and the surf-beaten beach of Lake Michigan only a step away, it remains pictured in the memory of the writer as a notable way-mark of one of the pleasant stages of a somewhat eventful life.

In the fall, the owner of the shanty having use for it, the Sunday-school had to be transferred to other quarters. Once or twice it was held in the dwelling of Mr. Robert Miller, and then for some time in the sitting room of an unfinished building owned by Mr. Althouse and kept by him as a house of entertainment for travelers. It only remains to add that from the organization of that school up to the time of the present writing, Charlevoix has never been without a Sunday-school in active operation, except on a single occasion when, one winter, there was an intermission of six weeks' duration.

In the fall of 1867, the Michigan conference of the M. E. church established Charlevoix circuit, and sent Rev. J. Gulick to take charge of the work. There was already a class there, consisting of thirteen members, who were scattered over the surrounding country, only one or two of them living in the village. The first quarterly meeting was held in the sitting room of the Althouse building, where the Sunday school had been in the habit of meeting. The quarterly conference consisted of only the presiding elder, the pastor in charge, and the class leader. Mr. Gulick immediately set about the construction of a small building to be occupied as a parsonage, which, by the willing aid of the people, was so nearly completed as to be comfortable when winter set in. During the year that followed, he was compelled to eke out his scanty salary by serving a part of the time as clerk in the store of Fox & Rose.

The first school house in Charlevoix, which has been already alluded to as standing on the grounds now occupied by the Charlevoix summer resort, was a log structure about sixteen feet square, with a floor of hewn planks, a roof of shakes, a door fastened with a wooden latch, three windows of six small panes each, seats of planks supported on rough legs, and writing tables of long boards placed edgewise against the wall around three sides of the room. In the fall of 1867 it began to be felt that the school house accommodations were too limited. There were perhaps a dozen white families in and around the village. As the legal voters did not seem inclined to move in the matter of building, the women took the affair into their own hands, and went about it in their own way. After consultation, they resolved to hold a fair to raise money as a nucleus for a building fund. The matter was pushed with such energy that three weeks after the inception of the project everything was ready, and the evening of the sixth of December was appointed for the gathering.

When the evening arrived, a general interest in the fair, if not in the object it was intended to promote, had been aroused, and, though a wintry storm was raging, nearly all the inhabitants of the settlement, old and young, were early at the place appointed, anticipating, and determined to have, a good time. The ladies had prepared a large number of articles—useful and ornamental—for sale. Most of them were first disposed of at private sale, and were then put up at auction by the first purchasers, the money in every case going into the common fund. After the sales were completed, the company repaired to the dining room, where, as a lady who was present has since expressed it, "they had oysters, real oysters, don't you think—a dish almost unknown in those days except in name—and they were dealt out by good big dishfulls—not a little soup with one poor little oyster swimming around all alone." Perhaps not the least enjoyable part of the amusement of the evening was the public reading of the letters received by individuals through the young ladies' post-office. Several persons whose turn of mind lead them to work in that direction, had employed their spare moments in providing material for that department, consequently almost every person got a letter—in prose or verse, witty, humorous, sarcastic, spicy or dull, according to the whim and ability of the writer. Of course the recipient was required to pay a small sum as postage, to help swell the receipts of the evening. One letter, in verse, addressed to Mrs. Fox, has been preserved, and may serve as a sample of the lot. It ran as follows:

> With wifely charm and loving care,
> When home affairs get in a box,
> With wisdom true and talent rare,
> Guide and control that sly old Fox.
>
> And when rude storms, o'er all the earth
> Sweeping, portend the equinoxes,
> Then, hovering near the homestead hearth,
> Nurse and protect the little Foxes.

The fair was a success financially, about $75 being realized. This was put into Mrs. Ainslie's hands as treasurer, and was expended the next spring towards building a school house. The new house, though not completed that season, was occupied for a three month's summer term of school.

CHAPTER XXVI.

Inception of the Benzonia Enterprise Preliminary Explorations—Influence of Deacon Dame's Article in the N. Y. Tribune—The Compact—Location Agreed on—Clearing the Betsey River—First Colonists—Incidents of Progress—The First Woman on the Trail—Other Settlements—Frankfort, Homestead, Joyfield, Pleasanton, Monroe Center, Wexford.

At this stage of our narrative, it becomes necessary again to turn our attention to a new point of interest. The establishment of the colony at Benzonia was an event in the settlement of the country of no small moment.

As early as the winter of 1855, the idea of a christian colony and college as one of the best agencies for laying a foundation for good to the world, took definite shape in the mind of Rev. Charles E. Bailey, a congregational minister of Medina, Ohio. Mentioning the subject to Rev. M. W. Fairfield, nearly a year later, he learned that some of the people attending the ministry of the latter were entertaining a similar project. A meeting for consultation was held at Mr. Bailey's house. A plan of operations was agreed on, and Messrs. Bailey and Fairfield undertook to find a suitable location and attend to the purchase of land. In the discharge of this duty, they performed a toilsome journey of exploration through a part of Iowa, only to learn at the last moment, on visiting the land office, that through the operation of some recent railroad land grant law, the government lands of Iowa had been withdrawn from market. As the plan which had been agreed to required the purchase of government lands in that state, the project had to be abandoned. Returning to Medina, Mr. Fairfield withdrew from the enterprise altogether. Mr. Bailey, though his ardor was somewhat abated, resolved to persevere.

As the original organization was now broken up, Mr. Bailey and his brother John, on their own responsibility, spent considerable time in visiting various portions of the west, hoping to find second-hand lands suitable for the purpose in view. After months spent in explorations, and the endurance of much hardships from winter travel on the unsettled prairies of Iowa, they found a location in the northern part of that state which seemed in all respects desirable. The owners or agents of the lands lived in Dubuque. Thither the brothers went with buoyant spirits, only to meet with another disappointment. A choice quarter section in the central part of the tract, at the point most suitable for platting a village, was found to be the property of minor heirs, and could not be purchased. This circumstance was afterwards looked upon as providential and fortunate, as, if the colony had been located there at that time, the enterprise would probably have been wrecked in the financial crash of 1857.

The remainder of the winter and the early spring were spent in discussing plans and the probable advantages of many widely separated localities. Some years before, Mr. John Bailey had clipped from the New York *Tribune* an article written by Deacon Dame, describing in glowing terms the country around Grand Traverse bay. This, which he had preserved in his pocket-book, was now read and re-read with a great deal of interest. While the brothers Bailey were discussing plans, at Grinnell, Iowa, Mr. Chauncey T. Carrier came from western New York to Ohio, on his way west in search of a home for himself and family. Calling on Rev. A. D. Barber, an old school friend, the latter informed him of the project in which the Baileys were engaged, and induced him to join them at Grinnell. Mr. Carrier had formerly known Deacon Dame, and had confidence in his statements. Comparing notes with the Baileys, he, as well as they, was favorably impressed in regard to northern Michigan. As Mr. Carrier had business in Minnesota, it was arranged that he should pursue his journey, and that the three should finally meet at the most northerly port in Grand Traverse bay, though none of them knew its name or had any definite notion of its location.

As the time for the appointed meeting approached, Mr. Carrier landed at Northport. The Messrs. Bailey landed on one of the Manitous, whence they passed over to Glen Arbor in a smal boat. While they were making their way to Northport on foot, Mr. Carrier visited a location on the east side of Elk lake, in Antrim county, which seemed to him to offer important advantages for the establishment of the proposed colony. Meeting his comrades at Northport, he induced them to visit it, it being stipulated, however, that the three should also visit and examine a tract of country of which the Baileys had heard favorable reports, lying between Traverse City and Glen Arbor and south of the latter place, before coming to a final decision. The tract near Elk lake not proving satisfactory to the Baileys, the party started in the direction of Glen Arbor, arriving at Traverse City on Saturday morning. It had been their intention to remain there over Sunday, but an incident, which in its results may to us of the present day seem amusing, caused them to change their minds. In those days the antislavery agitation was at its height, and discussions commenced in a friendly spirit not unfrequently ended in bitter hostility. Mr. Carrier was an earnest, outspoken, uncompromising hater of the system of American slavery, having no patience with its northern apologists. While waiting for breakfast in Hannah, Lay & Co's boarding-house, he fell into conversation with the landlord, and became so displeased with the latter's expression of proslavery sentiments that he refused to remain. Starting again about nine o'clock in the forenoon, the party pushed on as rapidly as they were able, on a trail so blind as to be followed with great difficulty, till darkness compelled them to encamp. They passed the night in great discomfort, without shelter, suffering from thirst, and a part of the time exposed to a drenching rain. In the morning they went on as far as the shore of Glen lake, where a deserted log cabin afforded them shelter for the remainder of the day and the following night. On arriving at Glen Arbor, the explorers were so well pleased with the country they had seen that they resolved to return at a future day, and make a temporary home at that place till a location suitable for their purpose could be definitely fixed on. As a matter of prudence, however, it was thought best to first take a look at Missouri. Mr. C. E. Bailey and Mr. Carrier accordingly visited the northern part of that state, but returned fully convinced that, all things considered, the Grand Traverse country offered more and better facilities for their contemplated enterprise than any other open to settlement.*

A decision having been reached, Messrs. John and Horace C. Bailey and H. A. Wolcott, with their families, moved to Glen Arbor in the fall of 1857.† Mr. C. E. Bailey remained for the winter in Illinois, where he was temporarily preaching, and where he prepared the articles of association for the colony. They are styled "Articles of Agreement and Plans for a Christian Colony and Institute of Learning, to be located in the Grand Traverse Bay country, Northern Michigan." To the original articles are attached the autograph signatures of Charles E. Bailey, John Bailey, James F. Bailey, Lorenzo Bailey, H. C. Bailey, H. A. Wolcott, R. A. Severance, Amzi D. Barber, C. T. Carrier, J. B. Walker, and Charles Burr. In them it was stipulated that all stock subscribed and paid in should be expended in the purchase of government lands, and that one-fourth of all the government lands obtained by the stockholders, either individually or jointly, should be devoted to the establishment and permanent endowment of a college or university, to be located on the lands of the colony. The college or university was to be of such a character as to afford to both sexes, without distinction of color, the opportunity of acquiring a liberal education. Provision was made for grounds for a church, a parsonage, a common school building, and a cemetery, and a tract was to be set apart for a college farm. All conveyances of colony lands were to contain a clause forever prohibiting on them the manufacture, sale or gift, except strictly for mechanical and medicinal purposes, of all intoxicating liquors.

During the winter, Mr. John Bailey made an exploring tour south from Glen Arbor, passing east and south of the point where the village of Benzonia was afterwards located. Traveling, by reason of the snow, was difficult and toilsome. Returning, Saturday night overtook him just west of the outlet of Crystal lake. Though within a day's walk of home, he chose to remain in camp till Monday morning, preferring to endure the discomforts of the situation rather than violate the sancity of the Sabbath by traveling.

As early the following spring, (1858,) as it was deemed safe to travel by water, Mr. C. E. Bailey and his family came to Glen Arbor. They were accompanied by Mr. Charles Burr and his two sons, of Bellevue, Ohio.

Immediately after the arrival of the new-comers, a party of six set out on an exploring tour, for the purpose of fixing definitely on a site for the colony and village. The place selected as the central point, was one mile south and two miles east of the present site of the village of Benzonia, though a minority of the party were at that time in favor of the present site. A location having been determined on and the lands selected, Mr. Burr and Mr. Wolcott were chosen delegates to visit the United States land office and make the purchase.

During the summer Messrs. John and C. E. Bailey made several visits to the proposed site of the colony. A small boat was constructed, that two men could carry, which was conveyed over the ridge that separates Lake Michigan and Crystal lake, and launched on the latter. The vicinity of the purchase could then be reached from Glen Arbor by coasting along the shore of Lake Michigan to the portage over the ridge, crossing it, and passing in the small boat up Crystal lake to its eastern extremity. Returning from one of these visits, they were once compelled by stress of weather to remain over Sunday near Point Betsey light house, when Mr. C. E. Bailey improved the opportunity to preach to a small audience in a fisherman's shanty. Capt. Emory and his son, of the peninsula, happening to be present, were among the hearers. The sermon was the first ever preached in Benzie county.

The lumber for the first house had to be transported from Glen Arbor to the mouth of the Betsey river in small boats, and then up that stream to a point as near the intended location as practicable. Several days were spent in clearing the river of obstructions. Becoming discouraged with the magnitude and difficulties of the work, Mr. Wolcott and the Baileys commenced explorations for an available land route for some part of the way. While engaged in this project, they had occasion to pass over the tract on which the village has since been built, and all became convinced that, all things considered, it was a more suitable location for the central point of the colony than the one already selected. A change was accordingly agreed upon, and the location of the future village, now Benzonia, was permanently fixed.

In the latter part of October, final preparations having been made for locating permanently in their new home, a vessel was chartered to convey their goods from Glen Arbor to the mouth of the Betsey, the women and children being provided with conveyance in a small boat. The party consisted of Mr. and Mrs. C. E. Bailey, Mrs. John Bailey and two children, Mr. and Mrs. Wolcott, Mr. and Mrs. Horace Burr, and Mr. Elijah Burr. Dr. B. A. Severance and Mr. Charles Burr, father of the Burr brothers, accompanied the party for the double purpose of rendering assistance and viewing the country. Mr. John Bailey and the widow of Horace C. Bailey, being in ill health, had gone to Cleveland, Ohio, for medical advice. It was eleven o'clock at night when they landed at the mouth of the Betsey, where the village of Frankfort now stands. There were three Canadian French families living there at the time—Wm. Robar and his son-in-laws John Greenwood and Frank Martin—with one of which the party found accommodations for the night. Then two days and a half were consumed in ascending the river. On the third day at noon, they landed in the vicinity of their future home, a little more than a mile from what is now the center of the village.

In the fall of the following year, (1859,) J. R. Barr and Edward Neil became residents of the colony. Among those who came in 1860, were L. W. Case, Rev. George Thompson, Joseph Carson, Wm. Weston, and a Mr. Risley. There were also, at this time, several young unmarried persons in the settlement. The first wedding took place in June, the contracting parties being Mr. Hugh Marsh and Miss Emily Burr. A church was organized, consisting of eighteen members. A district school was opened, taught by Miss Julia M. Case, in a part of the dwelling-house of John Bailey. In the winter of 1860 and '61, there were thirteen families in the settlement. From 1860 to '63 large additions were made to the population by the arrival of new settlers. In the early part of the latter year, about sixty came within a period of ten days. Among them were Rev. J. B. Walker, D. D., of Sandusky, Ohio, a theological writer of some note, and Rev. Reuben Hatch, who had been the first president of Olivet college.

On the 10th of June of this year, the first meeting of the board of trustees of the college was held. Dr. Walker was elected president of the college, and Mr. Hatch professor of languages. Under the charge of Professor Hatch, a preparatory department was opened on the first day of July.

This year, also, the first grist mill was got into operation. It was a log building, containing a single run of stones. The builder, Mr. W. S. Hubbell, who, with his sons, had come to the settlement the year previous, had been obliged to bring the millstones and the machinery from Glen Arbor, where they had been landed from a propeller, along the shore of Lake Michigan and up the Betsey river in a small boat.

During the first few years of the existence of the colony, great inconvenience was experienced in consequence of the absence of roads. All goods landed at Frankfort or brought from Glen Arbor, where the lake steamers more frequently called, had to be transported in boats up the Betsey river, at no small cost of patience and labor. Up to 1862 there were no roads from Benzonia to other settlements. The mail route from Traverse City to Manistee by way of Benzonia, was only a trail, or foot-path, marked by blazed trees. In summer the mail was carried on horseback; in winter on a sort of sled, not unlike the dog sledges in use in some arctic countries. It consisted of a single plank, eight feet long and a foot and a half wide, turned up in front like a sleigh runner. On this the mail bags were securely fastened by straps passing over them. The plank was drawn by a single horse, scarcely sinking into the snow and running over fallen trees without difficulty. The driver usually ran behind, but when fatigued sometimes rested himself by riding. When, as was sometimes the case, the mail carrier was an Indian, he used dogs for his team, in true arctic style. An incident or two will illustrate the difficulty of winter travel at that time.

Mrs. Jacob Barns was the first woman who passed over the trail. Her journey was accomplished, in company with her husband and others, in February, 1859. A party of eight, including two Indians with the mail, left Traverse City together, being conveyed over the first seventeen miles of the route in a sleigh, when they encamped for the night. The sleigh could go no further. The next day Mrs. Barns rode a favorite pony, sometimes being obliged to leap over obstructions in the path. They reached Benzonia the second night. On the morning of the third day they went down to the shore of Lake Michigan, at or near the present site of Frankfort, where Mrs. Barns exchanged the saddle for a seat on the dog train of the Indians. They traveled the remainder of that day and a part of the following night on the ice, encountering a terrific snow storm and finding considerable difficulty in passing a stretch of open water. It was midnight when they reached a place of shelter at the mouth of Portage creek. From Portage they were conveyed by teams to Grand Haven, arriving at that place ten days after leaving Traverse City.

In February, 1862, H. E. Steward and L. W. Hubbell went from Benzonia to Traverse City and returned, with ox teams and sleds, for the double purpose of carrying grain to mill and purchasing supplies. The snow was two and a half feet deep, and the track was little more than what had been made by the mail carrier's horse and plank sled. At that time the woods were more open than at a later period, and it was possible to get through with sleds by frequently running over the trunks of fallen trees. They were six full days in making the round trip, camping in the woods two nights both going and returning. On their way out a supply of fodder for the teams was left at each camping place, to be used on their return.

A road was cut through the woods from Benzonia to Manistee, by way of Bear lake, in January, 1862. In the fall of 1863, one was cut out and made passable for wagons between Benzonia and Traverse City, the citizens of each settlement by agreement doing the work on that half the route next their own locality.

Immediately after the establishment of the colony at Benzonia, Benzie county and the adjacent parts of Grand Traverse, Wexford, and Manistee began to be dotted with settlements. A company was formed for the purpose of opening business at Frankfort, who built a saw mill, established a store for the sale of goods, and engaged to a limited extent in the manufacture of staves from elm timber, and the exportation of hemlock bark. As early as 1861, besides the three families already mentioned as being there in 1858, there were living in that vicinity Richard Ball, Dr. A. J. Slyfield, Richard Weston, L. A. Dauby, Wm. Cogshell, and J. Hadsall. The first three were located at various points north of what is now the village, Mr. Hadsall a short distance south of it, and Messrs. Dauby and Cogshell at the mouth of the river. Mr. Dauby was employed as the business agent of the company, and Mr. Cogshell kept their boarding-house.

Mr Wm. Steele came to Benzonia in 1861, and soon afterward settled in Homestead. In 1863 John Hunt settled near Herring lake; Rev. A. Joy, a baptist minister, in Joyfield, after whom the township was named; and George B. Pierce in Pleasanton. In 1859, Wm. Monroe established his home at the place since called Monroe Center, twelve miles south of Traverse City, and was soon followed by several of his brothers. The next year Charles Downs located two miles south of Monroe's. In 1862 John Cotton settled on a homestead claim a mile beyond Downs, and in 1863 A. B. Davis located a mile farther on in the wilderness. In June of the same year, (1863,) Lewis Cornell, Elon Cornell, James Wart, and Wm. Masters selected lands in Wexford, and in the following fall brought on their families, forming the nucleus of what has since been known as the Cornell settlement.

* Mr. Carrier never became a resident of the Grand Traverse country. At the breaking out of the war of the rebellion, he was living in Duplain, Clinton county. He enlisted in the first regiment of Michigan cavalry, and laid down his life in the service of his country. It was my good fortune to know him intimately, both as a citizen and a soldier, and I take pleasure in adding my testimony of his worth to that given by Mr. C. E. Bailey in a manuscript narrative I have been permitted to examine. Mr. Bailey says: "I have seldom, if ever, met a man who in so short a time so endeared himself to me as he. True to principle, active, decided, though never captious, he was always ready to be governed by a good reason. A sincere friend of the oppressed and a lover of his country, he early offered himself in their and her defense, and laid down his life during her struggle with the rebel foes of liberty." Some time after the close of the war, Mr. Carrier's family became residents of Benzonia. M. L. L.

† Mr. Horace C. Bailey was not permitted to become a resident of the new colony, but died at Glen Arbor in June, 1858. M. L. L.

CHAPTER XXVII.

War History—Imperfection of the Record—Probable Number of Grand Traverse Men in the Service—The First Martyr—Lists of Volunteers—Honorable Mention—Lieutenants McClelland, Brooks and Holden—War Meetings—Local Bounties—Lieut. Graverat.

At the time of the present writing, scarcely twenty-three years have passed since the first gun fired upon Sumter sent a thrill of excitement throughout the loyal north, and called her patriotic sons to battle, yet it is impossible to give anything like a full history of the part the people of the Grand Traverse country took in the war that followed. Those who make history by their deeds, usually do not write history. Some one who comes after, gathers up the fragmentary records, traditions, and recollections, and fits them together as best he may. Fortunate is the writer whose chain of narrative is not made conspicuous by the great number of its missing links. In studying the records of the "boys in blue" who volunteered from the Grand Traverse country, industrious research enables the writer to do little more than give names and dates. The list of volunteers is so incomplete that to publish it seems almost like an act of injustice to those whose names do not appear. The regiments in which they served, are often a matter of conjecture, and the fate of many, some of whom may have fallen in battle, perished in hospitals, or been starved to death in rebel prisons, is involved in obscurity.

To avoid misunderstandings, it should be remembered that at the breaking out of the war, the unorganized counties of Antrim, Leelanaw, and Benzie were attached to Grand Traverse for civil and judicial purposes. When, in this chapter, Grand Traverse county is mentioned, the territory of the three referred to is intended to be included. Grand Traverse county as thus defined, was divided into nine townships—Meegezee, Milton, Whitewater, Peninsula, Traverse, Leelanau, Centreville, Glen Arbor, and Crystal Lake.

The number of men in the territory alluded to of an age suitabbe for military service, making no allowance for exemptions on account of disability, could not have exceeded six hundred, and probably fell short of that number. From this territory, it is believed, more than two hundred went into the service within the next four years. Of course considerable accessions to the population resulted from immigration, during that period, thus increasing the number liable to military duty.

One of the first to volunteer was Curtis Fowler, jr., son of Hon. Curtis Fowler, judge of probate for Grand Traverse county. Fighting bravely in the ranks of the gallant First, he was wounded at the battle of Bull Run, in July, 1861, was discharged from the service on account of disability from the wound, and returned home. His brother, Francis Z. Fowler, considering it a matter of honor as well as of patriotism that the family should be represented in the ranks of the defenders of the country, volunteered in his place, and laid down his life in the second battle of Bull Run the following year, "the first martyr from Grand Traverse to the slaveholders' rebellion."

Thirteen volunteers started from Traverse City on or about the 13th of September, 1861. Their names were as follows: Martin A. Hopper, Andrew McKillip, Isaac Winnie, James Nicholson, James Fitzpatrick, Wm. E. Sykes, Samuel A. McClelland, E. J. Brooks, Lewis Steele, Frank May, Aaron Page, Orselus Evans, and Thomas Lee. Of these the first five had been for a long time in the employ of Hannah, Lay & Co. On settling with them, Mr. Hannah made each a handsome present, and told them that if they were ever in distress or in need of funds, to draw on him at sight, and their drafts would be honored. Wm. E. Sykes was sheriff of the county. McClelland, Brooks, Steele, May, and Page were from Northport, Evans was from Whitewater, and Lee from Centreville.

At the time of leaving Traverse City, it was the intention of several of these men to enlist in Chicago, in Capt. Busteed's company of light infantry. We afterwards find some of them in the First New York Artillery, one of their number, McClelland, holding the rank of second lieutenant. At the battle of Malvern Hill, the first of July, 1862, the "Grand Traverse boys" received special commendation from their officers for bravery and good conduct. Of the thirteen mentioned above, the following

Wm. Callison, George Flack, Benjamin Rattelle, Dudley Wait, John O'Leary, Patrick Graham, George Askey, John Rodart, John Williams, Lewis Stevenson, Andrew Anderson, and Edward Dewaire

On the 15th of August, 1862, John Lewis Patrick, a young man who had been for two years an apprentice in the office of the Grand Traverse HERALD, started for Chicago, where he enlisted in the Mercantile Battery. Not long after, it fell to the lot of the paper on which he had wrought to publish his death, which occurred in the hospital at Memphis, Tenn, on the first of February, 1863 The editor of the HERALD, Morgan Bates, afterwards Lieut. Governor, speaks thus tenderly of his young friend "He was one of the noblest and purest young men we ever knew, and it caused a heart-pang when he left us to volunteer for the defense of his country ' All who knew him loved him, and his early death will cast a gloom over many hearts."

In August, 1862, recruiting was lively. Capt E. S Knapp, (called L. Edwin Knapp in "Michigan in the war,") assisted by Lieutenants Jacob E Siebert, of Manistee, and Charles H Holden, of Northport, raised a company in a short time, in Manistee and Grand Traverse counties, to which was given the name of the "Lake Shore Tigers." The following is an imperfect list of the men enlisted by Lieut Holden, in Grand Traverse, with the names of the townships to which they were credited

Whitewater—P. D Greenman, Francis Hopper, C R Lackey, Horace Phillips, John A. Brainard, Milton Stites, John Duncan, Henry Odell, Oscar Eaton, George Allen.

Traverse—Elias Langdon, jr., Thomas Bates, Giles Gibson, Asa V Churchill, George Moody.

Peninsula—Gilbert Lacnor, John A. Thayer

Leelanau—Wm. H Voice, Mortimer Boyes, Henry Budd, George W Bigelow, Wm W. Nash, Henry Holcomb, Charles E. Lehman

Centreville—George Ramsdell, Joseph Warwick, Melville Palmer, Wm Lawson, James Lee, Frederick Cook, Jacob Hans, Deidrick White, George W Miller, John Egler, James Adameson, L Grant, H. Dunckelow, Thomas McCreary, Charles E. Clark, George H Mills.

Capt. Knapp's company had originally been intended for the Twenty-first, but on arriving at Ionia, that regiment was found to be full. Application was next made to the Twenty fifth, then organizing at Kalamazoo, but that being full also, the company finally proceeded to Jackson, and was mustered into the service as company A of the Twenty-sixth, under Col Farrar

Lieut. Holden, was prosecuting attorney of the county at the time of organizing the company, and resigned his office for the purpose of entering the service He was mustered in as first lieutenant, and was afterwards made quarter master of the regiment. He resigned April 4th, 1864, and was honorably discharged The second lieutenant was Sewell S. Parker, of Monroe Lieut. Siebert, who helped to enlist the company, does not appear ever to have belonged to the Twenty-sixth According to "Michigan in the War," he belonged to the Twentieth, and was killed in action at Poplar Spring Church, Va, Sept. 30th, 1864 Of the enlisted men from Grand Traverse, Sergeant Wm H Voice died in camp at Jackson, Sept. 22d, 1862, P. D Greenman at Fairfax, Va., March 27th, 1863, and George Moody at Yorktown, Va, July 15th, 1863

In the summer and fall of 1863, from the early part of July till late in October, Lieut. Edwin J Brooks, of Northport, was engaged in recruiting for the Tenth Cavalry, under Col Foote, having its rendezvous at Grand Rapids Unfortunately there is at hand no list of Grand Traverse men who volunteered for that regiment under Lieut Brooks. Lieut. Brooks was mustered in as first lieutenant of Company E. He was promoted to a captaincy April 25th, 1864 March 13th, 1865, he was made Brevet Major of U S volunteers "for gallantry in action at Strawberry Plains east Tenn., Nov. 17th, 1864". On the same day he was further promoted to Brevet Lieut colonel U S volunteers, "for gallant and meritorious conduct through four years of active service." He was mustered out and honorably discharged Nov 11th, 1865

In September, while Lieut. Brooks was recruiting, the citizens of Traverse, anxious to make up the full quota of the township by voluntary enlistment, raised by subscription a fund for the payment of fifty dollars bounty to each recruit enlisted and credited to the township before the expected draft should take place

On the 12th of October, official information having been received that the draft would take place on the 26th of that month, and that only eleven men were needed to fill up the quota of Grand Traverse county, the board of supervisors appropriated eleven hundred dollars to a fund to be called the military bounty enlistment fund The chairman and clerk of the board were authorized to draw orders on this fund for one hundred dollars each in favor of the first eleven men who should enlist and be sworn into the service of the United States prior to the 23d of the month, provided they should be accredited to the county in the coming draft.

During the following winter, additional calls for troops made it necessary to hold out additional inducements for voluntary enlistment. In the month of February a series of war meetings was held in Traverse, which resulted in the calling of a special township meeting, to authorize the issuing of bonds for the purpose of raising money to pay bounties to volunteers

The efforts at enlisting were successful. On the second day of March, forty-two recruits left Traverse City for the rendezvous at Grand Rapids, constituting the full quotas for Traverse, Peninsula, and Centreville. On the evening previous to their departure, the ladies gave them an entertainment, providing a bountiful supper, at the boarding-house of Hannah, Lay & Co., at which a large proportion of the population of the village and surrounding country was present. Mr. Hannah presided, brief addresses were made by Hon. Morgan Bates and Rev J H Crumb, and the scene was enlivened by patriotic and soul-stirring music, under the direction of Mr. Charles H. Day

The following is a list of the volunteers.

Traverse—Albert S Brooks, Earnest Crain, Wm W Bradley, George L. Smith, Edward Beavis, Aaron Mettes, Myron A. Moody, Paul Gravel, Robert Myhill, James Lynch, Tobias F. Houghtaling, John Sutherland, Wm. W. Johnson, Henry C. Fuller, Sands Moon, Alonzo F. Hopkins, John Flannery, James Monroe, George W. Hargraves, Wilson P Johnson

Peninsula—James Birney Lancaster, Charles Lonkey, Columbus Winnie, Richard W. Smith, Abram D. Langworthy, Francis L. Bourasaw, Wm. B. Munn, John M Allison.

Centreville—Thomas Harmer, Adam Cook, James Manseau, Isaac Clark, James Mason, Jacob Burger, Clouve Warren, Martin Novotney, Ferdinand Kord, Philip Egler, Albert Norris, Henry Lemmerwell, James Clark, Martin Wachall.

Several of these men found their way into the Fourteenth regiment, and first entered upon active duty at the front in the vicinity of Nashville, Tenn. Those known to have been in that regiment are Crain, Mettes, Gravel, Lynch, Lancaster, Lonkey, Winnie, R. W. Smith, Langworthy, Bourasaw, and Allison. The names of the regiments in which the others served are not known. Myron A. Moody died in hospital at Grand Rapids, March 26th, 1864.

In the summer of 1864, the call for troops taxed to the utmost the patriotism and ability of Grand Traverse, as well as most other sections of the loyal north. On the 10th of June a draft was had, in Grand Rapids, for Whitewater, Elk Rapids, Milton, Centreville, Glen Arbor, and Leelanau. In August the township board of Traverse offered a bounty of two hundred dollars for recruits. On the 30th of the same month a meeting of the enrolled men of the township was held to raise funds to pay an additional bounty. Three thousand dollars was subscribed on the spot. With this sum the aggregate of bounties to each volunteer was raised to nearly six hundred dollars. Twenty-three men, under the calls of the president, were due from the township. Eight had already been obtained, eight more came forward at this meeting, and the remaining seven were obtained within the next forty-eight hours. The names of all but one are contained in the following list: Wm. Tracy, Adolphus Payette, Harvey Avery, Ira Chase, Joseph Kunn, Nelson C. Sherman, Edward Morgan, Ora E. Clark, Wm. Sluyter, George Sluyter, Barney Valleau, Zodoc Wilcox, James Mason, John Reynolds, John Fairue, Leander Curtis, Alburn Atwill, Abram Adsit, Marcus Lacore, Michael Gallaghn, Austin Brunnon, David Sweeney. All of these except Clark went into the Tenth cavalry, and got their first experience of active war at Strawberry Plains, east Tenn.

We close this imperfect war record of the Grand Traverse country with the following melancholy items:

Daniel Carmichael, of Traverse City, who was a member of a Wisconsin regiment, died in hospital at Lake Providence, May 6th, 1863.

George Leslie, of Traverse township, died in the Shenandoah valley, Sept. 22d, 1864.

In the fight before Petersburg, on the 17th of June, 1864, Lieut. G. A. Graverat, a gallant young officer from Little Traverse, laid down his life for his country. He was the second lieutenant of Company K., First Mich., sharp shooters. While fighting by the side of his father in the trenches, he saw his parent shot dead. Bearing the body to a safe spot, weeping bitterly, he dug a grave with an old tin pan in the sand, and buried it. Then drying his tears, the devoted son returned to the battle. His rifle told with terrible precision among the rebel officers, till he was disabled, wounded in the left arm. He was brought to Washington, where the arm was amputated at the shoulder, resulting in his death on the 10th of the following month. Lieut. Graverat was partly of Indian descent. He was but twenty-four years old, was highly educated, being master of several modern languages, besides being a fine portrait and landscape painter and an accomplished musician.

CHAPTER XXVIII.

Hinderances to Early Settlement—Ignorance and Misrepresentation—Indian Reservations—Railroad Land Grants—Beneficial Effects of the Building of the Railroad—State Swamp Land Roads—The Homestead Law—Indian Reserve Lands in Market—Winchell's Report—Pioneer Fruit Growers—Benzie County Leads in Agricultural Fairs—Agricultural Societies Organized—Reputation of the Country Established Abroad—Meeting of the State Pomological Society at Traverse City—The Triumph of the Pioneer Fruit Growers.

There were several reasons why the Grand Traverse country was not settled sooner, and why, when settlements were once commenced, its development was not more rapid during the period gone over in the preceding chapters.

One reason was that little or nothing was known abroad of its attractions and advantages. It was not readily accessible by land. Until the government lake survey furnished reliable information in regard to the hydrography of the region, the masters of vessels were generally unwilling to enter Grand Traverse bay, supposing it to be shallow and dangerous. It was for the interest of those engaged in the carrying trade on the great lakes, to decry Michigan and eulogize Illinois and Wisconsin, thus securing the profit of conveying emigrants as far west as their steamers and vessels sailed. Capt. Blake, once well known on the lakes, is said to have been the only one of his time who knew the Grand Traverse country, and was disposed to do it justice. He frequently told his passengers, when off the bay, on the way to their more distant homes in the west, they were passing the most beautiful country ever beheld. As late as 1859, Horace Greeley, in the *New York Tribune*, spoke of the northern half of the lower peninsula as being cold and uninviting to the cultivator, diversified by vast swamps, sterile, gravelly knolls, and dense forests of but moderately valuable timber not yet readily accessible, so that its settlement was likely to be slow, and its population sparse for generations.

Another reason was that, in accordance with treaty stipulations, several townships of choice land were withheld from market for Indian reservations.

Another and more potent reason, and one which for many years seriously retarded the development of the country, was the granting of every alternate section of extensive tracts of land as subsidies to certain railroad companies, for the building of railroads into the country from the south. The original intention of the general and state governments, no doubt, was to speedily open the northern wilderness to practical settlement and improvement. Such would have been the result, had the companies been held to strict compliance with the terms of the grant. But they were allowed to hold the lands, or, more strictly speaking, the lands were held for them by the state, being kept out of market, for a long term of years after the expiration of the time in which the roads were to have reached the heart of the northern wilderness, while in road-making practically nothing was done. The citizens of the northern counties regarded the course of the national and State governments as unjust and oppressive to their section of the state. There were some exciting contests in the State legislature, in which their representatives vainly strove, against overwhelming odds, to induce that body to compel the fulfillment of the terms of the grant or cause the lands to be restored to market. Among the earnest advocates in that body of the interests of the northern counties, was Mr. Dixon, of Charlevoix, and, later, Messrs. Dunlap, of Grand Traverse, and Utley, of Newaygo. Failing to secure justice to their constituents, Messrs. Dunlap and Utley recorded their formal protest against what they conceived to be the perpetration of a great wrong by the legislature in legalizing an extension of the time allowed the companies in which to build their roads. It was not till 1869, when the Grand Rapids and Indiana Company had extended their road to Cedar Springs and were rapidly pushing it northward, that any degree of confidence in the company or any expectations that the road would be built within the life of that generation began to be felt by the people of the Grand Traverse country. When, however, a litttle later, it came to be generally believed that the company were now working in good faith, and that railroad communication with the south and east was sure to come at no distant day, its healthful effect in promoting improvements was speedily felt throughout the region. As the road was pushed northward, settlers flocked in, dotting the wildernes in advance of it with their log cabins, clustering around, and giving new life to, the little villages already in existence, and founding new ones along the line of the road, even in advance of its completion. The good time long waited for had come, and the injustice of the past was nearly forgotten in the prosperity of the present.

There remained, however, one subject of contention between the people of the northern counties and the railroad companies. Thus far the railroad lands had been exempt from taxation. This was regarded by the people as unequal and unjust. The hardy pioneer, enduring the privations of backwoods life while toiling to hew out of the forest a home for his family, could not understand why his new farm, on which was only a log cabin and a few acres of improvement, should be taxed, while the lands of a great and rich corporation adjoining his own, which were constantly increasing in value from the improvements he and his neighbors were making, should be exempt. In the legislative session of 1871, the Grand Traverse country being represented in the House by Mr. Mitchell and in the Senate by Mr. Moffatt, the latter moved an amendment to the general railroad bill then pending, subjecting the lands of railroad companies to taxation, which, after a warm debate and in the face of powerful opposition from a strong railroad lobby, finally prevailed.

Looking back from our stand point of a later date, we can see that though the people had good cause to complain of the delay, the building of the road, even with the concomitant hardship arising from the earlier proceedings, has been, on the whole, an agency of no small importance in developing the resources of the country. Its population, wealth, and business interests are far in advance of what they could by any possibility have been at the present time, if the road had not been built at all.

An agency that contributed largely to the settlement and improvement of the country, the influence of which began to be felt immediately after the close of the war, was the policy of the State in regard to the swamp lands within its borders. These lands had been granted to the State by an act of congress, on condition that their proceeds should be applied to their drainage and reclamation. As the most direct means to the execution of the terms imposed on the State, the legislature wisely determined to appropriate a considerable portion of them to the construction of roads through the less improved sections of the country, thus opening to settlement the tracts in which the lands were principally situated, and bringing them into the possession of actual settlers, whose interest it would be to improve and cultivate them. In accordance with this policy, from 1863 to 1868 roads were opened by State authority and with trifling expense to the people, intersecting various portions of the Grand Traverse country, the principal ones running from Manistee by way of Benzonia to Traverse City, from Newaygo to Northport, from Traverse City by way of Elk Rapids and Charlevoix to Little Traverse, and from Traverse City by way of Houghton lake to Midland City. The opening of these roads was everywhere attended by an influx of settlers to the localities thus made accessible. It is not easy to conceive of a plan by which the disposal of the swamp lands could have been made to contribute more directly and more efficiently to the development of the newer sections of the State, and especially of the region of country we are considering.

The homestead law, giving to every actual settler from eighty to one hundred and sixty acres of land for a merely nominal sum, which took effect on the first of January, 1863, contributed not a little to hasten the settlement of the country. The entries of homesteads for the first month at the United States land office at Traverse City, numbered one hundred and twenty-eight, and for the first eight months five hundred and twenty-eight. For several years afterwards they varied from fifty to eighty per month, with the exception perhaps of two or three months in the dead of winter of each year. It should be understood, however, that the Traverse City land district, throughout which these homestead entries were scattered, embraced a territory much larger than what is being treated of in this work as the Grand Traverse country proper.

On the opening of the Indian reserves to homesteaders, in the spring of 1874, there was a scramble for choice locations. Soon after daylight, on the 15th of April, the day on which the arrangement was to take effect, although the rain was falling fast, and the office was not open till eight o'clock, men began to gather about the land office building. So great was the crowd that it was found impossible to admit them to the office. At eight o'clock a window was thrown open, and business commenced. The first three applications were made by widows, after the reception of which things became lively, and continued so during the forenoon. In one week one hundred and ninety-four homesteads were entered, and two hundred and fifty soldiers' declarations filed. The Grand Traverse HERALD of that date, facetiously remarks that "fifty-nine of the sixty men who came all the way from Petoskey to locate the 'N. E. ¼ of Sec and have gone home disappointed. Only one of them got it. It wasn't the man that vociferated the loudest. It wasn't the man that slept in the dry goods box. It wasn't the man that held on to the door knob of the office from midnight till eight a. m. It was the man that was lucky."

With a view to making the attractions and advantages of the country better known abroad, several prominent citizens employed Prof. Alexander Winchell, state geologist, to examine and report upon it, the expense being paid by subscription. The season of 1865 was spent in the examination, and the report was published the following year. It was widely circulated, and created a favorable impression in regard to the country for agricultural pursuits, and especially for the cultivation of fruit. Prof. Winchell characterized it as the most remarkable and most desirable section of country in the northwest, and expressed his opinion that as a fruit-growing region it was doubtful whether any other part of the United States could compete with it.

From the first it had been evident to those engaged in the study and cultivation of the soil that the Grand Traverse country, contrary to preconceived opinions and published reports, was well adapted to general farming, and especially to the successful cultivation of fruit. On its adaptation to fruit-growing, its reputation was now being mainly built.

As early as 1859, the Grand Traverse HERALD, then in the first year of its existence, published notices of apples grown by Rev. Geo. N. Smith, of Northport, that showed remarkable keeping qualities; other choice apples, from the orchard of John Garland, on the peninsula; and peaches from Mr. Norris's orchard, two miles from Traverse City, as good as the editor had ever tasted. Among the apples sent to the HERALD, in September by Mr. Smith, were Harvest, Tart Bough, Sweet Bough, and Summer King, of that season's growth, and with them Rhode Island Greenings and Blue Pearmains grown the previous year, but sound and fit for use.

Mr. Smith was one of the earliest pioneers of fruit growing, having brought a few small trees with him when he came to Northport in 1849, to which considerable additions were made the following year. Hon. J. G. Ramsdell, for many years circuit judge of his district, who came to Traverse City in 1861, and established a fruit farm on a hillside in the vicinity, did much toward making known abroad the capabilities of the soil and climate, and establishing a reputation for the excellence of the fruit. On the peninsula many of the settlers turned their attention to fruit-growing at an early day. Not one of the first in point of time, but the first among his fellows for scientific knowledge practically applied in his favorite pursuit, was Mr. George Parmelee, who had been a pioneer peach-grower in St. Joseph county. Mr. Parmelee came to the peninsula in 1867, for the purpose of establishing a fruit farm, with a view especially to the cultivation of apples. Both fruit-growing and general agriculture are largely indebted to him for their successful and profitable development.

The honor of leading in the matter of agricultural fairs belongs to Benzie county. The first was held at Benzonia, on the eighth of October,* 1864, several years before the organization of the county agricultural society. The previous notice was short, and the day was blustering and unpropitious, yet the fair was not a failure. The grains and vegetables exhibited were, for the most part, first crops from new ground imperfectly worked. There were no premiums, the only award being an honorable mention by the committees, the merit of the article being classed as extra, good, or fair. There was but little fruit. Of live stock of all kinds, only three animals were mentioned by the committee, presumably the only three present.

In 1868 county agricultural societies were organized in Leelanau and Benzie counties. In Grand Traverse county a union society was organized, intended to embrace, besides Grand Traverse, Leelanau, Antrim, and Emmet, including in the territory of the last what is now Charlevoix. Of the Leelanau society A. B. Dunlap was elected president, John T. Miller vice president, and John E. Fisher secretary. Mr. Dunlap soon resigned, and was succeeded by Rev. George N. Smith. Of the Benzie society W. S. Hubbell was president, E. P. Smith secretary and W. J. Young treasurer. The Grand Traverse union agricultural society, having its headquarters at Traverse City, elected A. B. Dunlap president, R. Hatch, Jr., secretary, D. C. Leach treasurer, and several vice presidents, distributed among the counties represented in the society. Successful fairs were held by all these societies in the fall following their organization.

Closely following the organization of the agricultural societies, came that of the Peninsula Farmers' Club, at Old Mission. This club was fortunate in having enrolled among its members several men of talent and education, who were also practical farmers, often performing the hardest labor of the farm with their own hands. Its weekly discussions, which, except for the first year or two, were published in the HERALD and the *Eagle*, did much toward raising the agriculture of the region to a high standard of excellence.

Through the systematic and persevering efforts of several enterprising persons, earnestly seconded by these societies, the Grand Traverse region at last came to be well known abroad as an agricultural and fruit-growing country. Its repeated successes in competition with other sections at the meeting of the state pomological society and at the state fairs, attracted the attention of the leading agriculturists and fruit men throughout the state. As a result an appointment was made for a meeting of the state pomological society at Traverse City, at the time of holding the union fair at that place, in October, 1873.

This opportunity to show to appreciative visitors the products of the country, was not lost upon the citizens. The fair was a grand success. Never before had such a display of fruit been seen in northern Michigan, and seldom in any western state. The sight was truly magnificent. The pioneers had good reason to be proud of their work. Their visitors were astonished.

Two evenings during the fair were occupied by meetings of the state pomological society, at which the merits of the several kinds of fruit on exhibition were freely discussed, and much interesting information elicited from residents in regard to the topography of the country, its soil and climate, and its adaptation to the production of fruit. A committee visited by invitation several of the principal orchards in the vicinity of Old Mission, speaking in glowing terms in their published report of the fruit and fruit-growers of that neighborhood.

The next year, (1874,) the society offered premiums for the more meritorious orchards in the state, of several classes designated. The awarding committee having in the discharge of their duty visited Old Mission, in their report made to the society at its October meeting awarded seven first and four second premiums to orchards in that vicinity. The reputation of the Grand Traverse county for its fruit was established. The triumph of its pioneer fruit-growers was complete.

CHAPTER XXIX.

Division of the Grand Traverse Region into Counties—Organization of Grand Traverse—First Election—First Circuit Court—First Meeting of Board of Supervisors—First Equalization of Taxes—Emmet—Manitou—Leelanau—Antrim—Benzie—Wexford—Charlevoix—Kalkaska—Missaukee.

In 1840 the territory now constituting Grand Traverse, by an act of the legislature was "laid off as a separate county, to be known and designated as the county of Omena." The territory now constituting Leelanau and Benzie counties, with the Manitou islands, was "laid off as a separate county, to be known and designated as the county of Leelanau." Wexford, Antrim, Charlevoix, and Emmet, were also "laid off" as counties by the same act. Within the territory thus designated there were neither county nor township organizations. The new counties remained attached to Mackinac, and the first settlers, if they desired to vote, were obliged to perform a journey to Mackinac for the purpose.

An act for the organization of Grand Traverse county was passed in 1851. The territory included within its boundaries was the same that had constituted the county of Omena, except those portions of the present townships of East Bay and Whitewater lying north of the north line of township twenty-seven, which, for some unknown reason, were left out. The act established the county seat "at Boardman's Mills, on the east fraction of section number three, in township twenty-seven north, of range eleven west, until otherwise provided." Provision was made for holding an election for county officers on the first Monday in August, the officers then elected to remain in office until the general election in 1852, and until their successors were elected and qualified.

On the day designated, the election was held at the house of Horace Boardman. The whole of the newly formed county constituted the township of Omena, but it does not appear that there was an existing township organization. The inspectors of election were Horace Boardman, George N. Smith, Hosmer K. Cowles, and Luther O. Scofield.

The number of legal voters present was twenty-eight, which was also the highest number of votes given for any office. The following is the list of officers, nearly all of whom were elected unanimously: Prosecuting attorney, Orlin P. Hughson; county judge, Joseph Dame; second judge, Martin S. Wait; county clerk and register of deeds, Luther O. Scofield; judge of probate, George N. Smith;* sheriff, Wm. H. Case; treasurer, Horace Boardman; coroners, Alanson Canfield and Richard W. Smith.

At the legislative session of 1853 an act was passed "to complete the organization of Grand Traverse county." It annexed to the county those portions of the former county of Omena that had been omitted by the act of 1851, provided for a special election of county officers, to be held on the first Tuesday of May, and divided the county into two townships—Peninsula and Traverse. Peninsula consisted of the same territory as at present; all the remainder of the county was comprised in the township of Traverse. The first township meeting in Peninsula was to be held at Old Mission; that of Traverse at the county seat. The unorganized counties of Antrim, Kalkaska, Missaukee, Wexford, Manistee, and Leelanau, the last including Benzie and the Manitou islands, were attached to Grand Traverse for judicial and municipal purposes. Antrim county constituted a single township. For township purposes, Kalkaska and Missaukee were attached to Antrim, and Wexford to Traverse. Leelanau, with it attached territory, was erected into a township of the same name, the first township meeting of which was to be held at the house of Peter Dougherty. Practically, then, in 1853, Grand Traverse county consisted of five township organizations, embracing the following territory—Antrim, the whole of Antrim, Kalkaska and Missaukee counties; Peninsula, that part of the peninsula in Grand Traverse bay lying north of the line between township twenty-seven and twenty-eight; Traverse, all of Grand Traverse county not included in Peninsula, with the attached county of Wexford; Leelanau, the territory now comprised in Leelanau and Benzie counties and the Manitou islands; Manistee, the whole of Manistee county.

There had been no election held in the county at the time for holding the general election in 1852. In accordance with the act of 1853, a special county election was held on the first Tuesday in May of the latter year. The board of county canvassers met at the county seat on the 9th, and organized by electing Thomas Cutler chairman and Theron Bostwick secretary. The canvass showed that the whole number of voters who had participated in the election was seventy-one. The following is a list of the officers elected: Judge of probate, George N. Smith; sheriff, Norman B. Cowles; county clerk, Thomas Cutler; county treasurer, Hosmer K. Cowles; prosecuting attorney, Robert McLellan; register of deeds, Thomas Cutler; county surveyor, Abram S. Wadsworth; coroners, Lewis Miller and Luther O. Scofield.

The first session of the circuit court in the newly organized county, which was also the first in the Grand Traverse region, commenced on the 27th of July, and closed the following day. A part of the unfinished dwelling of Thomas Cutler, the same in which Mr. Cutler's family now reside, was used as a court room. Hon. George Martin was the judge. The only lawyer present was Ebenezer Gould, of Owosso, who had come with Judge Martin. Mr. McLellan, recently elected prosecuting attorney, had not been admitted to the bar. Mr. Gould was appointed by the judge to act as prosecuting attorney for that session and Mr. McLellan, on application and examination in open court, was admitted to practice. As the court had no seal, it was ordered that the temporary seal should be the eagle side of the American half dollar. There was but little business requiring the attention of the court.

The first meeting of the board of supervisors was a special one, held pursuant to a call of three of their number—Robert Campbell, John S. Barker, and S. G. Rice. Responsive to the call, the board convened at the store of Cowles & Campbell, in Peninsula, on the 27th of July. There were present Robert Campbell of Peninsula, John S. Barker of Antrim, and Wm. M. McKillip of Traverse. After organizing, by electing McKillip chairman and Campbell clerk, they adjourned to meet at the store of Hannah, Lay & Co., at Traverse City, the following day. On the second day, in addition to those already mentioned, there was present Samuel G. Rice, of Leelanau. Manistee was not represented.

The first equalization of the assessment rolls of the several townships, as shown by the records, occurred at the regular meeting of the board in October, 1854. The taxable property of the county amounted to $204,854.97, distributed as follows:

ANTRIM.		
Real	$38,925 38	
Personal	6,948 00	$45,873 38
PENINSULA.†		
Personal		15,205 50
TRAVERSE.		
Real	40,641 62	
Personal	15,315 00	55,956 62
LEELANAU.		
Real	8,411 47	
Personal	14,704 00	23,115 47
MANISTEE.†		
Real		64,704 00
Total		$204,854 97

An act was passed by the legislature of 1853, which received the approval of the governor on the 29th of January and took immediate effect, providing for the organization of Emmet county. The Mormons, as we have already seen, had at this time a strong and flourishing settlement on the Beaver islands. There were a few families of the same sect at Pine river. Mr. Porter was quietly conducting his mission work among the Indians at Bear Creek. There were a number of whites at Little Traverse, and fishermen were scattered here and there on the islands and at various points on the shore. The new county included within its limits the present county of Emmet, all of that part of the present county of Charlevoix lying north of township thirty-two, together with the Beaver islands and, in the language of the act, "all the islands, bars, rocks, and lands under water, contiguous to the said counties of Emmet and Charlevoix, and within the said state of Michigan, not heretofore by any legislative enactment included within the body of any county in the state." It was divided into three townships—Peaine, Galilee and Charlevoix. The first election for county officers was to be held on the first Tuesday in the following May. The location of the county seat having been left to the board of supervisors, was afterwards fixed at St. James. As already stated in a previous chapter,‡ an act was passed for the reorganization of the county in 1855. At that time the boundaries were so changed as to leave out the Beaver and Fox islands.

The act for the re-organization of Emmet received the approval of the governor on the 13th of February, 1855. On the 12th an act had been approved for the organization of Manitou county. It consisted of "the islands in Lake Michigan known as the Beaver group, the north and south Fox islands, and the north and south Manitou islands." The Beaver islands were divided into two townships, Peaine and Galilee, the Fox islands constituted the township of Patmos, and the north and south Manitous that of Manitou.

No further changes of counties were made in the Grand Traverse region till 1863, when the legislature passed acts for the organization of Leelanaw and Antrim. The old county of Leelanaw was divided on the south line of township twenty-eight north, that part lying north of the line constituting the new county of the same name, and the territory south of it the county of Benzie. The latter remained attached to Grand Traverse for judicial and municipal purposes. It was provided that the county seat of Leelanaw should be determined by a plurality vote of the electors, the law requiring a choice to be made between Glen Arbor, Leland, and Northport. The election resulted in favor of Northport, where the county seat remained till 1882, when it was removed to Leland. The county at the time of its organization consisted of three townships—Centerville, Glen Arbor and Leelanaw. The first election for county officers was held at the time of the township meetings, on the first Monday in April. The following is a list of the first county officers: Sheriff, Edward Friend; judge of probate, John E. Fisher; county treasurer, John I. Miller; county clerk, Gerhard Verfurth; register of deeds, Gerhard Verfurth; prosecuting attorney, Eli C. Tuthill; county surveyor, Joseph Glen; coroners, George Ray and George N. Smith. The highest number of votes cast for any office was three hundred and thirty-eight.

The boundaries of Antrim, as defined in the act of organization, were the same that exist at the present time, except that they included the townships numbered thirty-two north of range five, six, and seven west, which have since been made a part of Charlevoix. The unorganized counties of Kalkaska, Crawford, and Otsego were attached to it for municipal and judicial purposes. The organized townships were Banks, Milton, and Meegezee, the name of the last being changed to Elk Rapids. The first election for county officers was held on the first Monday in April. J. W. Arnold was elected sheriff; Henry H. Noble, treasurer; James L. Gilbert, county clerk and register of deeds; Solomon Case, judge of probate; A. S. Wadsworth, county surveyor; Alexander Campbell and Gurdon Geer, coroners.

After the organization of Leelanaw and Antrim, a period of six years elapsed before it was deemed necessary to erect into organized counties any of the remaining territory of the Grand Traverse region. Then at the session of 1869, the legislature, by three several acts, provided for organizing Benzie, Wexford, and Charlevoix.

Benzie county as organized, consisted of the territory separated from Leelanaw and designated as Benzie by the act of 1863, which had since remained attached to Grand Traverse. It already contained eight organized townships—Almira, Benzonia, Crystal Lake, Gilmore, Homestead, Joyfield, Weldon, and Colfax. The first election for county officers was held on the first Monday in April. Addison P. Wheelock was elected sheriff; Roland O. Crispin, county treasurer; Theodore C. Walker, county clerk and register of deeds; Digby B. Butler, judge of probate; James B. Delbridge, prosecuting attorney; Wm. J. Young, circuit court commissioner; George E. Steele, county surveyor; A. E. Walker, superintendent of schools; A. J. Slyfield and L. Kenny, coroners. The organic act provided that the location of the county seat should be determined by a vote of the electors. For this purpose an election was to be held the first Monday in July. There was to be written on the ballots one of the following names of places—Frankfort, Benzonia, and the southeast quarter of the northeast quarter of section twenty-eight, township twenty-six north, of range fourteen west. The place last named was in the township of Homestead. If one of the places received a majority of all the votes, it was to be the county seat; if no place received a majority, then another election was to be held on the first Monday of the following October, at which the electors should designate by a majority vote one of the two places which should have received the highest number of votes at the July election. At the first election the vote stood for Benzonia 75, Homestead 237, Frankfort 194. As there was no choice, the second election was held, resulting in favor of Frankfort by 301 to 265. At a later date, the board of supervisors submitted to the electors the question of removal to a site near the village of Benzonia. The board of canvassers decided the result of the election to be in favor of removal, but the legality of their doings was questioned, and a long course of litigation ensued. In the mean time, the removal was accomplished in fact, and when a final judicial decision was reached the act of removal was sustained.

The act organizing Wexford divided that county into four townships—Hanover, Wexford, Springfield, and Colfax. The unorganized county of Missaukee was attached to it for municipal and judicial purposes, being, for township purposes, divided between the townships of Colfax and Hanover. The county seat was "located in township twenty-four north, of range twelve west, at or near what is called the Manistee bridge," now the village of Sherman. The list of the first county officers, elected on the first Monday in April, was as follows: Sheriff, Harrison H. Skinner; county treasurer, John H. Wheeler; county clerk, Leroy P. Champenois; register of deeds, Leroy P. Champenois; judge of probate, Isaac N. Carpenter; prosecuting attorney, Oscar H. Mills; circuit court commissioner, Oscar H. Mills; county surveyor, R. S. Clain; coroners, D. B. Davis and O. Morrell.

Charlevoix county was carved out of the southern part of Emmet and the northern part of Antrim, with a corner clipped from Otsego. It was described in the organic act as consisting of the following territory: "Townships thirty-two north, of ranges four, five, six, and seven west; townships thirty-three north, of ranges, four, five, six, seven, eight, and nine west; the south half of township thirty-four north, of ranges four, five, and six west; and all of townships thirty four north, of ranges seven and eight west." A special election was held on the first Monday in May, at which the first set of county officers was elected as follows: Sheriff, Richard Cooper; prosecuting attorney, Edward H. Green; county clerk, John S. Dixon; register of deeds, Morris J. Stockman; county treasurer, Jackson Ingalls; county superintendent of schools, John S. Dixon; county surveyor, Wm. Miller; judge of probate, Philo Beers; coroners, Lemuel W. Skinner and Solomon G. Isaman.

The counties of Kalkaska and Missaukee were organized in 1871, by virtue of acts passed by the legislature of that year. In each the special election for the first set of county officers was held, as was usually the case at the organization of a new county, at the time of the annual township meetings, on the first Monday in April.

Kalkaska, with the unorganized county of Crawford, which was attached to it for municipal and judicial purposes, was divided into three townships—Rapid River, Round Lake, and Kaska. At the first election sixteen votes were polled in Rapid River, sixty-five in Round Lake, and twenty one in Kaska, making a total of one hundred and two in the county. Wm. Sheldon was elected sheriff; O. S. Curtis, county clerk and register of deeds; C. Beebe, county treasurer; H. U. Hill, judge of probate; E. S. Pratt, prosecuting attorney and circuit court commissioner; Richard Towers, surveyor; Lorenzo Evans and Uriah Varguson, coroners. The county seat was to be located, in the year 1873, by three commissioners named in the act. The commissioners appointed the 20th of June for considering the subject, and requested the board of supervisors to meet them at the village of Kalkaska on that day. The board met as requested, but the commissioners were prevented by the illness of one of their number from being present. The supervisors, however, adopted a resolution, in the name of the people, requesting that the county seat be located at the village of Kalkaska, with which the commissioners complied.

Missaukee was organized with five townships—Reeder, Riverside, Clam Union, Pioneer, and Lulna, all of which except Reeder had been created by acts passed at the last session of the legislature. Gillis McBain was elected sheriff; Eugene W. Watson, county clerk and register of deeds; Ira Van Meter, county treasurer; John Vogel, judge of probate; Wm. H. Cavanagh, prosecuting attorney and circuit court commissioner; Abraham Stout, county surveyor; Marion D. Richardson, county superintendent of schools; Ezra F. Norton and Washington Reeder, coroners. The location of the county seat was determined by a special election, held for that purpose on the first Monday in June, which resulted in the choice of Lake City.

* How it was that Rev. George N. Smith, a resident of Leelanau county, was entitled to vote at this election and to hold a county office in Grand Traverse is not clear, as Leelanau was at this time, and until 1853, attached to Mackinac county. See Session Laws of 1840 and 1853, also Table LXXXVI, on page 98 of the supplement to the auditor general's report for 1870. M. L. L.

† It will be observed that no real estate appears on the roll of Peninsula, and no personal property on that of Manistee. M. L. L.

‡ For further facts connected with the re-organization of Emmet, see chapter XX.

CHAPTER XXX.

Grand Traverse Politically—Influence of the Grand Traverse Herald—Morgan Bates, its Founder—The Traverse Bay Eagle—The Charlevoix Sentinel—Brief Mention of Other Newspapers.

At the presidential election in 1856, the first that occurred after the organization of Grand Traverse, four hundred votes were polled in the county—one hundred and fifty-seven for Fremont, the republican candidate, and two hundred and forty-three for Buchanan, the democratic. The county at that time, it should be remembered, included within its limits, not only all of the Grand Traverse region except Emmet, but Manistee also. Four years later, in the same territory, except Manistee which had been detached, there were four hundred and seven votes for Lincoln and one hundred and ninety-eight for Douglas, showing a radical change in the political views of the voters. From that time on, not only Grand Traverse, but also the newer counties from time to time organized out of its attached territory—the whole Grand Traverse region except Emmet—have remained steadily republican.

Perhaps among the agencies that brought about the change and contributed to maintain the republican ascendency, none exerted a more potent influence than the first newspaper, the Grand Traverse HERALD, established by Morgan Bates, and conducted by him during the first nine years of its existence.

Mr. Bates was born at Queensbury, Warren county, N. Y., near Glen's Falls, on the 12th day of July, 1806. At an early age he entered a printing office as an apprentice, at Sandy Hill. At the age of twenty he established a newspaper at Warren, Penn., called the *Gazette*. Here Horace Greeley worked for him as a journeyman printer, and a strong friendship grew up between them, which continued till the close of Mr. Greeley's life. Afterwards he worked for Greeley as foreman, in New York, as Greeley had worked for him at Warren. In Greeley's office he was associated with several other young men who afterwards made their mark in the newspaper world, among whom were Elbridge Gerry Paige, better known by his *nom de plume* of Dow Jr., and George Wilkins Kendall, the projector and first publisher of the New Orleans *Picayune*.

In 1833 Mr. Bates came to Detroit, and was employed as foreman in the office of the *Advertiser*. In 1839 he purchased the *Advertiser*, in company with George Dawson, since connected with the Albany *Evening Journal*. Mr. Dawson soon retired from the firm, and Mr. Bates becoming the sole owner, conducted the paper till 1844, when, in consequence of the defeat of the whig party, whose policy he had ably advocated, regarding the future prospects of his paper as not flattering, he prudently sold out.

In 1849 he joined the army of gold seekers, and went to California, by way of Cape Horn. After two years, he returned by way of the Isthmus. In 1852 he again sought the land of gold, going again by way of Cape Horn. He remained in California till 1856. During this period he was for more than a year sole owner and publisher of the *Alta California*, daily and weekly. The daily was at that time the only one published west of the Rocky mountains.

Returning to Michigan, he was employed for some time in the auditor general's office, at Lansing, till he removed to Traverse City, in 1858.

To most men Traverse City would have seemed the most unpromising place for establishing a newspaper, while in reality it was the most eligible in the state, a fact Mr. Bates's experience and knowledge of the business enabled him to see.

The first number of the HERALD made its appearance on the 3d of November, 1858. This was just before the breaking out of the great civil war, when the question of the supremacy of the slave power was already convulsing the political fabric of the nation to its center. In his salutatory Mr. Bates defined his position and outlined the character and course of his paper in terms not to be misunderstood. "In politics we admit no such word as neutrality. We hate slavery in all its forms and conditions, and can have no fellowship or compromise with it. We entertain no respect for any party or any religion which sanctions and supports it, we care not from what source they derive their authority; and regard that politician, minister, or layman, who advocates its extension and perpetuity, as an enemy to the human race, and false to the God we worship. Entertaining these views on what we regard *the* great political issue of the day, we shall support, with zeal and firmness, to the best of our ability, the republican organization, so long as that party shall be true to the principles that now govern it."

When the control of the general government passed into the hands of the republicans, in 1861, Mr. Bates was appointed by President Lincoln to the registership of the land office at Traverse City. He held the office till 1867, when his outspoken condemnation of the policy of President Johnson's administration was followed by his removal. On the accession of Gen. Grant to the presidency, he was re-appointed, and continued to hold the office till his death. He was four times elected treasurer of Grand Traverse county, and would, no doubt, have been again the choice of the people, had he not declined the honor. In the fall of 1868, he was elected lieutenant governor, on the republican ticket. The office came to him unsolicited; he was not the man to ask for it. His nomination and election were a spontaneous recognition of his worth as a man and a citizen, and of his services in the interests of humanity and just government.

Mr. Bates was twice married. His first wife died in 1855; the second preceded him to the grave by a little more than a year. His own death occurred March 2, 1874, at the age of sixty-eight.

Intimately associated with Mr. Bates in the work of aiding the anti-slavery movement, was his twin brother, Merritt, without a brief notice of whose career our sketch would be incomplete.

Rev. Merritt Bates the twin brother of Morgan Bates, was a prominent clergyman in the methodist church in eastern New York and western Vermont and Massachusetts, and was an active member of, first, the New York and, later, the Troy conference, for 36 years. He was an outspoken anti-slavery man all his life, and for many years at Albany and Troy, N. Y., Burlington, Vt., Lowell, Mass., and other points, his house was a headquarters for the great anti-slavery leaders during the exciting times of a quarter of a century preceding the war of the rebellion. His own life was in jeopardy many times from the infuriated mob. In Lowell, Mass., the church doors were closed on him and he preached from the steps, and from thence was driven into the streets and imprisonment and personal violence threatened if he did not desist from his treasonable anti-slavery preaching. He was mobbed in the streets of Troy, N. Y., in 1844, and threatened expulsion by the Troy conference because he would not withdraw his subscription from an anti-slavery paper. But still he preached and taught anti-slavery doctrines, aided the fugitive slave on his way to freedom, openly defied the fugitive slave law and refused compliance to its mandates, and was recognized as one of the ablest and most daring advocates of free speech in that section of the country. He lived to see slavery abolished and, upon the occasion of his retirement from the ministry the bishop in attendance and the leading members of the conference, who had for years and years opposed him in his views on this question, took him by the hand and asked forgiveness, saying, "You were right, and we were wrong. You have fought a hard fight but have won a glorious victory for the right." Mr. Bates removed to Traverse City in May, 1863, to spend the remaining years of his life near his twin brother, between whom and himself there existed an unusually strong attachment. He bought a farm near Traverse City, and the next few years were spent in the improvement of his place, and during this time he took an active interest in the development of the entire region. His death occurred in August, 1869. His wife, the faithful companion and sharer of all his toils and triumphs for 35 years, followed him to the grave a year later.

At the close of the ninth volume of the HERALD, in December, 1867, Mr. Bates sold it to D. C. Leach. Mr. Leach conducted it till May, 1876, when it passed into the hands of the present management, Thomas T. Bates editor and manager.

Besides exerting a powerful influence on the politics of the region in which it has circulated, the HERALD has been an efficient agent in the development of the material interests of the country, making known abroad its resources, advantages, and attractions, and drawing to it the immigration that otherwise would have passed on to more remote regions.

The HERALD was the first newspaper published in northwestern Michigan. At its first appearance it was a modest four-column folio. It was enlarged at different times, as its patronage increased, till its present size and form were reached—an eight-column quarto, and it is to-day the largest paper in the state.

The Traverse Bay *Eagle* was the second newspaper published on the lower peninsula north of Big Rapids and Manistee. It was started at Elk Rapids, Antrim county, the last of March, 1864, by E. L. Sprague, the present editor and proprietor, under the name of the Elk Rapids *Eagle*. It first appeared as a very small folio sheet, the size being only fifteen by nineteen inches. At the end of the first year James Spencer became part owner and publisher, and the paper was enlarged to twenty by twenty-six inches. January 1st, 1866, the name was changed to Traverse Bay *Eagle*, and the paper was enlarged to twenty-two by thirty-two inches. In the spring of 1866, a power press was purchased, the first in the Grand Traverse region. In the fall of the same year, the paper was moved to Traverse City, and Lyman G. Wilcox was admitted as a partner, the firm being Sprague, Spencer & Wilcox. The paper was at this time enlarged to an eight column folio. One year later, Mr. Wilcox retired, Sprague and Spencer purchasing his interest. At the same time, a steam engine and boiler were purchased, to drive the press. Previous to this, however, at the time Mr. Wilcox became a partner, a job press was addad to the office, the first ever brought into this region. In 1872 Mr. Spencer's health failed, and the management of the office devolved entirely upon Mr. Sprague. The first of January, 1880, the paper was again enlarged to its present size, a nine column folio. In July, 1882, Mr. Spencer sold his interest to Mr. Sprague, the original owner and publisher. Mr. Sprague has been connected with the paper since its establishment, and is now the oldest editor who has been continually in the business in this part of the state. In politics the *Eagle* was republican up to the time of the presidential campaign in which Greeley was a candidate, since which it has been independent or democratic.

The third newspaper in the Grand Traverse region was the Charlevoix *Sentinel*, established at Charlevoix in 1869. It was published by W. A. Smith, for the proprietor, D. C. Leach. E. H. Green was the first editor. Mr. Smith purchased the paper in 1871, and remained the sole publisher and editor till August, 1883, when a half interest was sold to E. F. Parmelee, who became equal partner and associate editor. At first a five column folio, the *Sentinel* was enlarged to a six column folio in 1871, to a five column quarto in 1875, to a six column quarto in 1878, and to a seven column quarto in 1883. During the early period of its existence, it was for some time the official paper of six counties, including two in the upper peninsula. In politics it has always been staunch republican. Not a little of the credit for the prosperity of Charlevoix county and the northern part of the lower peninsula, is due the *Sentinel* for making known the resources and attractions of the country.

Since the appearance of the *Sentinel* the establishment of newspapers in the Grand Traverse region has fully kept up with the development of the country, if, indeed, it has not got in advance of it. A few have failed. Of those that remained, only a minority may be presumed to be receiving a liberal support. The fact that so many are able to maintain an existence at all, speaks well for the intelligence of the communities in which they are published, and for the hopeful enterprise of their publishers. A brief mention of each may not be out of place at this stage of our history.

The *Weekly Express*, Frankfort, Benzie county, was established in June, 1870, by W. F. Cornell. The following persons have been owners, wholly, or in part, at various times since its establishment: W. F. Cornell, O. V. Hosmer, W. F. Francis, A. Brewer, J. A. Brewer, S. A. Brewer, and A. B. Carrier. It was at first a seven column folio, and was enlarged to an eight column folio in 1874. Politics republican. The paper was burned out in 1881, and its publication resumed in January, 1882.

The Benzie County *Journal*, Benzonia, Benzie county, was established by a joint stock company, in 1872. The *Journal* has not been published since March, 1883. The editors were, in order of time, R. H. Brainard, James A. Pettitt, Bailey & Betts, and John B. Betts. Size, a six column folio. Politics, republican.

The Elk Rapids *Progress*, Elk Rapids, Antrim county, was established in 1872, by E. L. Sprague. Mr. Sprague sold it to H. E. Gemberling, and Mr. Gemberling to B. F. Davis. The editors have been F. R. Williams, James Parkinson, E. L. Sprague, Giles Danbeny, H. E. Gemberling, and B. F. Davis. The *Progress* was first published as a six column folio, was changed to a five column quarto, and then back again to its original form and size. It is independent in politics.

The Cadillac *News*, Cadillac, Wexford county, was established by C. L. Frazier, in 1872. It became successively the property of J. A. & O. Whitmore, Rice & Chapin, Chapin & Terwilliger,

C. T. Chapin, and J W Giddings. C. T. Chapin was editor from 1877 to 1882, since which time it has been under the editorial control of J. W. Giddings. It was started as a five column folio, enlarged to a six column quarto in 1877, and to a seven column quarto in 1883. Politics, republican

The Wexford County *Pioneer*, Sherman, Wexford county, was established by Cooper & Fuller, in 1872. It subsequently passed into the hands of Charles E. Cooper, who sold it, in 1877, to Charles S. Marr In 1878 it became the property of Campbell & Wheeler, and afterwards of J H Wheeler From its original dimensions of a five column folio, it has been enlarged to a five column quarto. Politics, republican.

In 1873, S W Davis started a paper in Missaukee county, called the Missaukee County *Reporter*, which he published for two years, doing the printing on a wooden press of his own construction. In size it was first a six column and afterwards an eight column folio.

The Leelanau *Tribune* was started by A. H. Johnson, at Northport, in June, 1873. In the winter of 1877 and '78 Mr. Johnson removed it to Suttons Bay In 1880 it was sold to the Tribune Publishing Company, who changed its name to the *Tribune*, and removed it to Traverse City, where, after a short time, its publication was discontinued. Mr. Johnson was the editor during the whole period of its existence. Size at first a seven column folio, which was changed to a five column quarto in the fall of 1880 Politics, republican while owned by Mr Johnson, democratic after sold to the company.

The *Kalkaskaian*, Kalkaska, Kalkaska county, was established by C. P. Sweet, about the first of March, 1874, It was the first newspaper on the line of the Grand Rapids and Indiana railroad north of Cadillac. Commenced as a seven column folio, it was enlarged to an eight column folio in 1878. Mr Sweet has been sole owner, publisher, and editor. Politics, republican.

The Emmet County *Democrat*, Petoskey, Emmet county, was established April 30, 1875, by Rozelle Rose, who has been its only publisher and editor. The size at first was twenty-one by thirty-one inches, increased to twenty-four by thirty six inches in September, 1875, and again to twenty-six by forty inches in April, 1882. Politics, democratic.

The *Republican*, Harbor Springs, Emmet county, was established by Warren Bowen, in 1876. After conducting the paper about three months, Mr Bowen sold it to L. A. Clark, who has since been sole proprietor and editor The size at first was a six column folio. In September, 1878, it was enlarged to a seven column folio, and again to a six column quarto at the close of 1879 In politics it is republican.

The *Journal*, Lake City, Missaukee county, was established by L. A. Barker, familiarly known in newspaper circles as "Ren" Barker, April 27, 1877, who was publisher and editor up to April 22, 1884, when it was sold to H. N McIntire, and consolidated with the Lake City *Leader*, a paper which Mr McIntire had established in 1883. In May, 1884, the name of the consolidated papers was changed to *New Era*. The *Journal*, started as a seven column folio, had previously been enlarged to eight columns. In November, 1882, the office was burned, but the *Journal* continued its weekly appearance without missing a number.

The Leelanau *Enterprise*, Leland, Leelanau county, was started at Northport, in 1877, by E. H Derby, and afterwards removed to Leland. In 1879 Mr. Derby sold it to W. C. Nelson Mr Nelson sold a half interest to George A. Cutler, but re-purchased it at the end of a year. The editors have been B. H. Derby, W. C. Nelson, George A Cutler, and, lastly, Mr. Nelson again It was at first a five column folio, but was enlarged in 1877. Politics, republican.

The Petoskey *Record*, Petoskey, Emmet county, was established by George Mosher and James Buckley, June 20, 1878 It was afterward successively the property of Mosher & Gibson, Mosher & Pray, Mosher & McManus, George Mosher, Mosher & Freeman, and finally, April 1, 1883, passed into the hands of J. C. Bontecou. The editors have been George H. Mosher, F S. Freeman, and J. C Bontecou. From a seven column folio it has been enlarged to a six column quarto, and lastly, June 1, 1883, to a seven column quarto. Politics, republican.

The *Northern Independent*, Harbor Springs, Emmet county, formerly the Emmet County *Independent*, was established by Charles S. Hampton, in 1878. For the first three years Benton Bement had an interest in it, but Mr. Hampton has always conducted the editorial department At the beginning of the fifth volume, when the name was changed, it was enlarged from a seven to an eight column folio. The *Independent* is national in politics, advocating what is popularly known as the greenback policy. During the summer of 1883, the *Daily Resorter*, a six column folio daily, was published by Mr. Hampton in connection with the *Independent*. The printing of the *Independent* has always been done at home.

The Kalkaska *Leader*, Kalkaska, Kalkaska county, was established by E. B. Dennis and J W Tinklepaugh, in May, 1878. Mr Dennis was editor till June, 1882; since that time it has been under the editorial management of Mr. Tinklepaugh Size, seven column folio, enlarged in March, 1882, to a six column quarto. Politics, republican

The Mancelona *Herald*, Mancelona, Antrim county, was established by Edwards & Slussar, in 1879 On the first of April, 1882, C S. Edwards retired from the business, and L. E. Slussar became proprietor and editor The size at first was that of a seven column folio, which was enlarged to an eight column folio in 1881, and in 1883 to a six column quarto Politically the *Herald* is republican.

The Manton *Tribune*, Manton, Wexford county, established in October, 1879, remained only a short time under the control of its founder, Marshall McLure, when it passed into the hands of A J Teed, and soon afterwards became the property of C E. Cooper In September, 1883, it passed into the hands of H. F Campbell. The publishers have been the editors At first a five column folio, it was enlarged to six columns at the time Mr Cooper took control.

The *Statesman*, formerly the *Standard*, Boyne City, Charlevoix county, was established by Wm Mears. The first number made its appearance March 11, 1881 The name was changed at the beginning of the third volume. It was purchased by the present publisher, P. A Badour, at the beginning of February, 1883 The editors have been Rev. T J Hill and P. A. Badour. The size and form have been successively a six column folio, and a five column quarto.

The Bellaire *Breeze*, Bellaire, Antrim county, was established September 29, 1881, by Albert S Abbott, by whom it has ever since been owned, edited, and published. It was commenced as a five column folio, and was enlarged to a five column quarto February 9, 1882. Politics, republican

The Cadillac *Weekly Times*, Cadillac, Wexford county, was first started, under another name, at Mendon, St Joseph county, in June, 1882, and was afterwards removed to Cadillac. The founder, Alf Rindge, has been the only publisher and editor. It was commenced as a seven column folio, and was enlarged to a seven column quarto in August, 1882. Independent in politics.

The *Enterprise*, East Jordan, Charlevoix county, was established by E N Clink, in April, 1882, who sold a half interest in it to W. F. Palmiter, a year later In November, 1883, the office was totally destroyed by fire, and the paper was suspended till February,

1884, when its publication was resumed by Palmiter & Nelson. Size at first a six column folio, enlarged to a five column quarto in June, 1883, and soon afterwards to a six column quarto.

The Elmira *Gazette*, Elmira, Otsego county, a six column folio, was established by C. S. Edwards, in October, 1882. A year from that date, it was purchased by M. W. Newkirk, the present owner. The proprietors have been the editors. Politics, republican.

The Fife Lake *Eye* was established at Fife Lake, Grand Traverse county, in September, 1881, and discontinued publication a year later.

The Fife Lake *Comet*, E. B. Dennis, publisher, Fife Lake, Grand Traverse county, a five column quarto, was established in November, 1882. E. D. Fuller was the editor till March 1, 1884. Politics, republican.

The Charlevoix *Journal*, Charlevoix, Charlevoix county, was established by Charles J. Strang, July 19, 1883. There have been no changes of publisher or editor. The *Journal* is a five column quarto. Politics, democratic.

The Antrim County *Record*,* Alba, Antrim county, was established by Justus L. Hissong, who is both publisher and editor, Nov. 7, 1883. Size, a five column quarto. The *Record* is non-political in character.

The *Northwest Farmer*, Traverse City, a sixteen page monthly, devoted to farming and rural affairs, made its first appearance in May, 1882. Publisher, D. C. Leach; editors, D. C. Leach and M. L. Leach.

The Benzonia *Citizen* was established at Benzonia, Benzie county, about May 1, 1870. It was a two column quarto and was discontinued in the summer of 1871. A. Barnard was publisher until March, 1871, then a Mr. Kingsley until the publication was dropped. Jas. B. Walker, editor. In politics it was anti-masonic.

*CORRECTION—In chapter XXVII, in speaking of the enlistments in Grand Traverse in 1864 the name of Marcus Lacore should have been Marvin Lacore. It is there stated that Mr. Lacore joined the 10th Michigan cavalry. This was a mistake. Mr. Lacore tells us he was assigned to the Mississippi squadron. Adolphus Payette was also in the Mississippi squadron. The amount received in bounty by Mr. Lacore and others who enlisted at that time was but $300. Those who entered the service a little later received more.

CHAPTER XXXI.

Conclusion—Topography—The High Central Plateau—The Grand Traverse Region on the Northwestern Slope—Surface of the Country—Population—Villages—Traverse City—Industries—Summer Visitors.

In bringing to a close this imperfect history of the Grand Traverse region, perhaps we cannot make plainer the changes that have been wrought since the white man first settled within its borders, or present anything of greater interest to the reader, than by giving a brief chapter descriptive of the country as it is, not forgetting its natural features—its topography, surface configuration, soils, lakes, streams, and climate.

In order to make clear what we propose to present, it is necessary to extend the description of the make of the country beyond the boundaries of the region we are considering.

The high central plateau of the northern part of the lower peninsula of Michigan is often referred to by writers who have occasion to speak of the topographical features of the country. To get a clear understanding of what is meant by the high central plateau, it is necessary to glance briefly at the general surface configuration of the lower peninsula.

The peninsula presents two grand swells, or regions of elevation, separated by a broad valley, each having its long axis running in a northeasterly and southwesterly direction. The long axis of the more southerly of these swells may be indicated somewhat accurately by a line drawn from Port Austin, near the mouth of Saginaw bay, to the southwest corner of Hillsdale county. In the northern part of Oakland county, this swell attains an elevation of 529 feet, but the highest summit is in Hillsdale county, where it reaches an elevation of 613 feet above Lakes Huron and Michigan.

The valley separating this region of elevation from the more northerly one, may be traced by following up the Saginaw and Bad aivers, and then down the Maple and the Grand. The highest part of this valley is a flat, swampy tract, in the southeast corner of Gratiot county, where the head waters of Bad river start within three miles of the Maple, and is not more than 72 feet higher than Saginaw bay.

The long axis of the more northerly swell may be indicated approximately by a line drawn through Gaylord, near the center of Otsego county, and Bond's Mill, in the eastern part of Wexford county. The broad, undulating summit of this swell is the plateau alluded to. In some places it presents the appearance of an extensive plain; in others it is a confused assemblage of hills and valleys. The hills are generally broad, smooth, and rounded, but there are exceptional cases in which their sides are too steep for tillage. The elevation of several points on this plateau has been ascertained with accuracy in the surveys of the Jackson, Lansing and Saginaw and the Grand Rapids and Indiana railroads. Gaylord is 778 feet above Saginaw bay. A mile and a half north of Bond's Mill, the road-bed of the Grand Rapids and Indiana is 832 feet above Lake Michigan, but the summits of the ridge on each side of it are nearly or quite a hundred feet higher, being fully 900 feet above Lake Michigan. It has been supposed that some of the hills of the plateau reached a height of 1,100 feet or more, but as yet the Wexford summit is the highest the elevation of which has been determined by actual measurement, and it is probably the highest land in the lower peninsula.*

The ascent to the plateau is gradual, but more or less irregular. Its borders are scarred by the streams that have their sources in its higher parts. Sometimes the rivers are found flowing through deep and narrow ravines; sometimes the ravines have been widened into broad valleys, as in the case of the Muskegon and the Manistee.† The northwestern slope is more abrupt in its northern than in its southern portion, and is generally more abrupt than the southeastern slope. In some places it shows an ascending series of terraces, well defined and regular; at other points the regularity entirely disappears. The thriving village of Mancelona is situated on one of these terraces, which is there several miles wide.

The country known as the Grand Traverse region occupies, with a portion of the summit of the plateau, the northwestern slope, between the summit and Lake Michigan. As a whole is is comparatively elevated, its surface being greatly diversified with hills and valleys, table lands, lakes and streams. The hills are heavily timbered. The streams are usually clear, cold, and rapid. The swamps do not give rise to malaria. The air is pure and bracing. The climate, modified by the influence of Lake Michigan, is more equable than that of the southern part of the state. The soil is variable, but in general terms may be described as a sandy or gravelly loam, containing a large percentage of calcareous matter. Not unfrequently the best soil for general farming is found on the tops of the highest hills.

By the census of 1880 the population of the nine counties of Emmet, Charlevoix, Antrim, Kalkaska, Missaukee, Wexford, Grand Traverse, Benzie, and Leelanaw was shown to be 46,384. Judging from the past rate of increase and from observation extending through a series of years, it is believed that the population at the present time (May, 1884,) does not fall short of 70,000. The valleys, plains, and hill-tops are everywhere dotted with the clearings of settlers. The busy hum of industry is heard where, in security, the wild beast but yesterday made his lair The merry school bell calls the children together from humble cabins hidden in the forest The resounding echoes of the steam whistle proclaim that the inland waters have been converted into highways of commerce

The Grand Rapids and Indiana railroad crosses the southwestern prolongation of the plateau in Osceola and Wexford counties, and then, rising over the gently swelling hills and descending in to the river valleys, runs along its northwestern slope, through the whole length of the region we are considering, to the straits of Mackinac Thriving villages have grown up all along its course, centers of local trade, where the settler can sell the surplus products of his farm and purchase his supplies on terms scarcely less advantageous than those offered in older communities

Arriving at Cadillac, in a northward journey on this road, one may consider himself as fairly within the borders of the Grand Traverse country Cadillac has already been incorporated as a city Farther north he will pass Manton, Walton, Fife Lake, South Boardman, Kalkaska, Mancelona, Alba, Elmira, Boyne Falls, and Petoskey, with other stations of less note, most of them possessing real advantages and enjoying solid prosperity, and all of them indulging in great expectations. From Walton a branch railroad leads to Traverse City, and from Petoskey another curves round the head of Little Traverse bay to Harbor Springs. The last three villages named enjoy the double advantage of both railroad and water communication with other localities If, in the season of navigation, the traveler prefers a journey by water along the shore, following the sinuosities of the coast, he will find evidences of enterprise and thrift at the numerous lakeport villages—Frankfort, Glen Arbor, Leland, Northport, Traverse City, Old Mission, Elk Rapids, Torch Lake, Norwood, Charlevoix, Petoskey, and Harbor Springs At Elk Rapids he can take passage on the line of small steamers plying on the chain of beautiful inland lakes in Antrim county, visiting several points of interest and penetrating the interior to the vicinity of Bellaire. At Charlevoix some of the large lake steamers pass through the harbor into Pine lake, on which are situated the thriving villages of Ironton, South Arm, East Jordan, Boyne City, and Bay Springs. If he chooses to leave both the railroad and the navigable waters and plunge into the interior, though he can not get far away from one or the other, he will still find prosperous villages at central points, as, for example, Lake City, Sherman, Wexford, Williamsburg, and Benzonia.

To give in detail a description of the business of the several villages, is the proper work of the gazetteer rather than of the historian, but for the purpose of showing the progress of improvement it may be allowable to mention concisely a few facts, taking one village as a representative of several.

Traverse City, the initial growth of which has been described in the earlier chapters of this history, is now a village with 3,000 or 3,500 inhabitants It has six churches, well attended Its graded school will compare favorably with any in the state It has three printing offices, two weekly newspapers, and a monthly agricultural magazine It has probably one hundred and fifty places of business, counting the offices of professional men Not less than a million and a half dollars worth of merchandise is sold in its stores and shops annually Hannah, Lay & Co. its founders, besides conducting one of the largest mercantile establishments in the state, manufacture annually 20,000,000 feet of lumber, the greater part of which is dressed before shipment. There is daily communication by railroad with all points north and south During the season of navigation, there is direct communication weekly by steamer with Chicago and Milwaukee, and daily with all the principal ports in northwestern Michigan.

The industries of the Grand Traverse region are more varied than those of new countries in general Farming, in some of its branches, will, in the course of time, become the principal employment of the people. At present, while new farms are everywhere being cleared of the primitive forest and brought into a condition for cultivation, the pine and hardwood timber is being put to profitable use Besides being manufactured into lumber, large quantities of hardwood are converted into charcoal for use in the smelting of iron. It having been found more economical to bring the ore to the charcoal than to carry the charcoal to the ore, smelting furnaces have been established at several points—Frankfort, Leland, Elk Rapids, Ironton, and Mancelona. Large quantities of cordwood, posts, railroad ties, and hemlock bark are shipped to various ports on the lakes, and ship timber is sent to Montreal and Europe.

Another fact in regard to the Grand Traverse country remains to be noticed, the importance of which is only just beginning to be understood. Its pure water, healthful atmosphere, and, more than all, its beautiful scenery, are attracting large numbers of summer visitors—pleasure seekers, invalids, wearied workers with hand and brain—who find here relief from the ennui, the ills, and the grinding toil of daily life. The region is rapidly becoming one grand summer resort

* The summit a short distance southeast of Mancelona probably has about the same elevation M L L

† The road bed of the Grand Rapids and Indiana railroad at the crossing of the Manistee, in the northeast corner of Wexford county, is 350 feet above Lake Michigan M L L

[THE END]

In the preparation of the History of the Grand Traverse Region, I am indebted to Parkman's valuable works for much of the information relative to the exploration and occupation of the country by the Jesuits, and the early wars affecting both Indians and white men. I have drawn to some extent on the earlier numbers of the Grand Traverse HERALD and the Charlevoix *Sentinel*. Most of the facts, however, I have obtained from individuals who were personally cognizant of the events and familiar with the scenes described. For the descriptive parts I have consulted Prof. A. Winchell, profitably I am under special obligation for valuable assistance to the persons named in the following list

Rev. Peter Dougherty, Mrs. O M Salisbury, Lewis Miller, E P Ladd, J. M. Pratt, S. E Wait, G A. Craker, Mrs. George N Smith, Andrew Porter, Wm. Gill, Mrs Wm Thomas, Fred. F. Cook, Mr. and Mrs John Lerue, Mr. and Mrs. T. A Hitchcock, Mr. and Mrs H. D Campbell, Mr and Mrs. J. K. Gunton, Perry Hannah, A. T. Lay, R. McLellan, J B Spencer, Mr and Mrs. Jacob Barns, Mrs D C. Goodale, Rev S. Steele, Rev J J McLaughlin, Rev. D R Latham, Rev J W Miller, E. S Noble, Mr. and Mrs J S Dixon, Louis Gebou, Capt McCausland, Mrs Ruth Bedford, Orson Campbell, Mrs. Polly Preper, Richard Cooper, H O. Rose, Wingfield Watson, Mr and Mrs. John Miller, D. H Pierce, Rev. Charles E. Bailey, W S Hubbell, Charles Downs, Wm Masters, Mr. and Mrs Michael Gay, A J Blackbird, Robert Dailey, Mrs M A Wadsworth, Rev. Leroy Warren, David J Parish, Jr., Mr. and Mrs W B Stiger, Rev H. C Scofield Mrs. Nelson Ainslie, M. M. Stinson, chief engineer G R. and I. railroad.

M L LEACH.

Traverse City, May, 1884

CPSIA information can be obtained
at www.ICGtesting.com
Printed in the USA
LVHW081746300722
724790LV00004B/49

9 781362 863120